Moving the Goalposts

A history of sport and society since 1945

Martin Polley

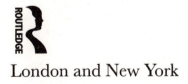

London and New York

First published 1998
by Routledge
11 New Fetter Lane, London EC4P 4EE

Simultaneously published in the USA and Canada
by Routledge
29 West 35th Street, New York, NY 10001

© 1998 Martin Polley

Typeset in Baskerville by Routledge
Printed and bound in Great Britain by MPG Books Ltd,
Bodmin Cornwall

British Library Cataloguing in Publication Data
A catalogue record for this book is available from the British Library

Library of Congress Cataloguing in Publication Data
A catalogue record for this book has been requested

ISBN 0–415–14216–4 (hbk)
ISBN 0–415–14217–2 (pbk)

For Catherine and James

Contents

Acknowledgements

This book would not have been started without the interest and enthusiasm shown by Heather McCallum at Routledge, and I am grateful for her consistent patience and support.

My colleagues in History at King Alfred's University College, Winchester, deserve my thanks. In particular, I am indebted to Roger Richardson and Michael Hicks for encouraging my teaching in sports history upon which this book is founded. They also helped the project by providing me with a period of study leave in the final stages. Chris Aldous, Neil Curtin, and Colin Haydon have always been ready with advice and reassurance. My colleagues in Sports Studies have given me opportunities to extend my teaching across disciplinary borders: particular thanks go to Barry Fry and Alastair Loadman. The students who have taken my various sport and leisure history modules have been influential in helping me to clarify and develop my interests and ideas. I am also grateful to the librarians at King Alfred's, particularly Wendy Hall and, on the inter-library loans desk, Andrea Hockings and Sarah Green. Their speed and efficiency in tracking down increasingly obscure items has been remarkable.

Beyond King Alfred's, I am indebted to Malcolm Smith, who supervised my first research in sports history, and to Peter Beck. Bob Harrison of Southern Oregon University promoted my sports history contributions during my exchange visit in 1995. As a work of synthesis, this book is to a great extent dependent upon the primary research that other sports historians and sociologists have carried out. My indebtedness to all of them is self-evident. More specifically, I am grateful to Wray Vamplew, Garry Whannel, and Raymond Boyle for supporting the project, and to Charles Korr, Daryl Adair, and Norman Baker for helping with information on sports history courses.

On a personal level, I would never have developed an interest in the history of sport without an earlier interest in sport, and this has been nurtured and enhanced by many people. Within my family, my grand-fathers Victor Bennett and the late Len Polley were major influences on my early awareness of both contemporary and historical sport: in particular, Len Polley's photographs and ephemera from his footballing days with London Schools and Dulwich Hamlet in the 1920s were a source of childhood fascination and pride. My brothers, Richard and David, played key roles, through football with 'jumpers for goalposts' and the legendary cricket matches featuring Angus, Headley, and Timmy. David also introduced me to Brentford FC, where my support has not only provided me with many moments of great pleasure – particularly in the promotion seasons of 1977–8 and 1991–2 – but has also given me an insight into the role of history in sport: following a club that had its best season thirty years before I was born has tended to develop my sense of the past. I would also like to thank the many friends with whom I have played, watched, and talked sport, including Stephen Brooke, Sean Ryan, Tony Furlong, Andrew Metcalf, Jonathan Larwood, and James Guariglia. James also deserves thanks for suggesting the title for this book.

My parents, Brian and Jean Polley, have my gratitude for the constant encouragement and unconditional support they have provided over the years.

My biggest personal debt is to Catherine. She has provided practical support, critical encouragement, and a tolerance of my absence in the study for this project, as for previous ones, and she has managed this with great patience through a period of major change in our lives. It is to her, and to James, that I dedicate this book.

The author and publishers would like to thank the following for permission to quote extracts from copyright works: *New Statesman and Society* for Tony Blair, 'Stan's my man'; Frank Bruno and Weidenfeld and Nicolson for Frank Bruno, *Eye of the Tiger: my life*; Falmer Press for John Coghlan, *Sport and British Politics since 1960*; Robson Books for Rogan Taylor and Andrew Ward, *Kicking and Screaming: an oral history of football in England*; HarperCollins Publishers for Neil Macfarlane and Michael Herd, *Sport and Politics: a world divided*. The extract from Alison Dewar's 'Sexual oppression in sport: past, present and future alternatives' is reprinted by permission, Alan G. Ingham and John W. Loy, 1993, *Sport in Social Development* (Champaign, IL, Human Kinetics).

Abbreviations

AAA	Amateur Athletic Association
AAM	Anti-Apartheid Movement
AELTCC	All England Lawn Tennis and Croquet Club
ASH	Association of Sports Historians
ATV	Associated Television
BBBC	British Boxing Board of Control
BBC	British Broadcasting Corporation
BLBA	British Ladies' Boxing Association
BOA	British Olympic Association
CA	Croquet Association
CCPR	Central Council of Physical Recreation (from 1944)
CCRPT	Central Council of Recreative Physical Training
CRE	Commission for Racial Equality
DES	Department of Education and Science
DNH	Department of National Heritage
DoE	Department of the Environment
FA	Football Association
FAI	Football Association of Ireland
FIFA	Fédération Internationale de Football Association
GAA	Gaelic Athletic Association
GHS	General Household Survey
GLC	Greater London Council
IOC	International Olympic Committee
ISL	International Sport and Leisure
ITV	Independent Television
MCC	Marylebone Cricket Club
NF	National Front
PFA	Professional Footballers Association
QPR	Queens Park Rangers

RAF	Royal Air Force
RFL	Rugby Football League
RFU	Rugby Football Union
SDA	Sex Discrimination Act
SNP	Scottish National Party
SRU	Scottish Rugby Union
STST	Stop The Seventy Tour
TOP	The Olympic Programme
UEFA	Union Européenne de Football Association
UN	United Nations
WCA	Women's Cricket Association
WFA	Women's Football Association
WRU	Welsh Rugby Union
WSC	World Series Cricket
WSF	Women's Sports Foundation

Introduction

Sir Stanley Matthews is a culture in himself, a culture that in all too many areas of the game has been eroded. Never booked, let alone sent off. Always able to find time for the children crowding around the players' entrance, for he knew that without them and their enthusiasm, the game's future was bleak. . . . Now I would be the last person to call for a return to . . . the slave wage structure of those days. But given the kind of adverse publicity the game got itself last year, and given the sums of money now involved in transfers and salaries and all the stories I keep reading in the newspapers, and all the various allegations kicking around, it is little wonder that the public might be concerned that the sport is too much driven by money and too little driven by sporting spirit.[1]

Three lions on the shirt
Jules Rimet still gleaming
Thirty years of hurt
Never stopped the dreaming
. . . Football's coming home.[2]

These two quotations offer us a way into the different roles that history plays in popular discourses on contemporary sport. The first comment, taken from Labour leader Tony Blair's speech to the Football Writers Association to celebrate Sir Stanley Matthews' 80th birthday, is an example of a prevalent popular view of past sport that is based on nostalgia and a belief in a golden age. It is underpinned by the assumption that sport in the past was better than sport in the present; that it was purer, unsullied by various pressures believed to be extrinsic to sport that have come in to corrupt it, including money, politics, drugs, violence, commercialism, and professionalism. As with all golden age versions of history, it is in many ways an unhistorical view, one that fails adequately to see past sport in the context of its time. For this reason, it has been chosen to open this historical study of sport in the UK since 1945. For a period of frequent and major change, this view offers common-sense solace that sport used to be better, and that it has been marred by the strains and stresses of modern society.

This ideology can frequently be seen in sports journalism, commentary, and debate. It was present in the police campaign against football hooliganism in the build-up to the 1996 European Championships, where one poster headed 'Spot the Difference' juxtaposed a picture of a peaceful crowded football terrace from the 1930s with one of fighting hooligans from the 1980s. It was present in the long and heated debate over the role of professionalism in rugby union that reached a head in 1995, and in the resistance to change from rugby league clubs and supporters when the sport was dramatically reconstructed in the interests of satellite television. Cricket has witnessed it consistently throughout the post-war period, with recent examples including traditionalists' expressions of antipathy towards advertising in the game: Scyld Berry, for example, called for a boycott of the companies whose logos were painted on the pitches, as the game's 'whole raison d'être is violated by reality's intrusion into the escape world of play'.[3] It is a view that could even be detected in some of the throwaway comments made by BBC television's anchorman, Des Lynam, during the 1996 Olympic Games, such as his observation that while going down to the pub is not yet an Olympic sport, beach volleyball is. In short, whenever aspects of social life have been perceived as corrupting or even just changing the certainties and traditions of a sport, from drugs to violence, all-seater stadia to shirt-front sponsorship, an unspecified past is readily mobilised as a golden age.

The second way in which the past can be mobilised in sport's present is exemplified here by the notion of 'football coming home' in the Lightning Seeds' anthem for England's 1996 European Championship team. Rather than being nostalgically backward looking to a golden age, and resistant to contemporary trends, it revisits and recycles past sport in a celebratory manner as an inspiration for the present. To a degree, it is based on trends that we could label as post-modern, as it uses irony and self-deprecating humour in its celebration of local, national, and international images. It can be seen most clearly in the spate of 1960s and 1970s footballing references in pop music from the mid-1980s onwards, references that ranged from the ironic to the iconic, the authentic to the surreal. Many bands, particularly those that were part of the guitar-based independent music boom of the 1980s, used such references. The Wedding Present named their album *George Best*, Half Man Half Biscuit paid homage to European football and Subbuteo with 'I Was a Teenage Armchair Honved Fan' and 'All I

Want For Christmas is the Dukla Prague Away Kit', while The Dentists pre-dated the recent fashion for quoting Kenneth Wolstenholme's most famous words by naming their 1985 album *Some People Are On The Pitch They Think It's All Over It Is Now*, and sampling the original commentary at the start of the record.[4] Beyond pop music, this drawing upon past sport to set both context and inspiration for present sport can be seen in media and popular comparisons, such as those drawn in lawn tennis between Fred Perry and Tim Henman during the latter's relatively successful 1996 Wimbledon Championships, and between the 1996 England football team and their World Cup winning counterparts of 1966. The 1966 victory was a constant theme in media coverage of the 1996 tournament, and as the semi-final pairing of England and Germany became imminent, images from the past dominated coverage. The match was set up, particularly in the tabloids, as a revenge for the 1990 World Cup semi-final, a replay of the 1966 World Cup Final, and, by extension, a rerun of two world wars. Headlines included 'Achtung! Surrender: For you Fritz, ze Euro 96 Championship is over' (*Daily Mirror*) and 'Let's Blitz Fritz' (*The Sun*). Tabloid stunts included a successful attempt to get the 1966 match ball back from Germany for hat-trick scorer Geoff Hurst, and, allegedly, abortive attempts by the *Daily Mirror* to organise a 'Spitfire flypast over the England team's hotel . . . and . . . to stage a reunion of *Dad's Army* actors'.[5]

Although both types of usage of the past share some common ground in a sense of nostalgia, they differ in their orientation. The former is essentially sentimental, backward looking, and potentially reactionary, assuming that the past was simply a better place; the latter is focused on the present while being aware of its links to the past. Throughout the world of sport, they are supplemented by other forms of historical narratives of the past. This has been described in a rugby union context by Adam Robson, President of the Scottish Rugby Union 1983–4, as the 'traditions and folklore [that] stimulate reminiscence and anecdote'.[6] The honours list and the trophy room; the collection and worship of records and statistics; the sense of place and local rivalry present in derby fixtures; the ritualised traditions around Wimbledon, the Ashes, the FA Cup Final, and the Boat Race; even the mediocre club runner's insistence on maintaining an account of personal best running times – all of these are examples of how the sporting present is related to the sporting past. Throughout sport, at the levels of participation, administration, media coverage, and reception, the past looms large: as a golden age, a storehouse of images, a cautionary tale, or just as an account of where we have come from. Whatever the immediate usage of such images, they are unavoidable in contemporary sport, and, while they often rely heavily upon a rather uncritical and unsophisticated sense of history, all informed followers of sport are aware of the importance of the past in shaping their sporting present. Midwinter has provided a neat summary of the relationship in his defence of county cricket's continued appeal: 'it speaks to us of past sensibilities; it is a bolt-hole during a cruel present; and it is a tiny part of the dream of a bright future'.[7] Without even the most basic acceptance of history, sport as an organised phenomenon is incomprehensible.

This is a historical problem with which this study of the post-war British experience aims to engage. If the past, as Hartley put it in the frequently quoted opening of *The Go-Between*, is 'a foreign country' where 'they do things differently',[8] then why is sport's past so often seen as so important for its present, as well as more attractive? How closely are the problems that are supposed to have corrupted sport related to wider changes that the UK has experienced since 1945 in its polity, economy, world position, social structure, demography, and gender relations? Why did they make themselves felt in sport, so long held in common-sense ideology to be somehow separate from the society in which it takes place? Are these corruptions solvable from within sport, or could new change come only from wider developments? This list of questions is extensive and challenging, but if we doubt the need for such critical interrogation, we need only reconsider the assumptions about sport and history behind the 'Let's Blitz Fritz' headlines of 1996. If historians, and their colleagues in sports studies, cultural studies, and media studies do not ask these questions, then such ahistorical and mythological invocations of the past will continue to inform our everyday awareness of sport. We need to ask critical questions of the history of sport precisely because, as Mason put it, 'the notion that sport has nothing to do with anything else has a long and revered history as well as an extremely energetic present'.[9]

Thanks to Mason and a number of other pioneering sport and leisure historians, including Brailsford, Mangan, Vamplew, Bailey, Cox, and Holt, the discipline of history is now in a position to challenge this popular notion, and to make the connections between sport and 'anything else'. This historiography assumes that there are links between the sport practised in a given society and the social, political, economic, and cultural conditions of that society. The point was neatly summarised by Hermas Evans of the Welsh Rugby Union (WRU) in his Foreword to that organisation's official centenary history. He justified the WRU's decision to commission two academic historians to write the book by succinctly pointing out that a history of rugby in Wales 'must . . . be more than a mere description of great matches, famous players, and the administration; it must also attach itself to the social, industrial and religious life of Wales'.[10] The notion of attachment is a useful one. It goes beyond the more simplistic idea that sport 'reflects' the society it is played in, exemplified in Perkin's huge claim for sport's historical significance: 'The history of societies is reflected more vividly in the way they spend their leisure time than in their politics or work.'[11] Using examples from our period, the presence of black athletes in contemporary British teams 'reflects' the fact that the UK is a multiracial society. Similarly, the growth of mass participation in non-competitive sporting activities linked to personal fitness, such as aerobics and jogging, 'reflects' the fact that many people are increasingly concerned about their personal health, and see a link between exercise and physical well-being.

This is a starting point for critical thought about sport in society, but we need to go further. Rather than thinking purely in terms of reflection, which implies passivity on the part of sport, it is more useful to see how sport is shaped and constrained by the wider forces, and how it interacts with them and reproduces them. To return to the example of black athletes, the presence of Linford Christie, Colin Jackson, Tessa Sanderson, and others in British athletics teams would not have been possible without post-war trends in Commonwealth immigration, but beyond the mere fact of the presence of a black population, we cannot explain their success unless we look at such issues as education, integration, career opportunities, and institutional attitudes, as well as less tangible and constantly shifting cultural notions of British identity, national representation, and popular approval. In other words, we need to see how sport works as a part of British society, not just how sport reflects demographic trends. Similarly, the growth of the personal fitness trend is not merely a reflection of people's concerns about health: it is integrally linked to such varied influences as increasing leisure time and disposable incomes, the marketing strategies associated with the 'international community of step-aerobics',[12] and changes in gender relations and women's perceived roles. These examples will be developed elsewhere in this book. They serve here simply to highlight the complex relations that exist between sport and its society, and to stress the need to think beyond reflection. Houlihan presents a useful way of looking at this question: he outlines the 'cultural contours' of British society – including deference, democracy, and 'social divisions along racial, sexual, religious and class lines' – and asks how far sport 'reflects and confirms' these features.[13] Sport can be called a reflection of society in so far as recognisable characteristics of the society are discernible in sport, but it must also be seen as part of that society. Sport is not passive: it co-exists with its society, and, for post-war Britain, is an important component of that society.

THE POST-WAR SETTING

The primary aim of this book is to provide a critical historical introduction to a number of important themes in post-war British sport, offering an overview of major developments, and raising the main issues that have drawn the attention of historians and other academic commentators. It is a work of synthesis rather than a work of primary research. The themes have been chosen as ones that will bring out the relationship between sport and society, and as ones that are crucial for us to engage with if we are to see contemporary sport as more than just a matter of performance. The first three chapters will explore broad contextual areas of continuity and change in British sport: first, the role of the state; second, the different elements of national identity in sport; and third, the development of sport's commercial character. They will be followed by three chapters exploring the historical development of three crucial areas of constraint and opportunity in sport: gender; social class and status; and ethnicity.

The major themes have been chosen for the light they can shed on the specific post-war development of British sport. They relate to areas in post-war society in which there have been major changes, as discussed by various social and political historians.[14] It is not the task of this present text to duplicate this historiography, but it is worth noting the widespread view that this has been a revolutionary period in British history, described by Royle as a time characterised by 'an accelerating discontinuity with the past'.[15] If we think purely about the developments most pertinent to the themes of this book, we can see at a glance some of the changes. It has been a period of increasing state intervention in people's lives, ranging from the growth of the welfare state to less welcomed growths in areas as diverse as taxation and surveillance. In another area of politics, the post-war period has seen the acceleration of the growth of regionalism and nationalism, to the degree that by the mid-1990s, Irish Nationalists are regularly joined by Scottish National Party and Plaid Cymru representatives in the House of Commons, and devolution is seriously on the agenda. The social structure has changed, with increasing mobility between classes helping to blur some of the more traditional distinctions, and politicians welcoming a mythologised classless society: even if it does not exist, the fact that politicians aspire to it suggests a shift from pre-war rigidity. Gender relations, building on the developments earlier in the century based on women's enfranchisement and increasing role in the workplace, have continued to shift, with the post-war development of career women, househusbands, and an equal opportunities machinery dedicated to ameliorate barriers based on gender in the workplace and elsewhere; again, even if the reality is not as equal as it might be, the aspiration is a sign of a shift. The equal opportunities culture also covers ethnic issues, and this has been one of the major areas of change in post-war society: the growth of a multi-ethnic population based on Commonwealth immigration. The economy has gone through various transformations, linked to the post-war nationalisation and subsequent reprivatisation of key industries, the decline of the manufacturing industry, the growth of the service and leisure sectors, and the growth of consumer expenditure and leisure time. Linked to this is the huge growth of the broadcasting media, based upon technological improvements which have put television sets and latterly video recorders in the majority of homes, with satellite receivers in many. These developments have all had an impact on sport, for the basic reason that sport is part of its society. If the society changes, then sport cannot remain the same. Changes in political, economic, and social structures influence the opportunities and constraints that face people making decisions about sports participation, what Gruneau called the 'choices and possibilities' that are 'expressed in and through play, games, and sports'.[16] However, the emphasis on change should not disguise the period's connections with the past. Continuities, in the same areas mentioned above, have also shaped the period, most obviously in the survival of class divisions, patriarchal values, and a white English hegemony within the UK. Sport is one way into the dynamic relationship between survival and reconstruction that has characterised the period.

This study is needed because, despite the growth of critical academic study of sport and its history, the post-war period has been relatively underdeveloped in its own right. This is due largely to its proximity: one of the major drawbacks of contemporary history is the lack of perspective that standing so close can bring. The period that has probably attracted most attention has been the industrial revolution and its immediate aftermath, a time when traditional games and sports were transformed, under economic, temporal, and spatial pressures, into modern sports, with rules, regular competitions, and bureaucracies.

Holt has successfully challenged the notion of this 'apparently simple model of "modernization" of sport',[17] and has demonstrated various continuities between pre-industrial, industrial, and contemporary sport, a theme that Brailsford also developed in *Sport, Time and Society*.[18] The simple model should also be challenged on the grounds that different sports have 'modernised' at different times: Maguire's discussion of English basketball's development from a minority school and university sport into an Americanised spectacle in the 1970s and 1980s is a case in point.[19] However, a great deal of British sports historiography is primarily concerned with the emergence of sports in the recognisable modern forms from the eighteenth century to the late nineteenth century.[20] As a result, there are a number of gaps in the coverage of twentieth-century sport, particularly the post-1945 period. It has by no means been neglected, as the sources for this book prove, but it has frequently slipped into the grey area between contemporary history and the more present-centred disciplinary approaches of cultural studies, sports studies, gender studies, and media studies. For example, Leicester University Press's major series of sports monographs, which cover a great deal of historical material in such areas as Scottish sport, world football, and football support, is marketed as 'Sport, Politics and Culture'.[21]

General historians of post-war British society have not always paid sport the attention that we might wish for. The reasons for this are obviously linked to the long-term hostility and indifference of the academic community to the serious study of sport. The 1979 Pelican edition of Calvocoressi's *The British Experience 1945-75* managed to include Roger Bannister's moment of triumph on its front cover photomontage, along with images of Aneurin Bevan, Harold MacMillan, and other politicians, but sport was not covered in the text. Marwick, in his 1982 volume for the Penguin Social History of Britain, offered some passing references to sport – darts and football both got brief coverage. However, his decision to exclude 'football and holidays' from the section on culture, and not fully to include them elsewhere, showed how marginal sport can appear. Arnold's *Britain since 1945* included a large section on the media but did not touch upon sport, while Pugh's political and social history of the period 1870–1992, *State and Society*, discussed the emergence of organised football in the late nineteenth century, but did not cover post-war sporting developments.[22] Whannel's 1983 observation that 'general histories tend to ignore sport'[23] was accurate, although an exception appeared that year in Robbins's *The Eclipse of a Great Power*, which gave sport significant space.[24]

By the late 1980s and early 1990s, however, the sporting history of the post-war period found itself covered more and more in general texts. Morgan's *The People's Peace* included amongst its plates, alongside images of striking miners and The Beatles, a photograph of the England World Cup winning football team from 1966. The text gave a respectable amount of coverage to sport, including discussions of the links between football and permissiveness in the 1960s, and how Commonwealth relations have occasionally seemed to exist only on the cricket pitch.[25] Marwick's third edition, published in 1996, contained contextualised coverage of sponsorship and football hooliganism.[26] Another clear indicator of sport's growing respectability is the inclusion of a chapter on 'Leisure, sports and the arts' in the third edition of Oakland's *British Civilization*, an introductory British Studies text, justified with the claim that the varieties of leisure activities reflect the 'diversity of life in contemporary Britain'.[27] Similarly, Obelkevich and Catterall included a chapter on sport and gender in their 1994 collection of essays, *Understanding Post-War British Society*. Sport's inclusion alongside demographic change, the family, education, and poverty was justified as follows:

> In the popular mind both sport and leisure are essentially minor issues – 'optional extras' which may enrich people's lives, but matter less than earning a living or raising a family. . . . In reality, both sport and leisure have major social, political and economic significance in contemporary society.[28]

Once again, this brings us back to the need to explore sport's recent history.

In such a setting, the disciplinary approaches of history can bring a number of insights. First, it can establish the wider contexts – social, political, cultural, and economic – in which the sport played at any time in the past took place. Second, it can offer a sense of long- and short-term trends that are not always visible to present-centred disciplinary approaches. Third, it can show both continuity and change at work in the field, demonstrating how some elements of sports have remained apparently unchanged across the period while others have apparently so radically altered. Finally, it can offer analysis, through primary evidence, of particular events and moments to illustrate and exemplify the wider points.

The sources used for the analysis of these themes have been many and various. The basic genre has been academic sports history: that is, history books and articles presented with references and bibliographies which 'attempt to set sport in its full cultural context', written by historians 'interested in sequence, tendencies, outcomes and change'.[29]

This subdiscipline has been charted and analysed in a number of studies,[30] and Cox's bibliographies and research guides give us access to the sources.[31] Related to this academic historiography have been studies written by academics from sports studies, media studies, sociology, and cultural studies. When dealing with the contemporary history of sport, it is impossible not to take account of these present-centred disciplines, and this work has helped to fill some of the gaps in the historiography. This is best exemplified by Maguire's work, which is based in the historically oriented figurational sociology.[32] A third type of source used has been the non-academic history book, those that tend to narrate the story of a particular sport without rigorously setting it within the 'cultural context' referred to by Mangan. These are problematic, particularly when they do not use the machinery of references and bibliographies which allow the reader to check, but they have been essential for two reasons. First, a number of sports simply do not yet have an academic historiography for this period. In 1995, Mason drew attention to athletics, bowls, motor sport, rugby league, and swimming as sports that 'largely await the scholar's scrutiny',[33] to which we could add badminton, fencing, squash, and many others. Until these gaps are filled, the synthesising historian is left with no option but to rely upon non-academic sources. Second, and more positively, they do provide us with insights into the cultures, practices, and ideologies of the sport's dedicated followers, for and by whom they are generally written. There may not be much genuine awareness of class as a problematic in Spencer's observation on the beauty of Cirencester Park Polo Club, where those 'who are able to compete and polo *aficionados* who can watch the game in such idyllic settings are indeed privileged', but the text tells us a great deal about the sport.[34] These three main types of source have been augmented where appropriate by media sources, sportsmen and women's autobiographies, and personal memory and observation. Taken together, these sources have facilitated the synthesis, and allowed a thematic view of sport and society in post-war Britain to emerge.

There are, inevitably, gaps in this synthesis. The chosen themes are not the only significant ones for this period, and we need to be aware of other important parts of sports histories that have not been given coverage here. As a work of synthesis, this book has concentrated on areas that are not just important in their own historical right, but have also received the bulk of historiographical and other academic coverage. As Holt put it after writing *Sport and the British*, 'There is nothing like attempting a synthesis to show up the gaps in a subject',[35] an observation we can only echo. The most obvious example for our period has been the media. While television's relationship with sport has been narrated and analysed in a number of texts,[36] there is no comparable historiography for the other media, particularly the press (both general and specialist) and the radio, but also, latterly, teletext and Internet-based communications channels. Sport for the disabled as an area of public achievement as well as one of personal therapy is an important development, and can be firmly linked to the post-war growth of an equal opportunities culture and the shifting discourse on the body and the treatment of the disabled. As yet, it awaits historical analysis to explore its development and context. Sport's relationship with environmental issues is similarly underexplored: debates on sport's spatial character and the pollution linked to many sporting events need to be seen historically, and while Bale's interdisciplinary insights, Allison's general essay, and Jarvie's work on Scottish land use have set up agendas, there is still much to be done here.[37] Even within the chosen themes, there were obvious gaps in the historiography. The most blatant ones are the paucity of material on sport in non-Afro-Caribbean ethnic minority communities; the relative underexposure of masculinity in comparison with women's history; the discussion of England and Englishness in sport to match those on Scotland, Wales, and Ireland; and the lack of work on sport and diplomacy based on government records, currently available up to 1966.

Alongside such gaps in the coverage, the use of certain case studies is acknowledged as a potential problem owing to their atypicality. However, the approach chosen has allowed for themes to be introduced and illustrated, giving the reader both a context for the sport of the period and a range of examples to see what happened within that context. Through this, we can gain an informed and critical view of the importance of recent history in shaping sport, which can act as a counter to the nostalgia that so frequently characterises discussion about sport's past.

Chapter 1

Sport, politics, and the state

INTRODUCTION

Neil Macfarlane, Conservative Minister for Sport from 1981 to 1985, opened his memoirs of his time in office with the following observation on the relationship between sport and politics:

> In the 1933 edition of the *Shorter English Dictionary* I keep on my bookshelf, politics are described as being 'the science and art of government', and sport as 'participation in games or exercises, especially those pursued in the open air'.
>
> I have no doubt that when the dictionary was being prepared by a Fellow of Corpus Christi, Oxford, he would have claimed with some justification that there was and should be no relation between politics and sport.[1]

He juxtaposed this time of apparent political neutrality for sport with the crises of his time in office, including the boycott of the Los Angeles Olympics of 1984, the debate over sporting links with South Africa, the Zola Budd affair, and the problems of football hooliganism. In following this rather simplistic and naïve approach that ignored a full historical relationship between sport and politics, Macfarlane was expressing a widely held popular belief: that sport and politics did not naturally belong together. The assumptions underpinning this stance tell us a great deal about popular attitudes towards both sport and politics. It assumes, for example, that sport is a free voluntary activity that works beyond the constraints of the prevailing political economy; that sport is a private activity in which political agencies have no business; and that when political agencies do get involved, they invariably damage, corrupt, or pervert sport. What this view ignores is the long-term, structural relationship that exists between sport and political agencies at the local, regional, national, and international levels, and that political involvement is not the same as political intervention. Houlihan has astutely observed that 'It is one of the common clichés associated with sport that "sport and politics should not mix". Showing the naivity of such a distinction is fast becoming a sport in its own right';[2] and in the face of observations such as Macfarlane's, it is difficult not to participate in that sport. What is clear for the post-war period is that the relationship between sport and politics – using here the rather narrow sense of state structures and administration rather than the more inclusive definition of power relations and contestation of resources – is increasingly public and generally acknowledged. By exploring the main themes in the development of this relationship in the UK since 1945, we can establish a context for the current debate.

This subject has been the focus of a great deal of academic work, which we can largely link to its contemporary significance. The period since the early 1980s has seen 'a considerable growth in interest in the relationship between politics and sport, the role of government in sport, and the way sport is organised',[3] which Hargreaves has linked specifically to the public debate over the 1980 boycott of the Moscow Olympics, which 'was to make inroads into the ideologically important notion that sport is "non-political" in Britain'.[4] Houlihan's main focus was contemporary, and we can see the growth he refers to exemplified in the essays collected by Allison in *The Politics of Sport* and *The Changing Politics of Sport*:[5] as Allison points out, the fact that the second book was 'a sequel' rather than 'a mere new edition' reflects the rate of change in the area.[6] These deal with a diverse range of issues in sports politics, from Thomas's essay on hunting through to Allison's work on the environment.[7] Surveys of the politics of leisure, whilst having a wider focus than just sport, have also been forthcoming, such as Henry's *The Politics of Leisure Policy*, which surveys the contemporary history of state involvement in leisure.[8] We can also see the growth of interest in politics from the discipline of history. This has included wide surveys, such as Hargreaves' *Sport, Power and Culture*, as well as micro-studies of specific events or themes, examples of which include Hart-Davis' *Hitler's Games* and Hill's *Horse Power*.[9] Finally, it is worth noting that a number of useful memoirs have been published since the mid-1980s, which serve not only to provide information on the careers of those directly involved in the relationship between state and sport, but also to formalise that relationship with the stamp of personal historical authority. Of particular interest here are the memoirs of two sports ministers, Denis Howell's *Made in Birmingham* and Neil Macfarlane's *Sport and Politics*, and the work of John Coghlan, a former Deputy Director-General of the Sports Council, whose *Sport and British Politics since 1960* is a history heavily informed by his personal involvement.[10] Add to this the increasing availability of primary sources from government archives through the annual opening of files under the 1968 Public Records Act,[11] and we can see why state involvement in sport has become such an important area of study. There are, however, some gaps in this literature. While the establishment of the Sports Council and high-profile problems such as football hooliganism have been explored in depth, governmental involvement in international sport for diplomatic reasons has been underexplored. In part, this is because the official records of the highest profile events, such as the 1977 Gleneagles Agreement on sporting links with South Africa and the boycott of the 1980 Moscow Olympics, are still closed under the 1968 Act, and any study based on published sources alone will be incomplete without them. However, there is plenty of material on the earlier part of the period: such key issues as sport and the development of the Cold War, and British reactions to South Africa's sports policies in the late 1950s and early 1960s, are already open to researchers' scrutiny. It is to be hoped that the historiography of sport and politics will soon embrace this aspect. Similarly, the issue of sport and the law has only belatedly been developed from an analytical academic standpoint, notably in the works of Foster and Grayson, and further historical research here will be beneficial.[12]

Despite these gaps, there is enough common ground in the existing historiography to allow us to see the emergence of a number of themes in the relationship between sport and the state since 1945. The basic issue is that, by the end of our period, the feelings expressed by Macfarlane were becoming increasingly difficult to support: such clear public examples of state involvement in sport as the existence of the Sports Council, the funding of sports projects with money from the National Lottery, the provision of sports amenities by local authorities, and the contested issues of sport and diplomacy over Moscow and South Africa could not be ignored. Whether we see this as a loss of innocence or simply a recognition that sport is about resources and representation and so inevitably falls into the state's remit is of secondary importance to the fact of a new public awareness and discussion. This is a view that is summed up well by Coghlan, who identified the 'ever-increasing threat of governmental interference'[13] as one of the dangers to the future of British sport, but appreciated that

Sport is a part of the social order of society and politics is very much about 'social order'; the way in which we wish to live and organize our affairs. The question, therefore, is not whether or not politics should be involved in sport but rather 'how' politics should be involved.[14]

We can survey the period with an analysis of two main themes. First, we will look at the reasons for the development of a relationship between sport and state: what contexts caused the formalisation and public acknowledgement of a relationship that had traditionally been informal and, at times, covert? Second, we can look at the ways in which the relationship has developed, with concrete examples of the forms of involvement that have been forthcoming. These themes will give insights on the effects that the sport–state relationship has had on the way in which sport is played, watched, and administered by the mid-1990s. The aim is to help us step back from the everyday common-sense assumptions about the relationship between sport and politics, and think more constructively about the links. There is nothing natural about the conflict between anti-hunt protesters and a hunt, or in the state's provision of sports facilities to improve the population's health: these are historically specific political aspects. As well as helping to guide us through the historical period, this critical approach can help us avoid the polemical reactions that frequently accompany new sport and political crises, summed up in various sportsmen's defences of their contacts with South Africa. Boxer Frank Bruno retrospectively justified his 1986 fight against Gerry Coetzee by saying that the anti-apartheid issue was 'a subject for politicians, not sportsmen';[15] while Mike Gatting's defence of the 1989 rebel cricket tour of South Africa was summed up in his observation that 'what goes on in the townships has nothing to do with us'.[16] As John Arlott wrote about an earlier run-in between English cricket and apartheid, those involved in politics 'think in broad terms', and see cricket as 'no more than another facet of human relations',[17] an observation that we can apply to all sports. Critical historical assessment of why and how the state has a relationship with sport helps to maintain this broad view that is so necessary for historians.

Before pursuing this thematic survey, it is worth noting the precedents upon which the post-war relationship was based. Taking a long historical view, the regular banning of popular games by medieval monarchs probably ranks as the first major form of state intervention, while the suppression of leisure during the Commonwealth period and the nineteenth-century outlawing of animal baiting sports must be seen as continuations of this trend.[18] Put simply, whenever sportive activity has posed social order problems, or has become identified with notions of indecent and uncivilised behaviour, it has found itself the subject of political action. As sport boomed in the first half of the twentieth century, so too did political involvement in sport. Various governments used sport for diplomatic purposes,[19] popular gambling remained a contested area,[20] and the state provision of amenities mushroomed. State involvement became more formalised with the establishment in 1935 of the Central Council of Recreative Physical Training (CCRPT) with state funding from the Ministry of Education to 'provide a national comprehensive stimulus for post-school sport'.[21] The National government extended its interest in these issues in 1937 with the Physical Training and Recreation Act, which formalised state grants to voluntary sporting and recreational organisations: this was 'the first statute dedicated exclusively and specifically to [the] activities identified in its title'.[22] Moreover, non-governmental political organisations became increasingly involved in sport during this period, notably in the battle for ramblers' rights that found its most famous public expression in the mass trespass on Kinder Scout in 1932,[23] and in British anti-Nazis' publicity on the politicisation of German sport as part of their wider campaign to isolate the Third Reich.[24] However, while there may be nothing new about the fact of a relationship between sport and politics, the post-war period has seen some major developments in that relationship.

CONTEXTS AND CAUSES

Before considering the specific historical contexts of post-war Britain, it is useful to consider Allison's general model for state involvement, what he has called the 'considerable and necessary politics of sport'.[25] First, sport creates 'politically usable resources',[26] such as physical health, social order, and local and national prestige, and as long as sport is organised on the basis of representation of clearly defined geopolitical entities, from village cricket eleven to national Olympic team, this aspect will be a part of sport. Second, linked to the question of organisation and ownership, Allison claims that 'sport is divisive':[27] it arouses conflicts between different interest groups over wealth, group identity, access to resources, and even over problems of individual and public morality, as in the debate over the use of animals for human sport. These insights provide a good basis for analysis of our period. We can identify three main related reasons why the state, at central and local levels, has developed the relationship with sport: first, as part of the general growth in welfarism and collectivism; second, as a response to general social, economic, and demographic trends; and third, in response to specific crisis situations. Moreover, when we appreciate the amount of revenue that government raises from sport, we can see a basic argument for the state reinvesting in sport: 1986 estimates showed that VAT, betting duties, and other sports-related revenues were bringing central government £2.4 billion annually.[28]

In the immediate post-war period, the Labour government built on pre-war and wartime innovations and established the machinery of a welfare state, based around public sector health care, education, unemployment, and sickness insurance, and the nationalisation of selected industries and services.[29] One of the underlying assumptions of this strategy was that the state had a right and a duty to attempt to improve individuals' lives, and so the further development of leisure and sport provision was to be expected. As Henry has shown,[30] from the mid-1940s through to the early 1960s, successive Labour and Conservative governments developed leisure policy based on welfarist principles, including the incorporation of the Arts Council in 1946 and the National Parks Commission in 1949. Sport and leisure became officially justified targets for public spending as 'an appendage to an expanded welfare state'.[31] Welfarism from then on increasingly embraced leisure, based on the predominant ideologies of the consensual collectivist state, and this is the key reason for the dramatic changes that have occurred in the sport–state relationship since 1945. However, this has obviously not been a static situation, and in line with changes in the politics of consensus associated with radical conservatism from the late 1970s, the contexts have changed. Under Thatcherism, collectivism as a predominant ideology has been replaced by a fragmentation of the welfare state and the privatisation of nationalised industries, and the development of neo-liberal and free-market strategies in welfare provision. Sport and leisure provision, as we shall see, has been affected by this new context.

However, the growth of welfarism alone is not sufficient to explain the reasons for the growth of the sport–state relationship: underlying trends in the social and economic structure of the UK, and in the UK's international position, were also responsible. With the structural changes in the workplace associated with a late industrial society and the reconstruction after the Second World War, increasing leisure time and expendable income were realities for many by the mid-1950s, setting up new kinds of demand on the sport and leisure infrastructures. In particular, the growth of private motoring, increased holiday time, and the development of television were impacting upon sport, with falling attendances at spectator sports but increasing participation rates in individual and family-based activities. In this climate, sports' governing bodies through the renamed Central Council of Physical Recreation (CCPR) were calling for a greater co-ordination of provision to ensure that demands could be met. But other, less pleasing trends were also being observed by planners that helped to set up reasons for structured intervention. Most obvious was a growing youth problem, associated from the mid-1950s with Teds, and later with Mods and Rockers, which commentators linked not only to high levels of free time and disposable income amongst young males, but also to the end of conscription, which was wound down from 1957. In this context, a pressing need for sport to be more widely available was felt, relying on functionalist readings of sport as a means of social control, socialisation, cohesion, and discipline. These feelings were expressed most publicly in the Albemarle Report, *The Youth Service in England and Wales*, and the CCPR's Wolfenden Report, *Sport and the Community*, both of which were published in 1960.[32] Both reports assumed connections between the inadequacies of the existing provision of sport and leisure and the problem of idle juveniles. As Wolfenden put it, 'there is a vast range of opportunity which is at present denied, especially to young people. . . . We want to see young people, particularly at the stage of adolescence, given the opportunity for tasting a wide range of physical activities.'[33] This aspect has remained one of the reasons for government involvement in sport since that time, as perennial youth problems, both in times of full employment and high unemployment, have brought state attention to sports provision.

This debate in the late 1950s was also informed by a popular feeling of national decline in the international arena, brought home to the British by the related processes of decolonisation and the Cold War, which found a contemporary focus in the Suez crisis of 1956. This renegotiation of a political world role was played out alongside an acceptance that British sporting superiority could no longer be assumed, particularly thanks to the famous defeats of the England football team by Hungary in 1953 and 1954, and the single gold medal won by the British at the 1952 Helsinki Olympic Games: as such, it helped to form the context for state intervention. This apparent decline was linked by commentators with the lack of state funding for sport in the UK, a point made strongly in 1956 by physical educationalists at the University of Birmingham in their influential pamphlet, *Britain in the World of Sport*. They asked whether, in a world which regards success in sport as an index of national vitality and national prestige and in a world which contains so many governments which are 'professionals' in the organisation of sport, the British government can remain 'amateur'.[34]

These post-war changes in the nation's international standing, and its citizens' perception of relative vitality, must be seen alongside the general growth of welfarism as reasons for the growth of state involvement in sport.

While these reasons can all be linked to changing structures, we also need to consider pragmatism and crisis management as reasons for involvement. Across the period, certain crises have occurred in and around sport that have required responses from the state, and the expedient nature of these responses cannot be ignored simply because a formal relationship with sport existed. In this category, we can place crowd disasters at football stadia (notably Ibrox in 1971, Bradford in 1985, and Hillsborough in 1989) which elicited government-backed investigation and action, as did football hooliganism at different points throughout the period. Much involvement in diplomatic issues around sport has also been based on pragmatic reasons: the Conservative government's backing of the American boycott of the 1980 Moscow Olympics, and the Labour government's action to cancel the 1970 South African cricket team's projected tour, were essentially crisis management situations owing more to short-term readings of particular problems than to any long-term structured involvement.

The reasons for the growing relationship, as far as the state has been concerned, have thus been varied, but the common thread is one of responsibility and answerability in a mass society. In the post-war period, the traditional amateurism and voluntarism of sport has been supplemented by successive governments in the interests of social cohesion, national identity, and popularity. But sport cannot be seen merely as a victim in this process: through its lobbying fora, notably the CCPR, the Sports Council, and the British Olympic Association (BOA), it has courted investment, publicity, and facilities from the state for reasons linked to the agendas of the various interest groups involved. With these contexts in place, we are able to examine ways in which the relationship between state and sport has developed over the period.

FORMS OF INVOLVEMENT

As with the reasons for involvement, it is worth modelling the general methods of involvement. These have been most comprehensively conceptualised by John Hargreaves' 'three modes of intervention':[35] state repression of sport, such as legal controls on certain activities; political ritual in sport, exemplified by the presence of governors at the sporting pastimes of the governed in capacities of patronage; and the 'programmed welfare provision' of sport, which covers state-funded sports facilities, such as municipal swimming pools and tennis courts. In addition to these modes, Whannel has identified the state's role in regulating and licensing sporting activities as a form of state involvement.[36] While this partially overlaps with Hargreaves' notion of repression, it is useful to distinguish as it allows us to see the legal accommodation of some sporting activities, such as betting on horse-racing, as distinct from the legal prohibition of others, such as cock-fighting. The agencies involved in this intervention include central government departments, local government, individual politicians and leaders, and quangos such as the Sports Council and the Countryside Commission. The most significant feature of this is that it does not, as such, include a ministry of sport. For the UK, this approach was never really an option: not only did welfarist political ideology not extend as far as running leisure pursuits from the centre, but the strong amateur and voluntary tradition in British sport militated against such an idea.[37] The social democratic model assumed by John Hargreaves thus has the state seeing itself as provider and facilitator rather than controller. Based on these insights, we can look at some of the methods used through concrete examples: first, the establishment of formal channels of communication between state and sport; second, the provision of amenities by local authorities; third, the control of sport through permissive and prohibitive legislation; and finally, involvement in sport for diplomatic reasons. The choice of these themes should not disguise other areas that could be considered in this connection, including the role of sport and physical education in state schools and the National Curriculum,[38] and the impact upon sport of broadcasting legislation.[39]

The most dramatic method used has been the formal establishment of a governmental body to act as an overseer of sport, and to provide a channel of communication between state and sport. The idea of a 'sports development council' as a centrally funded body that could invest in and develop elite and mass sport was one of Wolfenden's recommendations. The significance of Wolfenden in its context can be seen by that fact that it was debated in the House of Commons in April 1961. Labour, in opposition, immediately flagged their support of a sports development council and developed it as part of their manifesto for the next election, while the Conservative government made a number of initiatives, most notably the appointment of Lord Hailsham, the Lord President of the Council, as the Minister with Special Responsibility for Sport.[40] When Labour won the next general election, in October 1964, they immediately acted upon their commitment. The new Prime Minister, Harold Wilson, demonstrated his belief that sport, along with industrial training and the arts, was one of the 'subjects essential to Britain's economic and social development which had not been given adequate priority in the past'.[41] In February 1965, the Advisory Sports Council was established. This was backed up by the new government's public relations commitment to sport, seen most cynically in the use of the New Year's Honours List to decorate popular sportsmen and women: Stanley Matthews' knighthood, the first to an active footballer, is the classic example.[42] The Sports Council was constituted of various experts and specialists, including Sir Learie Constantine, Dr Roger Bannister, Walter Winterbottom of the Football Association as Director, and David Munrow of the CCPR and University of Birmingham's Physical Education Department.[43] Denis Howell, the new minister, took the role of Chairman, and Sir John Lang, his principal advisor from the Department of Education and Science (DES), became his deputy. The Council's four committees – international, research and scientific, sports development and coaching, and facilities planning – give a good view of its remit.[44] The structure chosen did not please all supporters of government involvement in sport: an influential pamphlet from Christopher Chataway and the Conservative Political Centre published the following year, for example, claimed that sport was too diverse to be run on an Arts Council model.[45] However, the fact that Conservatives were arguing in favour of continuing a state funding policy for sport helps to place this development firmly in the context of consensus politics.

The emergence of the state's machinery of Sports Council and ministerial responsibility can thus clearly be rooted in the wider political context of the late 1950s and early 1960s. The work of this machinery has shifted since in line with different political agendas and needs. Coghlan gives the best detailed summary of the administrative history, and Houlihan and Hargreaves both provide concise critical overviews, which need not be replicated here,[46] but some key features are worth noting. In 1972, it was restructured to meet the original vision of

Wolfenden by becoming an executive body by Royal Charter, which involved the effective assimilation of the CCPR and freedom from direct ministerial control. This technically gave the Sports Council more independence, although Howell has queried the 'independent' status of a body that was to be chaired and constituted by government appointees,[47] funded by government, and should, in the words of the Royal Charter, 'have regard to any general statements on the policy of Our Government that may from time to time be issued to it by Our Secretary of State'.[48] Clearly, this administrative step brought the Sports Council into a new relationship with government. While it was no longer chaired by the minister, as had been the case under Howell, the terms of the Charter ensured that wider government policy would be a consideration in the organisation's work. In practical terms, this has entailed the Sports Council's continued support for elite sport, particularly through the running of training centres at Bisham Abbey, Lilleshall, and Crystal Palace, and specialised outdoor centres at Plas y Brenin and Holme Pierrepont for mountaineering and water sports respectively. Other tasks have included the co-ordination of the various providers of sport, including the commercial, voluntary, and public sectors, and a strong emphasis on the development of 'sport in the community'. It is this latter aspect that shows most clearly that one of the Sports Council's functions from the government's perspective has been to promote sport as an agent of cohesion in otherwise fragmentary environments. This became apparent in various statements. The 1975 White Paper *Sport and Recreation* was particularly blunt on this, with its claim that 'by reducing boredom and urban frustration, participation in active recreation contributes to the reduction of hooliganism and delinquency among young people'.[49] This paper also made a link between elite sporting success and community provisions, seeing international victories as means of raising 'national morale' and stimulating 'the interest of young people to take part themselves'.[50] The emphasis on local sports facilities as diversions was also evident in the Sports Council's 1982 *Sport in the Community*, which declared a shift in policy from its heavy funding of elite sport, where 45 per cent of its budget was going, towards the depressed areas: 'The deteriorating situation in terms of unemployment, and the problems caused by social unrest in the inner cities have brought about a serious rethink by the Sports Council in terms of strategy for the future.'[51] The application of this policy of providing local sports facilities in order to deter social disorder was seen most obviously in Northern Ireland. In Belfast, for example, the population size warranted eight sports centres according to central figures, but was provided with fourteen, turning it by 1979 into 'one of the most well-endowed [cities] in western Europe'.[52] This provision was defended by planners within Northern Ireland who stressed the problems that differentiated their situation from that faced by their counterparts elsewhere in the UK: 'We set up 14 not 8, because the Sports Council in England who drew up the figures hadn't the problems we had, they didn't have the population massacring themselves.'[53] Although these centres generally became associated with republican and unionist users, and became the sites for symbolic battles over the issue of flag-flying, the actual provision was clearly motivated by a desire to divert young people from involvement in the sectarian violence.[54] The intensity of the violence, and the opportunities for young people to get involved in it, were greater in Northern Ireland than elsewhere, but while the provision there may have been quantitatively different from other inner city areas, it was not qualitatively so. This policy became apparent in government funding, most notably in the 1978–9 budget for the Sports Council which earmarked £800,000 for inner city work: 'Thus "sport for all" slowly became "sport for the disadvantaged" and "sport for inner city youth".'[55] However much politicians publicly present this as being about opportunity and excellence, the subtext of social control based on functionalist assumptions about sport is never far from view.

A related feature of this formalisation of the relationship between state and sport that is worth considering separately is the allocation of sport as a ministerial responsibility, first experimented with by Macmillan's appointment of Hailsham, and formalised by Wilson's choice of Howell. The informality of the first appointment has been stressed by his successor, who noted that as Hailsham 'was responsible for almost everything for which there was no specific ministerial responsibility, such as the North-east, no one expected much' from him.[56] Hailsham himself later described the appointment as 'bizarre': 'I am no particular admirer of organized and commercialized sport'.[57] He described his role as being 'more a liaison officer than a government spokesman',[58] and how he originally envisaged the need 'not for a Ministry but for a focal point under a Minister'.[59] The significant point, though, is that such an appointment was made as a crucial feature of the state–sport relationship. Wilson raised the profile of the post by appointing Howell, who had a good working knowledge of sport and had been a Football League referee. His sport work was part of his portfolio as a Joint Under-Secretary of State at the DES. However, the appointment has not remained static. It has moved departments in line with changing government thinking on sport's exact character. Grayson, who is highly critical of the post's fluctuating history, tabulates the incumbents, their dates of office, and their constitutional status. What emerges is a picture of shifting designations and definitions of what sport is and where it belongs.[60] The post shifted from the DES in 1969 when Wilson moved Howell and his post to the Ministry of Housing and Local Government. Sport stayed in the renamed Department of the Environment (DoE) under successive Conservative and Labour governments from 1970 to 1992, when it was brought under the auspices of the new Department of National Heritage (DNH). While the new designation was important in terms of flagging sport's significance as a part of national culture alongside the arts, tourism, broadcasting, and museums and galleries, this administrative arrangement has helped to perpetuate one of the major problems of ministerial responsibility: no minister has ever had control of all of the state's links with sport. In 1994, Grayson identified fifteen different departments apart from the DNH which were 'relevant to sport', including the DoE for the planning of playing fields, the Treasury for tax and VAT matters in sport, and the Foreign and Commonwealth Office for international and diplomatic issues.[61] This diversity was linked by Houlihan to the 'lack of a clear statutory base' for sport. His analyses of successive governments' attempts to develop and implement policy on football hooliganism and drug use in sport showed up the problems that this 'fragmentation of administrative and policy responsibility' caused.[62] The problems were shown up very clearly in the parliamentary debate on the proposed boycott of the 1980 Olympic Games, when the minister with special responsibility for sport, Hector Monro, was, according to his successor, 'not allowed to speak': 'It more than graphically illustrated the lowly recognition and, indeed, the lowly position of a Sports Minister in a Conservative Government.'[63]

While this 'current chaos which pervades Whitehall and Westminster's lack of a comprehensive and intelligent approach to sport and recreation'[64] is partially mitigated by the co-ordinating work of the Civil Service Sport and Recreation Division,[65] it does help to highlight the historical and continuing political reluctance to prioritise sport more fully as a single ministerial issue in its own right. Houlihan summarises the reasons against sole responsibility, not least the point made in the 1973 Cobham Report that for many of these departments, sport is a 'by-product of some primary function – forestry and education are examples'.[66] He also notes that some ministers have taken a very proactive role towards sport as a whole. The best example has been Colin

Moynihan, who held the post between 1987 and 1990, and, after Howell, was the incumbent with the highest public profile.[67] Like Howell, Moynihan had plenty of sporting experience: as a boxing blue at Oxford, and more famously as the cox to Oxford's victorious Boat Race crew in 1977, and to the British Olympic eight at Moscow in 1980, where they won silver, and Los Angeles in 1984. (The irony of one of Thatcher's later ministers having ignored her calls for a boycott of Moscow is an interesting one.) The debate over the exact role and function of the minister is unlikely to be over: its almost nomadic history should encourage us to expect future changes. However, the historical development of the position helps us to see the essential paradox at the heart of the state's links with sport: as a leisure time activity traditionally run largely on private and voluntary lines, there has been no commitment to a direct official takeover. Instead of a Ministry of Sport, there has been a quango, 'a typically British "non-political" form of intervention, similar to the BBC . . . , an institution poised between state and civil society';[68] instead of a Minister of Sport, a roving post with frequently redefined responsibilities, but (apart from the coincidental Cabinet representation during Hailsham's tenure) never of higher position than Minister of State.

While the establishment of the Sports Council and the allocation of ministerial responsibility have been amongst the most high-profile ways in which the relationship has developed, the role of local government has probably been as significant for everyday access to sport. Financially, local government 'is by far the most significant vehicle for the delivery of leisure services'.[69] In 1990, for example, 90 per cent of public money being spent on sport and recreation was from local authorities.[70] Houlihan has provided a good historical overview of the process by which local authorities developed their own leisure provisions.[71] The process began in the nineteenth century, with local authorities building sports amenities such as public baths and playing fields: these were rooted in a mixture of public health and paternalism, but they ensured access to sport for local populations. Throughout the twentieth century, the actual provision of amenities has remained localised, with central government, respectively through the CCPR and the Sports Council, providing policy frameworks and grants, although much has been developed at the local level without specific requirements. In the immediate post-war period, provision remained rather low and haphazard as the shift towards personal and private sport was absorbed, and as late as 1971, there were only 500 local authority swimming pools and twenty sports halls in the entire country.[72] With the shift to Sport for All acknowledged by the Sports Council, and the maturation of mass sport as a welfare issue, the 1970s and 1980s saw a burgeoning of provision by local authorities. This included the construction of swimming pools – 700 new ones between 1971 and 1989, a 140 per cent increase in eighteen years – and purpose-built sports centres – 1,000 new ones by 1989, a 500 per cent increase, with the new buildings generally offering flexible facilities for multiple sports and users from varied age, class, and gender groupings. By the late 1970s, the municipal sports centre was a common feature in towns and cities, taking its place alongside more traditional public amenities such as swimming pools, playing fields, and tennis courts. Again, the Northern Ireland example shows a different model in use: whereas the legislation governing local authorities' policies was permissive in England and Wales, it has been mandatory in Northern Ireland.[73]

However, with the changing context of funding for local government from the late 1970s, caused by strategic cuts and change in central government economic policy, the provision of these amenities was restructured in the 1980s and 1990s, with an emphasis on commercial provision on a competitive tendering basis that was formalised in the 1988 Local Government Act.[74] Tendering, unlike the more radical option of selling the amenities to the private sector, ensured a continued local authority answerability on provision, and kept local facilities within the wider framework of local strategic planning. It also allowed for the continued provision of subsidised services for users with special needs and on low incomes, groups unlikely to have been catered for under purely commercial management.[75] Alongside this, and growing out of what Henry has identified as the Gramscian cultural politics of the New Urban Left,[76] has been a commitment to the needs and differences of local users. Here, sports facilities have been targeted not just at different age groups, ethnic groups, and at women as in the Sports Council's agenda, but also at gay and disabled users; and, more radically, funding has been awarded to alternative sporting activities linked to different minority groups as a way of promoting diversity and cosmopolitanism. Labour's administration of the last Greater London Council (GLC), from 1982 until its abolition in 1986, has been held up as a model of this. Through funding and management strategies, the GLC signalled its recognition of sport and leisure as political issues linked to people's access to resources, and set up the 'specific aim . . . to increase participation among "underserved" groups'.[77] While some of these initiatives were damaged by the restructuring of local government in the 1980s, a legacy of this work has survived into the 1990s. Mixed with the liberal assumptions of Sport for All and the inherent commitment of local authorities to provide services for their electorates, the differential pricing for those on low incomes, special women's and pensioners' sessions, and childcare provision are all defining features of mass sport at municipal level. With the changing contexts since 1945, these different strategies have been forthcoming to keep the local provision of sport as a central part of the state–sport relationship.

Another form of response has already been touched upon: legislation. Linked to the various reasons why the state has intervened, we can see the law being used as a direct and specific way of controlling sport. Broadly, in the post-war period sport has been affected by permissive and prohibitive laws, which offers a continuity from the long-term historical record of the state both banning and accommodating sporting activities. With the increasing scale of sport, and the increasing amounts of money involved in it, the post-war period has seen an unprecedented range of legal interventions. By way of accommodation, one of the most important examples has been the gradual legislative acceptance of off-course cash betting in horse-racing, greyhound-racing, and other sports. The government had been raising revenue from on-course cash betting and off-course credit betting since the interwar period through taxation and the Tote, and its continued opposition to off-course cash betting became increasingly anomalous in the post-war period.[78] As an unquantifiable but significant illegal culture of street betting continued to flourish, the establishment of a legal basis was seen by many to be overdue when, in 1960, the Conservative government passed the Betting and Gaming Act. The first betting shops opened in May 1961.[79] Although these early shops were notoriously austere establishments, controlled by law to provide a minimum of comfort in order to prevent loitering, subsequent changes have shown a more liberal attitude as television screens, refreshments, and eventually Sunday opening have all been allowed. This major example of permissive laws helping sport can be backed up by others linked to Sunday trading, contractual regulation, sex discrimination, and fair trading. In part, they fit with the context of extended welfarism, but they have also been strongly connected to the development of commercial interests in sport which have required a firmer legal footing than in the pre-war period.

However, legislation affecting sport has also been passed in order to control and repress certain activities, rather than to accommodate them, and existing laws have been used against sports for the same end. Football supporters have been the most targeted group in this context.[80]

Crowd disasters at Ibrox, Valley Parade, and Hillsborough all inspired government investigations (by Wheatley, Popplewell, and Taylor respectively) which led to legal changes to the structures of spectating. Safety certificates, limited capacities, and eventually the introduction of all-seater stadia were used to deal with the specific problems caused by uncontrolled crowd movements, fire hazards, and overcrowding of terraces, but they have also had wider impact upon the autonomy of spectators, and current Labour party proposals to review the all-seater requirement show that this debate is not over. Hooliganism has also inspired legislation when it became clear that existing legal powers were not preventing football-related violence and disorder. For example, the Conservatives' 1985 Sporting Events Act, a pragmatic response to the Heysel disaster, made the possession of alcohol and offensive weapons at sports events specific offences, and the opportunity for restructuring behaviour after Hillsborough led to the 1991 Football (Offences) Act, which proscribed pitch invasions, the throwing of missiles, and obscene and racist chants.[81]

A different form of legal suppression has also been evident in animal sports, which have a long history of legal proscription. The survival of illegal cock-fighting has been claimed for our period, but new controls were brought in to deal with dangerous dogs in 1991, when the Dangerous Dogs Act prohibited the breeding and sale of such fighting dogs as pit bull terriers and tosas. Fox-hunting has also had its critics in Parliament and government throughout the post-war period, with various attempts to ban the sport being unsuccessful: as Thomas has shown, the Labour government's attempt to ban coursing and stag-hunting in 1949 failed, and was followed by the appointment of the Scott Henderson Committee to study the issue, which reported in 1951 that hunting was the best means of control. Another Labour bill against coursing in 1975–6, which got through the House of Commons, was rejected in the House of Lords.[82] These limited attempts at repression have come alongside growing public antipathy towards hunting: surveys carried out in 1978 and 1994 found those in favour of bans on fox-hunting and coursing at 54 per cent and 69 per cent respectively.[83] Successive governments have attempted, in the face of successful lobbying and vested interests, to repress this elite animal sport in a similar way to its historic repression of mass sports, with local authority action on banning hunts from their roads showing some success at county level. Debates over the safety of boxing, with calls from some medical professionals for it to be banned by law, show further evidence of the belief in the state's powers and rights to repress sporting practices deemed dangerous, inhumane, or uncivilised. Clearly, in the post-war period the mechanism of legal control, or at least its threat, has been felt in a variety of sporting settings. The criminal prosecution of sportsmen and women for actions committed during play is another part of this. High-profile cases in football have set the trend, where players accused of violent offences have been taken to law for resolution, rather than being left to the game's authorities for punishment. These have included Brentford's Gary Blissett, charged after breaking Torquay's John Uzzell's cheekbone with his elbow in 1991, and Manchester United's Eric Cantona for his attack on a fan in 1995. These cases have not always been successful, as intent is difficult to prove in a sporting context: Blissett, for example, was acquitted. While many in sport have resisted this development, arguing that governing bodies have their own rules and can control their own players, Foster has pointed out that it is an unavoidable situation given the economics of sport in the post-war period.[84] This form of state intervention to regulate and control behaviour in sport needs to be considered alongside other forms of repression.

The final method of intervention that needs to be explored is, in some ways, the most dramatic: the use of international sport as a medium for diplomacy. British governments have informally taken an interest in sport for this reason since at least the first Olympic Games in 1896, and throughout the interwar period they gradually became more interested in sport as a form of cultural propaganda. The popular platform that international sport offered, and the national representation that it rested upon, have historically made it tempting for the channelling of specific messages to other countries, and as sports organisations have actively courted support and assistance from governments, it has historically been a two-way relationship. The interwar precedents reached a peak when the National government persuaded London and the BOA to withdraw its bid for the 1940 Olympic Games in order to let Tokyo win the award in the interests of Anglo-Japanese relations.[85] The Labour government backed the 1948 Olympic Games in London, with both material and diplomatic support, both as an exercise in earning dollars through tourism, and to help reconstruct relations after the war; Italy's presence, and the absence of Germany and Japan, were significant here. The Foreign Office's support for the 1945 British tour by Moscow Dynamo was another part of this process of using sport to cement relations and promote understanding. Throughout the developing Cold War, British governments maintained an interest in Olympic politics, gathering intelligence on the German,

Korean, and Chinese issues. However, these situations were largely dealt with in a covert and semi-official manner, generally through private dealings between civil servants and Olympic administrators. However, since the late 1960s, a number of high-profile diplomatic interventions have taken place, and it is worth noting these.

The first concerned South Africa.[86] The policy of apartheid was first applied to sport in 1956, and, as Guelke has shown, immediately drew international attention to the institutionalised racism of the Nationalist party. Opponents of the South African government urged other nations to sever sporting contacts along with economic ones to show their disapproval. Trevor Huddleston made the case forcefully in his influential *Naught for your Comfort*, where he argued that isolation in sport would damage white South Africans' 'self-assurance', and could be 'an extraordinarily effective blow to the racialism': 'It might even make the English-speaking South African awake to the fact that you can't play with a straight bat if you have no opponents.'[87] South African sport soon found itself increasingly isolated, most significantly with the International Olympic Committee's exclusion of South Africa before the 1964 Tokyo Olympic Games. Some opposition also became apparent in the UK, notably during the 1960 visit by South Africa's cricket team, with some protests outside grounds and public statements of opposition by David Sheppard, who refused to play, and John Arlott, who refused to commentate on the matches.[88] It was, however, the crisis caused by the Marylebone Cricket Club's (MCC's) stance over Basil D'Oliveira in 1968 that brought the issue to a head in the UK.[89] D'Oliveira, a Cape coloured who had moved to England in 1960, was not named in the MCC's party for the winter tour of South Africa despite his merit, an omission that led to protests and allegations that the MCC had bowed to South African pressure. Learie Constantine encapsulated the arguments in his observation: 'Speaking as a cricketer, the omission of D'Oliveira is to be regretted. Speaking as a West Indian, the circumstances of this omission are positively suspicious.'[90] D'Oliviera was quickly included in the face of this pressure, and the tour was accordingly banned by the South African government: Vorster claimed that the team 'is not the team of the MCC but the team of the Anti-Apartheid Movement'.[91] The Labour government maintained an interest in this messy affair throughout. Howell raised the issue with the MCC as early as January 1967, and was assured that the team would be selected on merit, but was unable to intervene when the original team was named.[92]

However, the whole issue raised public awareness of apartheid sport:

Nixon claims that it 'catapulted the sports boycott out of obscurity, pitching the anti-apartheid cause with unprecedented force and regularity onto both the front and back pages of the British national press',[93] and when the next crisis occurred in 1969, the British government was forced to intervene pragmatically. Anti-Apartheid Movement (AAM) members and Young Liberals formed the nucleus of a new group, the Stop The Seventy Tour (STST) campaign, which focused opposition against the South African cricket tour planned for 1970. STST used various tactics to publicise the situation, and employed direct action against the visiting South African rugby union team in the winter of 1969, including pitch invasions and confrontations with the police. At their fixture in Swansea, for example, the Springboks were met with a pitch invasion and a police response that led to injuries to 200 demonstrators and ten policemen.[94] In this atmosphere, the MCC continued its planning for the 1970 visit, but the threats of disruption to the cricket matches mounted: plans to litter pitches with broken glass, saturate them with oil, and even release 70,000 locusts on to the grass all led to the erection of barbed wire around the cricket grounds. The risks involved in allowing the tour to continue were great, particularly as 1970 was a general election year. Most obviously, it could give rise to riots around the matches, and so presented law and order problems. Second, it would aggravate race relations in the UK if the government was seen to be tolerant of apartheid ambassadors: this point was made in a celebrity letter to *The Times* from a group including David Sheppard (by then Bishop of Woolwich), Learie Constantine (by then Trinidad's High Commissioner in London), as well as Jeremy Thorpe, Reg Prentice, Edna O'Brien, and Henry Moore, who claimed that the tour would 'damage the already strained racial situation in this country'.[95] Third, the prospect of the tour strained Commonwealth relations, both in sport, with a threatened boycott of the 1970 Edinburgh Commonwealth Games, and more generally. The situation set up a classic case of pragmatic crisis management from the government. Prime Minister Harold Wilson spoke on the issue a number of times in the spring, calling for peaceful demonstrations against what he saw as the uncivilised sporting practice of racial selection, and in May, his Home Secretary Jim Callaghan asked the Cricket Council to cancel the tour 'on grounds of broad public policy'.[96] The tour was duly called off. The whole issue aroused much debate on the rights of a government to cancel sporting fixtures, and on the role of public opinion in influencing sport. For our purposes, it provides an excellent example of the way in which post-war governments have been able increasingly to see sport as part of their remit when it mattered, and of the public way in which the debate took place. The next Labour government furthered official British opposition to apartheid sport in 1977 with the signature, along with other Commonwealth governments, of the Gleneagles Declaration to withhold 'any form of support for, and . . . [to take] every practical step to discourage contact of competition by our nationals with sporting organizations, teams or sportsmen from South Africa'.[97] Again, this must be seen in the wider context of the need to maintain Commonwealth unity.

As well as the South African situation, which has been so relevant because of Commonwealth links and race relations in the UK, Cold War politics were also played out in sport by British governments during this period. The boycott of the 1980 Moscow Olympics provides a classic example of pragmatic diplomatic response as a means of intervention.[98] In January 1980, President Jimmy Carter of the USA warned the Soviet government that its failure to withdraw troops from Afghanistan might lead to an American boycott of the Olympics; when the 20 February deadline was missed, the United States Olympic Committee, under pressure from the government, voted in favour of a boycott. In the UK, the new Conservative government showed its support for the Americans by backing the boycott: Prime Minister Margaret Thatcher later claimed that 'the most effective thing we could do [to take action against the USSR] would be to prevent their using the forthcoming Moscow Olympics for propaganda purposes'.[99] However, the idea was not presented well to the BOA. After a number of private contacts between Thatcher, the Foreign Secretary Lord Carrington, and the Environment Secretary Michael Heseltine who had Cabinet-level responsibility for sport, a parliamentary debate was held on the following motion put by Lord Privy Seal, Sir Ian Gilmour: 'This House condemns the Soviet invasion of Afghanistan and believes that Great Britain should not take part in the Olympic Games in Moscow.'[100]

The government won the debate, and proceeded to impose this decision upon the BOA, but, in a crucial break with tradition, the BOA refused to co-operate with this line. Despite an apparently large amount of diplomacy – the official records will not be available until 2010 – the BOA saw this as an infringement of its independence. Its line, followed by some in Parliament, was that it was being used as a high-profile pawn. The BOA refused to be used in isolation from other Anglo-Soviet contacts in trade and diplomacy that were not being threatened just because sport was so public and emotive. As Howell had put it during the Commons debate:

How can we tell Steve Ovett . . . and others that they ought not to be taking part in sport in Moscow at the same time as the Minister [for Trade] is delighted that we have a new contract to build a chemical plant financed by Morgan Grenfell, Barclays and other banks?[101]

The government threatened bullying tactics, including the refusal of leave to civil servants competing. There was a general pro-Olympic feeling that the government had steamrollered into a situation to add cultural support to the special relationship with the USA, and had failed to consult the sporting bodies in advance of announcing the boycott. All precedents in the archives suggest that the BOA has traditionally been amenable to informal advances from government, but this time, the public nature of the declaration made it push against the government. A British team duly went to Moscow, and while the team registered its symbolic condemnation of the Soviet government by marching under the Olympic flag rather than the national one, the successes of Daley Thompson, Alan Wells, Steve Ovett, Sebastian Coe, Duncan Goodhew, and others were classed as British victories. Thatcher's memoirs are again interesting on this point: having criticised the British team for going to Moscow, she claims disingenuously 'of course, unlike their equivalents in the Soviet Union, our athletes were left free to make up their own minds'.[102] However, sixty-two nations did follow the American line and stay away, including the major sports powers of Japan and West Germany, along with such varied nations as Canada, Israel, China, Chile, and a number of Islamic nations. In all, 5,353 competitors from eighty-one nations took part, compared with 7,147 from 122 nations at Munich in 1972, the last Games not to have been hit by a boycott.[103]

While there are obvious risks involved in writing history from case study, not least their atypicality, these examples of British governments using sport for diplomatic ends over apartheid and the Soviet invasion of Afghanistan deserve elaboration because of their scale. Indeed, the Moscow boycott debate has been credited with making sure that 'British sport could never again be politically innocent'.[104] They are also crucial because of their role in the whole sport and politics debate that has developed throughout the twentieth century, most notably since the Second World War. The popular perceptions of the debate, based around an idealist view that the two are separate spheres, are more commonly informed by high-level crises such as these than by the structural politics of municipal swimming pools and Sports Council grants. It has been these crises that have forced people to look at the common ground between sport and state, most obviously in terms of national representation and the role of the sports arena in the expression of opinion between two or more nations. This was why the AAM used sport as part of its wider campaign, just as the Conservative government used the Moscow Olympics as part of its wider policy. However, all of the responses discussed in this chapter need to be seen as part of the relationship between sport and the state. To separate the dramatic from the mundane is to reinforce the idea that formal channels of involvement are somehow less political than boycotts and protests. What the post-war history of the British experience shows is that, as a result of growing state interest, many sports are now on a firmer financial footing than they were at the start of the period; more people have access to locally run amenities; and sport has a permanent structure in Whitehall for support and co-ordination. As the terms of the Sports Council's 1972 Royal Charter show, it would be naïve for sports administrators to believe that there is no catch to this support.

Chapter 2

Sport, the nation, and the world

INTRODUCTION

The idea that representative sport acts as a public location for national identity is one with a long history and a powerful present. 'The nation' has been formally enshrined in sport, through the use of flags and anthems in ceremonial aspects, and through the widespread use of national colours in sports clothes. A national team can, in media and popular discourse, take on the guise of the nation itself. When we say, for example, that 'Great Britain always underachieves in the Olympic Games', we consensually cut out the qualifying reference to tiny numbers of sportsmen and women practising specific sports, and assume a link between nation and team: sport provides 'the metonym whereby the nation is presented as a single sentient being'.[1]

This assumption does not take place in a vacuum. It is one of the examples of everyday flag-waving that Billig has characterised as 'banal nationalism', where the symbols of national unity and identity are regularly rehearsed in the public eye, forming the basis for the hot nationalism of war or other national crises.[2] It can also be seen to be part of how the national community 'imagines' itself, particularly when sportsmen and women are seen to embody certain traits that are popularly held as national characteristics.[3] Newspaper coverage of the four British national rugby union teams, for example, takes us into a world populated by 'dependable' Englishmen, 'crafty' Irishmen, 'dauntless' Scotsmen, and 'poetic' Welshmen.[4] This link can make explicit the notion that the physical performances of a country's chosen representatives are structurally linked to the more general state of that nation, particularly its health, stability, and world position. For the post-war British period, this has given rise to the populist playing out of debates over decline and erosion in line with the UK's changing world position, with 'defeats on the playing field . . . represented as a kind of litmus test for the nation's decline'.[5] Some have dismissed this idea: Francis Wheen, for example, adapted Ruskin's idea of the 'pathetic fallacy' as the 'athletic fallacy . . . the tendency to see English sporting performances as somehow symptomatic of the nation's health'.[6] However, the popular perception that there is a connection makes this a real issue. This can perhaps be seen at its most obvious in the early to mid-1950s, when the UK's sporting 'decline' was placed alongside decolonisation and an obvious decline in international political stature, a context that helped to formalise state involvement. It has also been present in the 1990s, when press coverage readily placed Prime Minister John Major as an ineffective leader alongside similar descriptions of those in charge of the England football and cricket teams.[7]

However, while the basic notion of national representation in sport may seem a simple one, it is problematic for a number of reasons. First, it is complicated by the confusing and overlapping boundaries of national sport units. Owing to various accidents and traditions, different sports have developed different organisational models for national representation. At the Olympic Games, the UK has historically been represented by a team designated as Great Britain, and many performers from all parts have achieved excellence: in athletics alone, for example, Welshman Lynn Davies, Scots Alan Wells and Liz McColgan, Mary Peters from Northern Ireland, as well as numerous Englishmen and women, have all entered the pantheon of 'British Olympians', as, indeed, have many born in the British Empire and Commonwealth.[8] However, these same performers can also represent their country in other competitions, including the Commonwealth Games, where England, Northern Ireland, Scotland, and Wales have separate teams. In football, the four nations of the UK are separately represented.[9] In rugby union, the countries are split into England, Scotland, Wales, and Ireland, with Northern Ireland and Eire providing a joint team: this case of Ireland existing as a sporting entity over seventy years after it ceased to exist as a political entity is repeated in cricket, hockey, and croquet. Moreover, a rugby union team drawing on all of the UK plus Eire, the British Lions, also exists. In cricket, Scotland has been refused admission to the International Cricket Conference on the grounds that it is not a country, a decision that ought to raise questions about England's role, but does not because of tradition and practice.[10] English football teams located close to Wales, such as Shrewsbury Town, are allowed to enter the Welsh Cup, but if they win it, they are not allowed to represent Wales in the European Cup

Winners Cup.[11] The picture is further confused by the existence of European teams for the Ryder Cup and the Solheim Cup in men's and women's golf respectively. While this situation clearly allows for sportsmen and women, the media, and spectators to practise acts of dual or even triple nationality, it also highlights the fact that the apparently simple fact of national representation in sport is highly problematic in the British case.

A second complicating factor is the existence of a number of sports that operate at an individual, rather than national, level. Here, while an individual's success or failure may bring nationalist media attention, the competitor is essentially representing self or sponsor. Grand Prix motor racing, with multinational teams based around companies, is an example, as are golf, athletics, and tennis for certain events. In the last sport, the priority that a number of players place on the appropriate professional circuit over national representation has led to a decline in significance of the Davis Cup and the Wightman Cup in the post-war period. This trend could be linked to the wider state of post-nationalism, where an individual's nationality is seen as an increasingly meaningless label.[12] Linked to this is the whole problem of how nationality is defined for a sportsman or woman, and again, different sports and different countries have established different practices. Birthplace, parents' birthplace, grandparents' birthplace, residence, spouse's nationality, and political defection have all been foundations for individuals representing 'their' country in different settings. This was clearly illustrated by the Zola Budd affair around the 1984 Olympic Games. The South African athlete, unable to compete internationally because of her country's ban, was hurriedly made a British citizen on the strength of her British grandfather, and duly ran in the controversial 3,000 metres at Los Angeles.[13] It has also been seen in the highly effective use of the grandparental qualification that the Football Association of Ireland (FAI) used to recruit otherwise English players in the 1980s and 1990s, which quickly turned Eire into a significant footballing nation: the English joke that any player who had ever drunk a pint of Guinness could qualify as Irish had an air of envy about it, particularly during the 1988 European Championships. So, with nationality being less relevant in some sports than in others, and with nationality itself being increasingly blurred rather than fixed, we can see complications in the overall concept.

A final problem is the whole question of what national representation, even in its common-sense form, actually means. Who or what are the players representing? Work on Scotland and Ireland has shown how tensions over religious and ethnic differences can influence team selection as well as the symbolism of the sport. Taken further, this line of enquiry leads us into how different sports are linked to class factions and/or specific gender relations which may not offer a consensually agreed 'national' representation. Jarvie and Walker referred to the 'amorphous identities and expressions of nationhood'[14] that emerged from a study of sport and Scottish nationalism, where such figures as Denis Law, Nancy Riach, and Liz McColgan 'might all share the similar experience of representing Scotland in sport [but] are divided by a number of factors, the principal of which are gender, class, locality, and . . . the historical period through which they experienced a sense of Scotland'.[15] Also, as Maguire and Bale have suggested, the ties of gender, class, ethnicity, and sexuality that override nationality have created 'a new order of globally recognized sports migrants' who 'assume a transnational significance beyond their sporting prowess'. Citing Muhammad Ali, Arthur Ashe, Martina Navratilova, and Ruud Gullit, this idea confirms the difficulty of reaching an agreement on what national representation means.[16]

The issue is thus far from simple, despite the easy appeal of the familiar image of a national team in national colours singing the national anthem before a game; and while Hobsbawm was correct in his claim that the 'imagined community of millions seems more real as a team of eleven named people',[17] these complicating factors demonstrate the need for a flexible historical approach to the subject, and should be kept in mind throughout this survey. After a brief historiographical review, we will examine the growth of international sport, and the place that teams and individuals from the UK have held within it. We will then move on to examine sport within the UK, looking at ways in which Scotland, Wales, and Northern Ireland have maintained difference from England through sport.

The historiography of sport and national identity in the UK has emerged most conspicuously since the 1970s, and can, in common with many of the themes covered in this book, be seen as one of the areas that has been developed after the initial ground of sports history was covered. Moreover, the emergence can be linked to wider trends in political and sociological discourse relating to the structure and stability of the UK, most notably the theory and practice of separate identities for the peripheral nations of Northern Ireland, Scotland, and Wales. Before this – and, indeed, in much uncritical historiography since – the label 'Britain' was frequently used to mean 'England', thus maintaining cultural, economic, and political assumptions about power within the UK. Indeed, it is clear that while the marginal countries have all enjoyed a growing body of sports research, the specific study of England as such remains underdeveloped thanks to the longevity of such assumptions, popularly displayed by the use of the Union flag for followers of specifically English national teams.[18] In Holt's words, 'Englishness and English nationalism are unjustly neglected subjects, especially where sports are concerned.'[19] Politically, such assumptions were increasingly challenged from the late 1960s onwards, when the revival of Irish republicanism in Northern Ireland, combined with the electoral emergence of Plaid Cymru and the Scottish National Party (SNP), served to question the relationships between centre and margins. As we shall see, sport played a role in this process: for our immediate concern of historiography, we can see a gradual growth of differential and critical analysis. Primarily, it made itself felt in a range of official histories, such as Thorburn's on Scottish rugby and Smith and Williams' more critical book on Welsh rugby, both of which emphasised difference and separate development from the English game.[20] Short's work on the Gaelic Athletic Association (GAA) in Northern Ireland has had a similar emphasis.[21] By the mid-1980s, the academic work was being more influenced by the wider debate on relations and structures of power within the UK. Jarvie summarised the mood – at least for Scottish studies – in 1986 by calling for the analysis of sport to be included in the 'debate in Scottish politics which urges historians, educationalists, cultural critics etc to challenge the dominant cultural power, question its values and assumptions, enquire into its operations and generate alternative codes for understanding Scottish culture and history'.[22] This call, taken with the preliminary work that Moorhouse had conducted on how Scottish football did not fit into the structures assumed by analysts of the English game,[23] has led to a decade's worth of rich critical work on Scottish sport. Moorhouse has continued to stress the ways in which English assumptions and theories on football are historically and sociologically inapplicable in Scotland;[24] while Murray, Finn, and Bradley have explored various dimensions of Scottish football's ethnic, religious, and social dimensions, and Jarvie has explored issues of landownership, environmentalism, and class relations in Scottish field sports and Highland Gatherings.[25] This strand of research was consolidated in 1994 by Jarvie and Walker's *Scottish Sport in the Making of the Nation*, a collection of critical essays.[26] Moreover, Jarvie's 1986 criticism that mainstream academic discussion was not taking sport seriously has, to a degree, been met by inclusion of studies on Scottish sport in a number of non-specialist collections.[27] For example, Moorhouse's work on Scottish football supporters in a book on the sociology of Scotland, and Walker's essay on Glasgow Rangers in a collection on Scottish Protestant popular culture, have set analyses of sport alongside other areas of debate, such as religion and education.[28] Another sign of the acceptance of sport came with the inclusion of McCarra's essay on sport in a cultural history of Scotland, sharing space with such areas as art, rock music, and engineering.[29]

Scotland has had more critical sports analysis than Wales or Northern Ireland. The complicated issue of Irish sports history has given rise to a rich historiography, but the majority of it has been concerned with the period before partition in 1921, and specifically with the links between sport and Irish nationalism that found its organisational outlet in the GAA.[30] Given the overt links between sport, politics, culture, and nationalism that the GAA has embodied, it is not surprising that it should have enjoyed the greatest share of historians' attention. However, the post-1945 period, and the experience of Northern Ireland as opposed to Eire, has been relatively underexplored by historians. Sugden and Bairner's work has been exceptional here, offering explorations of central and local government sports provision, the relations between Gaelic and non-Gaelic sports in Northern Ireland, and the problematic relations between sports organisations in Northern Ireland and Eire.[31] While this body of research uses historical insights, it is rooted in the present-centred disciplines of sports studies and politics, and there is room for more specifically historical research to be conducted here. Wales has been less extensively explored, excepting the critical work by Smith and Williams (both collectively and singly) on rugby union and other sports,[32] and a wealth of localised studies of specific clubs and towns. This relatively low coverage is, in some ways, surprising. The language issue for some of the source material is a problem for non-Welsh speakers, but the scope for wider research is there.

Alongside this coverage, globalism has emerged as an area of investigation. This concept, developed in geography, cultural studies, media studies, and elsewhere, is based on the assumption that the world is developing an increasingly global culture, with television, advertising, corporate economic strategies, labour migration, political ideologies, and information technology all serving to create flows between nations, leading to a 'diminishing of contrasts'.[33] The use of this approach in sports studies and sports history 'is still in its early stages',[34] but it has already inspired a significant debate.[35] Significantly, it is one that has attracted some of the same individuals who have worked on Celtic nationalism within the UK. The crossover is seen clearly in Williams's and Moorhouse's essays on the flow of Welsh rugby union players to rugby league in England, and the dependency of Scottish football on transfers to England.[36] Maguire, in particular, has been very influential in broadening out the research agenda. His offerings have included theoretical discussions of globalism, as well as applied discussions of how basketball and American football in the UK have illustrated the trend.[37] Sugden has gone beyond his Irish work and collaborated with Tomlinson to explore global football, both as editors of *Hosts and Champions* on the 1994 World Cup, and in current research on world football.[38] Here, Tomlinson has extended his interests shown in his earlier editorial collaborations with Whannel on the Olympic Games and the football World Cup.[39] Moreover, the leading journals in the field have become increasingly cosmopolitan, and international debates on sports history have been encouraged by contacts through conferences and courses. At a time when English rugby league has been restructured to include a Paris-based club, and when overseas footballers are becoming commonplace at all levels of the professional game in the UK, we can see a clear context for this line of enquiry.

THE UK AND THE WORLD OF SPORT

International contacts in sport have been increasing since their formal emergence in the late nineteenth century. With strong connections to the predominant ideology of the nation state, and fuelled by British imperial and commercial expansion, the last decades of the century witnessed the establishment of a range of international contacts in various sports. Cricket contacts between England and Australia, New Zealand, and South Africa; football and rugby union representative matches between the constituent parts of the UK; and the Olympic Games are amongst the most famous and enduring of these contacts. This period has elicited a great deal of research, particularly on the roles of sport in imperial relations, and on British influences in 'teaching the world to play'.[40] It has been linked to the '"take-off" phase of globalization',[41] characterised by competition, regulation, and standardisation between sports in different countries. Moreover, it is clear that this period saw the consolidation of the idea in many countries that 'elite sports serve the purpose of national or political representation'.[42] The 'athletic fallacy' clearly has long roots. This development, with European nations predominant, continued through the interwar period, exemplified most obviously by the growth in size of the Summer Olympic Games, and the establishment of the Winter Olympic Games from 1924 and the football World Cup from 1930.[43]

With this amount of structural development before the Second World War, international sport came out of the war with strong foundations, and the different international climate of the post-war period proved fertile for sport's further growth. Two strands are crucial here: the Cold War; and European decolonisation. Both allowed forms of rivalry to find expression in sport, most obviously in the competition between the USA and the USSR that began to characterise the Olympic Games from the Soviet arrival in 1952, a process that found its end in the boycotts of the 1980 and 1984 Olympics, held at Moscow and Los Angeles respectively. Post-colonial conflicts also influenced sport. For the British, cricket matches between England and India, Pakistan, Sri Lanka, and the West Indies provided a focus for popular discourses about nationalism, independence, and historical ties. This changing international climate helps to explain the changing context of world sport, and the attitude towards it held by the British. Other influences, notably the international co-operation of the United Nations (UN), the growth of European federalism, and the realignment of national boundaries in Europe after the Cold War, have also played a part.

The number of international contacts and competitions has expanded since the war. A few examples can show the range and size of this trend. The Olympic Games have mushroomed, bringing in over 100 nations every four years since 1968, bar the boycotted Games of Montreal (1976) and Moscow (1980): even Los Angeles (1984), hit by a Soviet-backed boycott, attracted teams from 141 nations.[44] The football World Cup has grown from its Euro-American basis, now bringing in qualifying groups based on Europe, South America, Africa, Asia, Oceania, and Concacaf: in 1994, the finals in the USA involved Saudi Arabia, South Korea, Cameroon, Morocco, and Nigeria, as well as competitors from Europe and Latin America.[45] A significant future development here is that the 2002 World Cup will be co-hosted by Japan and South Korea, the first time that the tournament has left Europe and the Americas, and the first time that it has been shared. The World Cup has been underpinned by continent-wide events on an alternate cycle, including the African Nations Cup and the European Nations Championship, the latter instituted in 1958 by the European governing body, Union Européenne de Football Association (UEFA), founded in 1954. These representative tournaments have been complemented by club-based events, of which UEFA's European Champion Clubs Cup, started in 1955–6 and won by Real Madrid for the first five seasons, was the first and remains the most prestigious and lucrative.[46] Rugby league built on earlier contacts by establishing its first

International Board in 1948, with Australia, France, Great Britain, and New Zealand as founder members. This sport saw international competition regularised beyond tours in the 1950s with its first World Cup in 1954, won by Great Britain in France, and with an experiment in a European Club Championship involving the winners and runners-up of the domestic leagues in Great Britain and France. Spread over the season, and using home and away fixtures, Hull won the experimental 1956–7 event, also contested by Halifax, Albi, and Carcassone.[47]

Rugby union followed the trend towards formal international competition with its first World Cup in 1987, a development linked by various commentators to the sport's revolution that has also involved the open acceptance of professionalism: even as late as the mid-1970s, 'the idea of a rugby [union] World Cup would have seemed like the product of a fevered imagination'.[48] The three events so far, held quadrenially in Australia and New Zealand, the Five Nations, and South Africa, have demonstrated the sport's standing. Cricket also came to the idea of a regular international tournament relatively late, with the tradition of test matches proving an obstacle. The way was shown by the women's game, which organised its first World Cup in 1973 (won by hosts England), with the men's game holding its first in 1975. Similar tournament-based regular competitions can be seen to have started in numerous sports in this period, and women's football and rugby union have also developed their own world cups. This was not a planned process, and neither did it happen overnight: the thirty-three-year gap between the start of the world cups in rugby league and rugby union, for example, highlights the fact that variables beyond the notion of national prestige – in this case, based on class and amateurism – could delay the development of tournaments. Sport-specific differences apart, in a political context of shifting power blocs and contested nationalisms, and with media interest and sponsors' funds providing incentives, the spread of tournament play at international and continental levels has been a characteristic feature of the post-war period.

As can be seen from some of the examples already cited, teams and national organisations from the UK have been actively involved in these processes. When we note that numerous international and continental events in many sports have been hosted by the British, we can also see a high level of involvement. The biggest events have been the 1948 Olympic Games in London,[49] the Commonwealth Games of 1958 in Cardiff and Edinburgh in 1970 and 1986, the football World Cup of 1966 and European Championships of 1996 in England, and the 1991 rugby union World Cup, co-hosted by all of the game's Five Nations.

Alongside these heavily covered events have been a host of events in swimming, athletics, gymnastics, hockey, and others. However, despite the national approval that such exercises can indicate – particularly when they have received state funding and facilities – there has been a degree of ambivalence towards international competitions from various parts of the British sports establishment. This is famously illustrated by the debate over qualification for the 1950 football World Cup, the first for the British nations to enter. When the Fédération Internationale de Football Association (FIFA) declared the home international series as a qualifying group, and allowed for both winners and runners-up to proceed to the finals in Brazil, the football associations of Scotland, Wales, and Ireland declared that they would go only as champions.[50] England qualified, but the team's unhappy experiences in the finals underlined the gulf that existed between British football and the rest of FIFA. Attitudes have changed in different sports over the intervening period, and the growth of competition has had a number of implications for British sport, but it is worth considering the reasons for some of the resistance.

Essentially, it is a question of history. Britons, through military, educational, religious, and commercial contacts in the nineteenth century, helped to start organised sports worldwide. The number of sports clubs with English names, or with the name of their town or city anglicised in the club's name, is testimony to this proselytism: Sporting Gijon, Go Ahead Eagles of Deventer, The Strongest of La Paz, Newell's Old Boys of Rosario, Milan, and First Vienna illustrate this. The legacy of this proselytism has been, for much of the twentieth century, a frequently uncritical belief that as the inventors and developers of modern sport, the British should have an innate superiority in it. This can help to explain the aloofness that a number of British sports administrations showed towards the idea of international tournaments, such as the four football associations' attitudes towards FIFA in the 1930s, where the FA's 'main contribution to the early world cups was to pretend that they did not matter'.[51] British sports administrations already had traditions of their own forms of representative fixtures. Rugby union had the Five Nations championship; cricket had test matches with Australia (from 1880) and South Africa (from 1888), with other regular opponents gaining test status during the interwar period (West Indies in 1928, New Zealand in 1929, and India in 1932);[52] and football had its home internationals, formalised as such in 1883–4, making it the world's oldest football tournament.[53] The emphasis on this tournament above any wider international competition helped to promote an insularity about the representative game in the UK. While England played overseas opposition on a friendly basis from 1908 onwards, the other national sides were less cosmopolitan in their fixture lists. Scotland's first non-British internationals were played in 1929 during a short continental tour; Wales waited until 1933 before its first game with France; while Northern Ireland's first came as late as 1952, when France visited Belfast. Both rugby codes also had strong traditions of tour-based representative matches, where incoming touring sides from the other major playing countries would take on representative, regional, and club sides, and unified British teams would pay return visits. Finally, there were differences between the bulk of sports administrators in the UK, and their overseas counterparts. The issue of professionalism was the most divisive, keeping the four British associations out of full membership of FIFA from 1928 to 1947,[54] and setting up rifts between the four rugby union governing bodies and Fédération Française de Rugby between 1932 and 1939.[55] The strength of voluntary traditions in the administration of British sports helped to confirm the attitudes and assumptions behind British involvement in many international tournaments.

The post-war period has seen a marked erosion of this kind of resistance. Under the related influence of media coverage, commercial and financial rewards, and less tangible but still genuine notions of national prestige, individuals, clubs, and nationally organized representative teams have taken part in the growing world of sport. The success rates have been variable, but have tended on the whole to confirm that whereas the UK may once have held the balance of power in sport, it has diffused and shifted during the century. In the post-war Summer Olympics, Great Britain has never finished higher than seventh in the unofficial medal table, the position reached in 1956 at Melbourne (although it is worth noting that Great Britain has not finished inside the top four since Paris 1924, and has finished first only once, in London in 1908). While it has produced a number of athletes who have won Olympic golds, such as sprinters Alan Wells and Linford Christie, and middle-distance runners Sebastian Coe, Steve Ovett, and Steve Cram, the Olympic team as a whole has never had the strength in depth in all sports to match the teams from the USA, the USSR, and the other major post-war Olympic nations. In football, the only British representative team to win any international tournament has been England with the 1966 World Cup, and the British national sides have between them failed to qualify for the final stages of tournaments on a number of occasions. At the 1994 World Cup in the USA, none of the home sides were there, leaving it to Eire – most of whose players played professionally in the UK – to provide the focus for domestic attention in the UK. At club level, however, the English have been extremely successful in European competitions. At first, the Football League was resistant to the notion of European club football, for fear that it would interfere with the domestic scene: this classic case of isolationism was demonstrated when the League barred champions Chelsea from entering the inaugural European Cup in 1955–6. The following season, Manchester United 'defied the League'[56] and entered, getting as far as the semi-final where holders Real Madrid knocked them out. Between 1956 and 1992, despite the five-year European ban on English clubs after the Heysel disaster of 1985, England produced more winners of club competitions than any other country. The golden age here was undoubtedly 1977–82, when Liverpool (three times), Nottingham Forest (twice), and Aston Villa (once) kept the European Cup in England, joined by Ipswich Town as winners of the UEFA Cup in 1981. The difference between club and country, of course, is that club sides such as Liverpool had a 'long-term dependence on British players who were not English'.[57] Scottish clubs have made a smaller impact on European competition, although Celtic's 1967 European Cup triumph made them the first British team to win it, 'a triumph of will over infrastructure'.[58] In men's cricket, England's international fortunes have been generally low in the post-war period relative to the earlier years of the century, both in test and world cup events, although the national women's team has been more successful. Rugby league has seen British World Cup victories in 1954, 1960, and 1972, and while no British side has won the men's rugby union World Cup to date, England achieved respectable positions of second and fourth respectively in 1991 and 1995. What this brief summary of some leading sports should tell us is that the mixed fortunes of British club and representative teams in post-war international sport have confirmed that any historical supremacy has not stood the test of regular competition.

This was appreciated by some governing bodies sooner than others. The England football shocks of the early 1950s brought it home to the Football Association (FA), whereas the limited amount of international competition beyond the structures of the Five Nations and the British Lions allowed the four rugby unions to maintain a relatively isolationist stance into the late 1980s. The differential rates of facing up to a changing world of sport have not, however, disguised some common implications and responses. These have included the growth of a more professional culture, particularly in training and coaching but also in management and administration, and an increasing acceptance of non-British influences and personnel in sport.

The gap in training and coaching between British and non-British sporting cultures was evident in the interwar years, particularly when competing against rivals from Italy and Germany, where governmental backing had promoted sport. Changes were made in the UK after the war, necessitated by the increasing pressure of international events and the growth of British commitment to them. The example most discussed by historians has been the 'coaching campaign'[59] in English football, associated with the FA's appointment in 1946 of Walter Winterbottom as the Director of Coaching and the first manager of the national team. An ex-professional player and a qualified physical education instructor, Winterbottom helped to bring practical and theoretical work into the England team's preparation. Winterbottom has recalled the culture into which this scheme was launched, with its lack of ball practice, the 'stamina training' based on just six laps of the pitch, the minimal knowledge of the game's laws, and professionals' habit of keeping their skills secretive: 'we were so insular that we wouldn't believe that other methods could be used for doing things, other ways of playing the game could be better than ours'.[60] The changes were not, of course, instantly successful. The 1950 World Cup and the Hungarian defeats came during Winterbottom's tenure of office, and Meisl was able to claim in his influential 1955 critique of football that the manager 'often runs the team as the scarecrow runs an aviary'.[61] The role of selectors at international level and directors at club level continued to be questioned throughout the 1950s and 1960s, as it was increasingly felt that their lack of direct knowledge of the game was constraining the coaching and tactical side. This was attacked by Len Shackleton in his 1955 autobiography: the chapter entitled 'The average director's knowledge of football' consisted of an empty page, with a footnote stating 'This chapter has deliberately been left blank in accordance with the author's wishes'.[62] For England, the changes seemed to have been successful by the 1960s, with the increasing exposure to international competition in the 1950s helping to broaden out players' and coaches' awareness: the 1954 and 1958 World Cups, and the relatively successful entry of British teams into European club competitions, were influential here.[63] In 1963, the FA appointed Alf Ramsey as Winterbottom's successor. He was able to 'insist on the abandonment of an anachronistic selection committee' and gain 'full autonomy', which formed the basis for England's success in the 1966 World Cup.[64] Some commentators have noted how this success, based on workmanlike skills rather than flair, imposed a legacy of rigidity over the international team;[65] and the relatively brave appointments of Terry Venables and Glenn Hoddle as England coaches in the 1990s have been hailed as a break from this tradition. The improved relations between the FA and the league structures of the Premiership and Football League have helped here, providing limited programmes of domestic matches prior to internationals. While the impact of such a flair player as Hoddle on the England side remains to be tested at the highest levels, the growth of coaching and training culture in football since the war can be seen as part of the response to the changing international context of sport.

Other sports have also, at different speeds, embraced this cultural change, although the influence of international defeats was always a factor. The Scottish Rugby Union (SRU), for example, instituted its first regular coaching scheme in 1952 after the national side's run of poor performances.[66] In Wales, the downturn of the national rugby union side's fortunes in the early 1960s gave rise to a period of reconstruction, with the physical rebuilding of Cardiff Arms Park paralleling the development of coaching schemes and youth initiatives: by 1969, despite controversies over implications for amateurism, the national squad was using a system of full training sessions, which paid off in the successes of the 1970s.[67] This shift cannot be linked solely with the growth of international sport: the growth of domestic professionalism and sponsorship are two other related influences that have forced British sportsmen and women, and their governing bodies, to take preparation more seriously. The latter has been driven home by the lucrative deals that national governing bodies have been able to earn through selling shirt, tracksuit, and fixture name space to sponsors: the Bank of Scotland's deal with the SRU, Save and Prosper's contract with the Rugby Football Union (RFU), Green Flag's with the FA, and John Smith's beer with the England Rugby League team have all exemplified this. Indeed, the Rugby Football League's (RFL's) experience shows up the connections between professional administration and tactical development: in the same year, 1974, it set up its National Coaching Scheme and appointed its first public relations officer.[68] However, the international scene has been a significant influence here, as it has involved wide exposure for the commonplace links between sporting prowess and national prestige. Similarly, the increasingly professional attitude shown by the FA in shifting footballing matters to the paid rather than voluntary sector of its organisation has been mirrored in other sports; and again, this has been related to commercial and sponsorship needs as well as to purely sporting ones. Overall, the increasing kudos of international success in umbrella events such as the Olympic Games and in sport-specific tournaments has influenced the way in which British sports have been managed and administered. Successive governments since the early 1960s have had a role here, as discussed in Chapter 1. As well as providing funding and channels for communication between state and sport, this has involved active backing, at local and central levels, for bids to host tournaments. Hill has provided good case studies of this in his work on Birmingham and Manchester's unsuccessful Olympic bids for 1992 and 1996, showing how different state agencies could gain from the award: while local authorities would gain infrastructure and educational benefits, central government would gain from the international profile and tourist revenue.[69]

A final aspect of this more serious entry into the world of sport has been a British involvement in a growing international market of sports professionals.[70] Before the Second World War, the global flows of athletic talent migration as they affected the UK were largely constrained by imperial ties. After the war, the increasingly international character of sport facilitated a growth in such opportunities, with British sports featuring both as exporters and as importers. The export role essentially showed some continuity with the earlier phase of Britons teaching the world to play, as footballers, athletes, boxers, and others found coaching and playing positions overseas: 'the syndrome of "have boots will travel" was not new' in the immediate post-war years.[71] However, there were also some significant changes here, most notably in football in the 1950s as a number of professionals chose to move overseas rather than limit their earning potential under the maximum wage structure.

The movement of Charlie Mitten, Neil Franklin, and others to Colombia in 1950, discussed in Chapter 4, was a controversial example of this, not least because of the secrecy surrounding the moves and the fact that Colombia was so unknown to the British public.[72] Others in the 1950s and 1960s favoured Italy, including John Charles, Jimmy Greaves, and Denis Law, showing that it was not just the pre-1961 employment structure of domestic football that was a push factor, but that the wider opportunities and new experience offered by the continental game also acted as a pull. This was hastened in the 1970s, with the brief life of professional football in the USA also attracting many British professionals, including George Best and Rodney Marsh, while Europe became increasingly attractive in the wake of the ban on English clubs after 1985. The number of recent British internationals who have developed their careers with non-indigenous clubs suggests that this feature of world football has become a recognised option in British professional culture: Gary Lineker (Barcelona and Nagoya Grampus 8), Paul Ince (Internazionale), Mark Hughes (Bayern Munich and Barcelona), and Paul Gascoigne (Lazio and Glasgow Rangers) have all shown that the constraint of nationality has not prevented career development.

A number of cricketers have been part of the outward flow by taking advantage of the climate and the game's international structure and developed careers overseas during the British winter: a 1986 analysis of the winter activities of the 312 indigenous registered professionals showed that eighty four were taking coaching appointments overseas, a figure that was artificially depressed by the potential career restrictions that coaching in South Africa would have brought. Middlesex bowler Simon Hughes countered the glamorous image of this migration, claiming that overseas cricket in winter was as exciting as 'an evening in the laundrette'.[73] Although this sector obviously involves only those not selected for international winter tours, the Kerry Packer affair of 1977 showed that a number of top professionals were prepared to put career development and earning potential ahead of national representation by joining the Australian-based multinational World Series Cricket. England captain Tony Greig – himself a South African who qualified to play for England – and his colleagues effectively challenged the employment structures of English cricket by this defection, and the whole affair helped to stress the power of the broadcasting media in the game.[74] For our purposes, the example stands as another part of the global process in sport, whereby British professionals exported themselves, in this case into a contrived multinational setting rather than an existing overseas league. The whole issue of rebel cricket tours to South Africa during the apartheid period, where players jeopardised international careers, was another example of the complex nature of cricket's global character in the 1970s and 1980s.[75]

The UK has also been an importer of sporting talent. This trend has varied in intensity and influence from sport to sport, and across the period. In some sports, it has been an integral part of the commercial take-off in the UK. Maguire explored this in his case studies of basketball and American football, where he linked the importing of players to British clubs to the sports' wider commercial developments and 'transformations' along American lines.[76] By 1985–6, for example, when 33 per cent of the players in the English National Basketball League's Division One were either American or dual nationals, the sport had a large league complete with commercial sponsorship of the competition and of most clubs.[77] These trends have been resisted by some indigenous players and clubs, fearful that the game would move too far away from its amateur roots, and that the opportunities for overseas players would discourage local youths from taking up the game. The 'contested nature of the recruitment of sports migrants and the commodification and shift of the game towards spectacle'[78] was summed up by the calls of one English coach in 1982 for restrictions on highly paid overseas players: 'We sacrifice the future of the game for the Americans.'[79] The revival of British ice hockey in the post-war period has also been linked to the influx of Canadian players: between 1979 and 1989, 435 of the 3,508 Canadian transfers abroad moved to UK clubs, 12 per cent of the total number, placing the UK as the third highest importer of Canadians after West Germany and Switzerland.[80] Athletic migration apart, the developing interest in such sports, confirmed by media coverage, paying spectators, and sponsors' interest, is evidence itself of how global influences in general have affected British sport in the post-industrial period.

More traditional British sports have also been influenced by the increasing opportunities for overseas players, and while their presence has also been debated, they have been valued for the glamour and flair that they have often brought. An influx of Australasians hit English rugby league immediately after the war, including Cec Mountford at Wigan and Vic Hey at Hunslet. Many of these players were top names – Australian Brian Bevan of Warrington, for example, achieved the record number of tries in first-class British rugby league – and the sport's historians have specifically linked their presence with the high attendances of the period: they were 'the adventurously exotic element that leavened the resolutely and sometimes dully parochial'.[81] These migration routes were, however, periodically closed from 1947, as they were creating a drain on the domestic games in Australia and New Zealand. English clubs tapped other sources, including South Africa and Fiji: St Helens' Tom Van Vollenhoven and Rochdale's Laita Ravouvou were examples of this diversification in the late 1950s.[82] A settlement on the employment of non-British players was reached in the mid-1980s: after a brief free-market approach led to fifteen Australians in one English league match in 1985, a quota system of three players per side provided some stability without closing out external influences.

Football has provided the most high-profile examples of this form of import. For much of the period, the British associations have been operating within wider UEFA restrictions of the number of foreign nationals that clubs can play, and until the early 1980s there was little overseas presence on league pitches. The high-profile signing by Tottenham Hotspur of two Argentinian internationals, Osvaldo Ardiles and Ricardo Villa, helped to change this, and showed that the Football League could be an importer as well as an exporter of talent. Both had been members of Argentina's victorious World Cup squad of 1978, although Villa had not played in the final, and they made an immediate impact in Tottenham's FA Cup winning team of 1981. Villa scored the stunning winning goal in the final replay, prompting the television commentator tellingly to declaim that this was the first time that the Cup had been won by a man from the other side of the world. Although they were unsettled by spectators' reactions during the Falklands War in 1982, Ardiles went on to begin his managerial career in England, and their success helped to publicise the opportunities the League faced by embracing wider markets. Successive world cups and European championships helped to provide further exposure for British managers looking to break into this market. At the time of writing, the 1996–7 football season is the most cosmopolitan year to date, financed by television and sponsorship money, and leading *The Times* to speculate on how referees would be able to cope linguistically: ' "Ich bin sick as un perroquet" will not always be enough.'[83] With a handful of clubs employing continental coaches, such as Chelsea's Dutch manager Ruud Gullit, this influx has had an impact on playing styles and media discourse about the differences between British and overseas styles. The relaxation of UEFA's regulations on non-national players has been crucial here in opening up the market, linked firmly to a wider diminishing of difference between European Union member states, as has the impact of the Bosman case which has created a larger stock of players able to move clubs at the end of contracts.

Overall, then, the increased volume of British involvement in the world sport scene since 1945 has had a number of effects and implications. Driven by notions of prestige and of history, and by the commercial and political benefits that participation has brought in a mass media age, British individuals, clubs, and representative sides, as well as sports administrations and the media, have entered into a continuing debate about styles of play and training, the provision of facilities, the meanings of success and failure, and the notion of national identity. For the first time in history, they have had regular and frequent meaningful competition across all sports for this debate to take place in. The effects have included the growth of coaching cultures, experimentation with styles based on non-'traditional' British values that are currently being expressed in total rugby union, and the restructuring of some elite sports to allow a closer integration between British and non-British teams: the Super League in rugby league, the Europe-wide basis of American football, and the shift in football's European Cup from a straight knock-out to a league-based group system are signs of this development.

Media interest in world sport has helped to establish a wider knowledge amongst sports followers of international trends. For the UK, this was greatly helped by Channel 4, launched in 1982, with a remit to cover minority interests. Applied to sport, this channel has successfully brought American football, Australian Rules football, hurling, the Tour de France, American basketball, women's football, *sumô*, Italian league football, and a range of other less publicised events to British living rooms. The commissioning basis of the channel's output has allowed for flexible and creative developments in the style of showing these more cosmopolitan sports. The format for some sports has diverged from some established broadcasting norms specifically because the viewers were assumed to know little about these non-mainstream sports: coverage of American football, for example, started 'from an assumption of ignorance' and took viewers 'through detailed explanations of rules, tactics, and the culture of the game'.[84] This approach had helped to undermine the traditional way in which the sports media emphasised the 'exotic character' of such sports: the serious nature of the coverage manages to 'dislodge the smug patronising superiority of the old Empire mentality of the English'.[85] Satellite and cable broadcasting, while reliant on high-profile sports such as the cricket World Cup and the Carling Premiership, also broadcasts extensive minority sport from around the world to help fill specialist channel schedules: luge, surfing, beach volleyball, biathlon and others share space with the headline events. Viewer interest in such coverage, and increasing public knowledge about world sport, is perhaps the ultimate effect of the post-war trend in British sport away from isolation. However, the notion that this represents part of a globally homogeneous culture is still open to debate: as Briggs put it in his rejoinder to the idea of post-nationalism, 'the "nation", tribal or not, remains the main unit both in sport and in communications and . . . in each nation both are part of distinctive cultural complexes. This fact alone will keep historians busy as the millennia come and go.'[86]

SPORT AND THE 'UNITED' KINGDOM

While the globalisation debate is still relatively new in sports studies in general, let alone sports history, it is clearly a key area for research and analysis. The debate's emphasis is not just on the notion of sameness – of all sports watchers in all countries having access to the same wide range of events, and of major American events such as basketball and American football being imitated and homogenised globally. It is also about how local and regional differences survive and adapt in this setting. The point is put best by Jarvie and Maguire, who emphasise that globalisation is about 'a balance and blend between diminishing contrasts and increasing varieties, a commingling of cultures':[87]

> Though sport has reinforced and reflected a diminishing of contrasts between nations, the close association of sport with national cultures and identities also means that moves towards integration of regions at a political level are undermined by the role of sport.[88]

This insight is central to any examination of the history of sport within the UK, where sport has historically provided a key focus for the constituent parts to emphasise 'separateness and distinctiveness'.[89] Rugby union for the Welsh, football for the Scots, and Gaelic sports for the Irish have played out in emotive public ways the perceived independent national cultures that these nationalities have had from the English. As discussed above, this is not quite as simple as it seems, owing to the complicating factors of different practices between different sports, qualification rules, and the fact that the different sports frequently represent only specific groups rather than the 'nation' as a whole. Mainstream Scottish football culture, for example, tends to marginalise the Highlands and the Islands, while an emphasis on the difference of the GAA in Northern Ireland disguises the complexities of sport for unionists, whose affiliation to the UK does not prevent them taking pleasure in Northern Irish – or indeed Irish – teams from beating the English.[90] However, the public and media identification of sports with such alternative nationalisms has made the issue a key theme in post-war sports history. For our purposes, it can be studied through two themes: first, how domestic sports cultures and structures within Scotland, Wales, and Northern Ireland have maintained 'separateness and distinctiveness' from their English counterparts; and second, how representative sport has continued in its historical role of representing those countries as fully fledged nations, particularly in competition with England.

The domestic sports of Scotland, Wales, and Northern Ireland have obviously had variable and differential structures, but the general trend towards administrative distinction from England has been widespread. With the important exception of the BOA, which acts as an umbrella organisation for all UK Olympic participants, governing bodies have developed on national rather than unified lines. This has been confirmed in general in the organisational structures of competitions, the distribution of funding, the management of refereeing and coaching schemes, as well as the management of representative sides. Official recognition of this state of affairs was made by the institution of the Scottish Sports Council and the Sports Council for Wales as administrative units within the Sports Council's structure in 1965, with the Sports Council for Northern Ireland added in 1973.[91] The Sports Council apart, these separate structures generally pre-dated our period: the Scottish Football Association split from the FA in the 1880s, the Welsh Rugby Union (WRU) was established in 1881, and the GAA was formed in 1884, when Ireland was run as a single administrative unit. There has, however, been some change in this area during our period, but on the whole this has served to reinforce the national divisions rather than blur them. The long-running debate over which football organisation should run the association game in Ireland, for example, was gradually resolved by the 1960s, with the Dublin-based FAI taking charge of the Republic and the Belfast-based Irish Football Association running the game in Northern Ireland.[92] More recently, commercial incentives led the Football Association of Wales to establish a League of Wales, which involved attempts to pull a number of clubs out of the English-run leagues they were playing in. The biggest Welsh clubs – Swansea, Wrexham, and Cardiff City, all playing in the Football League/Premiership structure – managed to resist this development, but some larger non-league and semi-professional clubs were included, despite claims that it would limit their opposition. These examples of retrenched national structures help to stress the continuing debate in British sport over national ties, and have kept the issue alive.

The period has also seen a continuity, despite international influences, in the idea that Scotland, Wales, and Northern Ireland have distinctive ways of playing world sports. Social realities may not always have matched the image, and there is clearly an element of invented tradition here, but the mythology has been important in retaining an air of difference. Golf in Scotland is a classic example. Frequently held up as a national game that involves 'near-universal participation and a suspension of social differences',[93] the image of a classless golf culture has been an attractive one. It has helped to set Scotland apart as more egalitarian and tolerant than England, to show the snobbery of the English middle classes, with their emphasis on privacy and closure in sport, as something that somehow stops at the border. Lowerson has successfully challenged this myth, showing how the game in Scotland has not been free from class distinction – or, for that matter, from gender, ethnic, and religious distinction. He concluded that the greater opportunities for working-class golfers in Scotland than in England 'have proved far from sufficient to bear the weight of the label of "democracy" attached to them'.[94] Scottish football culture has prided itself for much of the post-war period, as before, on its vitality and fertility, and on its difference from the game in England. Moorhouse's body of work has demonstrated various ways in which the game has had a related but separate history in Scotland. He has rejected the simplistic notion of 'sectarianism' as a defining feature of the Scottish game: 'in modern Scotland *talk* about ethnic antagonism is rather more prevalent than evidence of meaningful ethnic division'.[95] However, the strand in popular and historical discourse that he was attacking, that of emphasising the role of pro-unionist and pro-Irish republican ideologies around Glasgow Rangers and Celtic, has played a key role in maintaining a different football culture to that in England. Its basis in such features as Rangers' mythologised but real long-term refusal to sign a Roman Catholic player, in Celtic's tradition of flying the Irish tricolour at its stadium, and in the songs of rival supporters has made it attractive for such analysts as Finn and Murray, and has certainly set it apart as uniquely Scottish.[96] There are no exact English parallels, for example, to the Celtic fanzine's assumptions about pro-Rangers bias in refereeing that led to a mock advertisement for officials, with the equipment needed including 'a sash and apron';[97] or to the Rangers' fans' song 'Billy Boys': 'We're up to our knees in Fenian blood surrender or you'll die.'[98] Beyond these signs of difference, Scotland has continued, in relation to its population, to maintain 'a larger professional game than any other footballing nation'.[99] That Celtic were the first British club to win the European Cup was also significant here. Scotland has also continued to provide a constant flow of elite players for the professional game in England (and, increasingly, continental Europe): John Charles, Pat Crerand, Peter Marinello, Billy Bremner, Kenny Dalglish, and Pat Nevin exemplify this outflow for our period. Despite the disappointment that this causes to club followers, knowing themselves as perennial suppliers due to economic, political, and demographic factors, it has helped to reassure Scots of their game's superiority: a 'fatalistic sense of loss mingles with the pride that the

English simply cannot get by without taking Scottish talent'.[100] The more recent trend of Glasgow Rangers in particular importing big English names, such as Terry Butcher and Paul Gascoigne, has not ameliorated this sense of difference.

In Wales, rugby union has historically prided itself on difference from the English version. As with Scottish golf, the distinguishing feature here has been social class, although the game has been more really 'thoroughly democratized'[101] than the more mythical Scottish case. The sport's development in mining communities in the nineteenth century, and its administrators' 'looser rein over such matters as expenses'[102] than their English counterparts, have given the game a social complexion very different from that played elsewhere in the UK (with the exception of the Scottish borders). The sport has retained both a genuine community spirit at the local level, and a national flavour that is more populist than that of Wales' regular opponents in the Five Nations. The WRU's antipathy towards rugby league helped to protect this distinctiveness. This was maintained through bans on the Welsh union players who defected to the professional code in the north of England and by the WRU's resistance to the rival code establishing itself in Wales. This had been attempted unsuccessfully in the 1920s, and was tried again by the RFL after the war. The RFL provided subsidies to clubs, and bought its own grounds, as the WRU was able to obstruct the rival code being played on its own clubs' and public playing fields. The WRU's official attitude was captured by former Swansea and Wales winger W. Rowe Harding in 1950: 'The Rugby League is only an infant, but it wants strangling.'[103] The experimental Welsh Rugby League started in 1949, and the best club, Cardiff, spent 1951–2 in the RFL, but low popular demand and the WRU's intransigence helped to finish the experiment in 1955.[104] The rugby revolution of the late 1980s and 1990s has softened this resistance, and has included amnesties for players who turned professional, but the emphasis on a populist rather than elitist union game helped to distinguish Wales for much of the period.

These examples of world sports having distinctive 'national' cultures in their Celtic versions provide insights into one way in which domestic sports have played a part in promoting difference from England. Another aspect of this has been in the survival of sports that are peculiar to their national setting. Owing to the indigenous nature of such events, they are often closely associated with a sense of 'national' – as opposed to 'British' – culture. The motivation behind the GAA, formed in 1884 as part of a wider growth of Irish political and cultural nationalism, was based on this distinction: that hurling, camogie, and Gaelic football were based on pure Irish games which helped to separate the Irish from the British. The movement was 'rooted in a vision of Celtic Ireland' with a 'high emphasis . . . placed upon the purity of the Gaelic race'.[105] The GAA not only promoted these distinctive sports, but also banned from membership anyone who played sports identified with the English. While the movement was born at a time of rising national consciousness that fed into civil war and partition, it has survived that context, and the post-war period has seen its role as a focus for distinction continue. While its work in Eire is beyond our remit, it is crucial to stress that it has also thrived in Northern Ireland.[106] Although it dropped its ban on players practising non-Gaelic sports in 1971, it has continued to pursue a 'broadly nationalist yet factionally neutral' line.[107] Thus, it has provided an umbrella organisation and funding channel for leagues and cup competitions in Gaelic sports, and has attempted to keep these sports' profiles high at a time of increasing competition from sports with higher media profiles.[108] While attempting to remain outside the violence that has surrounded republicanism and unionism in Northern Ireland for this period, particularly since 1969, the Ulster GAA has acted as a focus for the cultural politics of nationalism. For example, its constitution shares the Republic's official view that the division of Ireland is a temporary one, with the 1985 Handbook stressing that the Association's 'basic aim' is 'the strengthening of the National Identity in a 32 County Ireland',[109] and members of the Royal Ulster Constabulary and British Army were refused membership of GAA clubs. The GAA's role in the Troubles was clearly illustrated in the dispute started in 1971, when the British Army appropriated part of the training area of Crossmaglen Rangers' ground, St Oliver Plunkett Park. The playing area was damaged by vehicle movements and helicopter landings, and club members were charged with trespass when they attempted to train. The case fuelled popular debates about the army presence, and the club's legal victory helped to underline the potential power that sport could hold in the cultural battle.[110] The GAA's distinctive 'celebration of Irishness'[111] through sport has been a crucial part of the trend towards alternative nationalisms.

Although this is the most distinctive example, because of its specific linkage with wider politics, indigenous sports have elsewhere been maintained as a way of stressing difference. However, they have not always been resistant to external forces, and can sometimes be seen to have effectively become little more than heritage events. In Scotland, shinty and curling have continued throughout the post-war period. Both sports have been described by one Scottish sports historian as 'deeply enmeshed in our culture',[112] but Whitson's 1983 analysis of shinty showed it in a period of rupture as its traditional community basis was being undermined by inward and outward migration from its heartlands in the Highlands.[113] With incoming professionals and managers in Oban and Fort William, physical education teachers from Jordanhill with their emphasis on other sports, and potential players attracted by sports they could watch on television, the game's promoters were having to analyse their approach: 'Are we promoting a modern sport or preserving an aspect of Highland culture?'[114] Jarvie's work on Highland Gatherings and the Highland Games has shown up ways in which activities maintained as celebrations of national and regional cultural distinctiveness can become reconstructed to external values – such as professionalism and modernisation – until their distinctiveness becomes the basis of a tourist industry.[115] Overall, the complex issues surrounding regional and indigenous sports make simple conclusions difficult, and, clearly, the examples discussed have experienced both continuity and change in the post-war period. However, these survivals are crucial to our appreciation of sport's role in maintaining sporting cultures that are self-consciously different from those followed in England.

If sport has helped to define national cultures within these nations, then it has had an equally important role in forming a focus for arguments about national status within the UK. In particular, when national and club sides from Scotland, Wales, and Northern Ireland have met English rivals, the contests have been charged with emotions linked to alternative patriotism and nationalism. Football matches between England and Scotland, and rugby union internationals between England and Wales, have been – and continue to be – defining features of the UK's composition. This phenomenon clearly pre-dates our period, and its survival into the post-war period, particularly alongside genuine political discourses about devolution, has been striking. The deeper meanings attached to such rivalries have been read in three main ways: as a surrogate for nationalism; as the only real forum for national identity; and as a symbol of national difference. The former view is the 'ninety minute patriot' idea used by Jarvie and Walker as the hook for their collection of essays. The title was taken from a comment made by Jim Sillars of the SNP after the 1992 General Election: 'The great problem is that Scotland has too many ninety minute patriots whose nationalist outpourings are expressed only at major sporting events.'[116] Jarvie and Walker argue that this idea has 'virtually attained the status of another national myth',[117] but its longevity is part of this debate about the meanings attached to representative sport for the members of the UK. The second view is that of sport as the only area in which the marginal nations of the UK have meaningful separate identities. As Moorhouse put it, Scotland 'really only has sport with which to strut its independent existence on the world stage'.[118] This helps to explain the popularity of Scottish campaigns in the football World Cup, particularly – as happened in 1974 and 1978 – when England failed to qualify. Beyond this, sport has acted symbolically as a 'vitally important channel for [a] sense of collective resentment'[119] within the structure of the UK. Scottish rugby internationals against England in the early 1990s, according to one former international, were about 'life and politics in Scotland; the poll tax and Whitehall rule. Even the players say, while they like to beat anyone, even Japan, and love to beat the Welsh or the Irish, they live to beat the English.'[120] Similar themes have been evident in Welsh rugby discourse. This was captured by the Welsh captain, Phil Bennett, in his rousing comments to the team in 1977:

> These English you're just going out to meet have taken our coal, our water, our steel: they buy our houses and live in them a fortnight a year. . . . Down the centuries these English have exploited and pillaged us – and we're playing them this afternoon boys.[121]

These elements of debate are continually being developed. For our purposes, it is worth considering some examples of how sport and national identity have been blended in this period. The culture and behaviour of travelling Scottish football supporters has been an obvious example, one that shows both a sense of history and a sense of contemporary difference from the English. The England v Scotland fixture, discontinued after 1985, was a clear focus for this. Here, travelling supporters would descend on London as a self-conscious national grouping, sporting tartan and national flags, and appropriating the match as a symbolic contest with the 'auld enemy'. The London media, particularly during the moral panic about hooliganism in the 1970s and 1980s, were keen to portray the supporters as an invasion force, and when the 1977 Wembley fixture, won 2–1 by Scotland, ended with a mass pitch invasion, the breaking of the goalposts and the digging up of sections of turf, it was portrayed as a battle. Interestingly, whereas footage of this event is used in England 'routinely . . . as an illustration of "hooliganism"', it is shown on Scottish television as a significant event 'without a hint of censure'.[122] Beyond the emotional context of the England game, Scottish supporters have gone global with their distinctive styles, and have become a regular feature of international competitions with tartan favours and exuberant but friendly behaviour: the Tartan Army even won praise from UEFA for their excellent ambassadorial work during the 1992 European Championships in Sweden. Giulianotti has empirically analysed this behaviour, and the factors that may have dissuaded more violent supporters from travelling. However, despite his role in successfully challenging the comfortable image of carnival behaviour, he still discovered plenty of behaviour that stressed the supporters' self-perception as distinctly different from, and in opposition to, all things English. Examples from Sweden included the singing of 'We hate Jimmy Hill' and 'We Have-nae Paid any Poll Tax', and the self-policing of racist behaviour: 'Fans at the front of the Scottish support making ape-noises at the coloured players Gullit and Rijkaard were rebuked by Aberdeen casuals: "Fuck off with that racist shit, this is Scotland not England you're with".'[123]

While this behaviour represents a broad vision of national difference, there have also been occasions in the post-war period when sporting nationalism has become more closely entwined with more explicitly political forms. Welsh rugby internationals in the late 1960s and 1970s, for example, became a focus for the nationalist political movement that was being expressed through party politics, through the cultural politics of language and literature, and through minority violent activism. At Cardiff Arms Park, especially against England, parts of the crowd 'became more overtly nationalistic, from the T-shirts in praise of the "Free Wales Army" to the concerted booing of "The Queen"'.[124] Similar sentiments were present in Scottish rugby union in the early 1990s, with devolution once more on the agenda and a growing sense of hostility to such Whitehall-imposed burdens as the poll tax. A defining moment for many came at Murrayfield in October 1991, when the SRU chose 'Flower of Scotland' to be played as the Scottish anthem, and the emotionally charged afternoon was read by some as 'a message of Scottish identity and nationhood'.[125] The impact of nationalist politics on Northern Irish international sport has been more problematic, owing to the composition of representative teams from clubs divided in sectarian terms, although Sugden and Bairner have shown how players and spectators take pleasure in beating England despite, as well as because of, the debate over unionism.[126] Boxer Barry McGuigan perhaps encapsulated the complexities of the situation by attempting to divorce himself from the political and religious divisions: an Irish-born Roman Catholic with a Protestant wife, resident in Northern Ireland at the time of his 1985 featherweight world title, he boxed under the UN flag.[127] The meanings attached to international sport provided the IRA with some high-profile targets for attacks, such as their car bomb at Windsor Park just after Northern Ireland's World Cup qualifier against England in 1985.[128]

In the debate about the UK's solidity that has been an important feature of post-war politics, sport can be seen to have played a role. Symbolic or not, the emotions that such competitions can arouse, and the obvious linkage they have to national identity through flags, colours, and anthems, must be seen as a part of that debate. Sport has offered a popular cultural forum for the power relations between the centre and the margins, and in a culture where the failure of the 1979 referendum on Scottish devolution can be blamed on the national football team's poor performance in the World Cup,[129] it is a forum that historians need to take seriously.

Chapter 3

Sport, commerce, and sponsorship

INTRODUCTION

In 1963, a new cricket tournament was first contested at county level in an attempt to bring money into the game through commercial backing, increased attendances, and television fees. The competition was based on one-day, limited-over matches and was named the Gillette Cup, after the shaving product manufacturer that provided £6,500 in sponsorship to be divided between the counties involved. Gillette had gained experience of sports sponsorship in the USA since 1915, and the company's belief in the value of such enterprises had been bolstered by a 350 per cent rise in sales after their backing of the 1939 World Series in baseball.[1] Gillette withdrew in 1981, despite the tournament's continued popularity: the National Westminster Bank took over, and the competition's name was altered to the NatWest Trophy. Not only had the competition's success made sponsorship too expensive for Gillette, but also, according to Midwinter,

> It was reported that the label Gillette had grown too familiar, that no one associated it with the shaving product the competition advertised, and even that some believed the cup was named after a renowned cricketer, maybe a Dr. W. G. Gillette![2]

The development of this competition, and the way in which the advertising it entailed became so taken for granted that it was almost forgotten in everyday discourse, is an excellent example of one of the most influential themes in post-war British sport. The fact that Midwinter's book on the history of county cricket from which the above quotation is taken was itself sponsored by Bass Brewers is an ironic side-feature of this trend. Commercial interests have always been present in organised sport: as Cashmore put it, 'all sports that are watchable have potential for commercial exploitation'.[3] However, the qualitative and quantitative shifts in commercial influence over the last fifty years have been little short of phenomenal. Through advertising at sporting events, sponsorship of competitions, the use of sports professionals to endorse products, the emergence of business-oriented sports managers, the specific marketing of sports-related goods and services, and an increasing reliance upon associated broadcasting fees, organised sport has become firmly and undeniably linked to the wider economic setting. Moreover, these developments have helped to influence shifts in the professional cultures of professional sportsmen and women, explored in Chapter 4. As a result, commerce is now impossible to avoid in virtually any observation of organised sport. This was fully driven home in the mid-1990s when rugby union, which had officially fought a staunch battle against professionalism and commercial exploitation for a century, reorganised itself on professional and commercial lines. The fact that the Rugby Football Union almost destroyed the traditional Five Nations Championship in the process owing to its zeal in securing a divisive satellite television contract made it clear to all observers that sport and money were inextricably linked.

This historical development has, however, been contested by some of those involved in sport. The volume of money invested in sport is, of course, frequently questioned, often in polemical terms. Mason drew critical attention to this issue in *Only A Game?*, his introductory sports text, with the juxtaposition of photographs of millionaire boxer Mike Tyson and a nurse caring for a premature baby under the question 'Who should earn more?', and many would argue that in terms of 'contribution to society', sportsmen and women are overpaid.[4] The whole issue of sponsorship has been criticised on many counts, including the way in which it allows cigarette manufacturers openly to flout restrictions on advertising, the links it establishes between sport and certain products that can be inimical to the 'values' of sport (notably cigarettes and alcohol), and the fact that major sponsorship tends to be concentrated at an elite level and does not always benefit the grassroots, where money is most needed. The influence that commercial interests can have on the structure and form of play has also been attacked by traditionalists, most notably in cricket over the development of one-day matches – 'a biff-bang menu of instant cricket'[5] – and in rugby league over the switch to summer competition. Broadcasters' fees, particularly in football, are held to be responsible for increasing polarisation between large and small clubs: the splinter Premier League, which broke away from the Football League in 1992, secured £212.5

million over five seasons from BSkyB, plus an additional £40 million for
overseas rights and £50 million in related sponsorship.[6] At a more local
level, football supporters have been increasingly vocal over commercial
decisions affecting their clubs that they felt were not in their interests,
such as mergers, stadium redevelopments, and membership and bond
schemes. What all these examples of contested commercialism show us
is the strong sense of both history and community that informs many
followers' appreciation of their chosen sport.

Undoubtedly, some of the resistance is based on naïve readings of the
past that fail to see a historical presence of commercial interests through
investment, advertising, sponsorship, and gambling. Anyone bemoaning
the commercial exploitation of contemporary athletics, for example,
would do well to consider the 1908 Olympic Marathon, which had beef
extract manufacturers Oxo as its 'Official Caterers' providing various
Oxo products to the runners and using the race as part of its newspaper
advertisements.[7] However, the scale and form of the post-war developments in this area, and their essentially televisual nature, have made the
issues far more apparent and more public than for previous periods. To
continue the marathon example, the fifty-six male athletes who raced
from Windsor to White City in 1908 with their Oxo packs have been
replaced by the tens of thousands of competitors of both sexes and
varying abilities running in the London marathon annually on live
television as a mass advertisement for, currently, Flora margarine.

The commercial aspect of sport has been explored by a number of
historians, and, as with all of our themes, the analysis has tended to
come at least partially in response to contemporary developments. The
1960s were a key decade in the commercialisation of sport, both internationally and specifically in the UK. As we shall see, it was a decade
that began with professional footballers gaining the abolition of the
maximum wage that led to the pop age stardom of George Best and
others; it was also the period in which cricket restructured itself in the
face of falling income, in such areas as the abolition of the profes-
sional/amateur distinction and the introduction of various new,
commercially sponsored competitions. Cricketers and jockeys formed
their first trade unions in this decade. Other sports also changed in this
decade, including lawn tennis, which went open. Moreover, the historical links between sport and betting were relegitimised by the 1960
Betting and Gaming Act, which paved the way for the sports-related
businesses of Ladbrokes, William Hill, and others. The sports historiography that emerged in the 1970s and after was thus written within a
context of an increasingly commercial world of sport, and these

concerns were reflected in a number of texts. Wray Vamplew's 1976 history of horse-racing, *The Turf*, examined both social and economic aspects of the sport's development, and Vamplew was to go on to pioneer research in the economic history of sport in general: his 1988 *Pay Up and Play the Game*, for example, is an authoritative and comprehensive survey of professionalism and finance in sport in the late Victorian and Edwardian periods. Walvin emphasised commerce and professionalism in his 1975 general history of football, as did Mason in his seminal *Association Football and English Society, 1863–1915* of 1980. As the commercial revolution continued in sport through the 1980s and beyond, involving everything from shirt-front advertising in the Football League to sponsors' logos appearing on the pitch at Lord's, so too did the historical interest. The historiography has included localised studies, such as Arnold's work on football in Bradford, *A Game That Would Pay*, as well as works on specific aspects of sport's links with money, such as Clapson's history of gambling, *A Bit of a Flutter*.[8] The major works of synthesis have all approached this aspect of sport, although Harris's relatively early offering here showed his background in classical sport by tending to avoid commerce, offering limited discussions of professionalism and significantly indexing both betting and gambling under 'corrupt practices'.[9] Such qualms were not demonstrated by Mason, Holt, or Brailsford in their respective overview texts, all of which devoted significant amounts of space to the economic and commercial side of sport.[10] From a more contemporary perspective, Cashmore also devoted a chapter to 'commercialism and sports' in *Making Sense of Sports*, describing the scale of the issue quite bluntly: 'The business surrounding sports is very much bigger than what goes on in the ring, on the field, on the boards, or on the ice'.[11]

Overall, the historiography of sport has done a lot to uncover the commercial history of sport in all significant areas, including professionalism, sponsorship, investment and speculation, cartels and monopolies, gate money and other incomes, and the relation of sport to other commercial concerns, including media interests, betting concerns, and sports goods manufacturers. This history sets the context for our period, and it demonstrates the antiquity and continuity of some issues that may at first glance appear to be present in sport only through contemporary or recent financial developments. The size of the sports economy has never been larger than it is in the 1990s. A 1992 survey for the Sports Council found that in 1990, the value of 'sport-related activity' stood at £8.27 billion, 1.7 per cent of the gross national product, with consumer expenditure on sport and sports-related items accounting for £9.75 billion, and the sector as a whole accounting for 467,000 jobs – similar in size to the postal and telecommunications sector, and twice the size of agriculture, forestry, and fishing.[12] However, this contemporary scale should not blind us to history. Many sports had been run as commercial ventures since their formal origins; commercial decisions have historically influenced the establishment of sports clubs, as Arnold demonstrated for Bradford; and commercial decisions have also historically influenced the structure of play in some sports, such as the 1925 revision of the offside law in football designed to create more goals and win back crowds.[13] However, the widespread perception that sport is somehow only now run as a business is clearly linked to the major changes and developments that have taken place since 1945. The reasons for these changes have varied according to the sport and the circumstances, but there is enough commonalty to allow some related themes to be picked out and analysed. The most obvious change has been in the presence and the role of the commercial sponsor, which has literally changed the physical appearance of sports clothes, spaces, and media coverage. Second has been the organisational changes that have taken place within governing bodies and individual clubs to attempt to run sport on more commercial lines, which has led to rugby union clubs taking more notice of spectators' needs as well as a number of football clubs being floated on the Stock Market. Both of these changes need to be seen in the context of developments in media coverage of sport, particularly the growth of television from the 1950s, including satellite and cable systems from the 1980s. Television has offered new forms and a new scale of advertising space, and sport's traditional links with advertisers, and the positive image that it can denote, have made it an excellent vehicle here: Whannel claimed that the 'rise of television turned sport into a whole new cultural form, with extensive marketing potential'.[14] The increased opportunities for direct and indirect advertising that television has brought form a strong link between all strands of sport's post-war commercial history.

SPONSORSHIP AND ADVERTISING

The growth of sponsorship by private sector companies and agencies has arguably been the most obvious and public form of commercialisation in sport. Because of the actual physical presence that the name of the product or company now has on shirt-fronts, hoardings, and even playing areas it is, as Mason put it, 'the most visible relationship between sport and business in the modern world'.[15] The names of products and companies appear as prefixes to so many competitions that they have become commonplace. A glance at the lists of results and fixtures in a random late summer Sunday newspaper takes us through the Football Association's Carling Premiership, the Nationwide League, the Tennants Cup, and the GM Vauxhall Conference in football; the Texaco Cup, the AXA Equity and Law League, and the Britannic Assurance County Championship in cricket; the Johnnie Walker PGA Cup in golf; the Benson and Hedges Cup in ice hockey; the Auto Trader RAC Touring Car Championship in motor racing; the Courage Clubs' Championship National League in rugby union; and the Land Rover British Horse Trials in equestrianism.[16] Moreover, within each event listed, diverse other forms of sponsorship are present, such as shirt-front advertising in football, cricket, and rugby union, and the presence of sponsors' logos on the bodies of the cars in motor racing. The sums of money involved vary depending upon the size of the event or team, but some of the larger recent deals are extremely lucrative. A 1995 survey found that AXA Equity and Law were paying £1.2 million a year for their Sunday cricket league, Carling's Premiership sponsorship cost £12 million over four years, while Beefeater Gin's support for the Oxford and Cambridge Boat Race, an event that lasts for less than half an hour a year, cost them £1.35 million over three years.[17] While the historical links between sponsors and sport are well established, the volume and tone of this presence have become more notable in the post-war period. Some sports locations have also been renamed for sponsors: cricket grounds Headingley and the Oval have respectively been renamed Bass Headingley and the Fosters Oval, for example, while the post-Taylor Report phase of new football stadium developments has so far included Huddersfield Town's Alfred McAlpine Stadium and Middlesbrough's Cellnet Riverside Stadium.

These practices have developed over the post-war period, although, as the Oxo example showed, there were some earlier cases of company (as opposed to private or landowner) patronage. The *News of the World* had funded athletics as early as 1915, and continued to sponsor the sport after the Second World War, backing the 1946 British Games and helping to launch the Amateur Athletics Association's new coaching scheme with donations of £522 in 1946 and £1,000 in 1947. This sponsorship continued into the 1950s and 1960s.[18] In cycling, the Tour of Britain was set up by the *Daily Express* in 1951 and restarted in 1958 with funding from the Milk Marketing Board, giving it the popular name of the Milk Race.[19] In the same year, the brewers Whitbread funded a new trophy in horse-racing that bore their name. This practice was picked up by cricket in the early 1960s, when, as we have seen, the Gillette Cup was established as a new knock-out competition which drew in, at first, £6,500 from Gillette for the counties involved. It was followed in 1969 by the John Player League, the same cigarette manufacturer sponsoring a new rugby league trophy from 1971 for £9,500.[20] More tobacco interests were brought into cricket in 1972 when the Benson and Hedges Cup was established. Football survived without major tournament sponsorship into the 1980s, although a number of small-scale events had been set up through sponsorship in the early 1970s, notably the Watney Cup and the Texaco Cup. Apart from these small-scale events, sponsorship 'found football in the 1980s'.[21] The first major event to take a sponsor's name was the League Cup, which became the Milk Cup in 1982, later to be competed for under the names of sponsors Littlewoods, Rumblelows, and Coca-Cola. The Football League became the Canon League in 1983; subsequent sponsors have included *Today*, Barclays Bank, and, after the restructuring of 1992, Endsleigh Insurance and the Nationwide Building Society, while the splinter Premier grouping was backed by Carling. The year 1983 also saw the arrival of shirt-front sponsorship in football. In Scotland, the League was backed by Finefare from 1985, while the Scottish Rugby Union's club championship was sponsored for the first time in 1977–8, when Scwheppes provided backing. The Rugby Football Union had already strayed from its amateur ethos by this time, having accepted perimeter advertising at Twickenham from 1973, and having sold its National Knock-Out Competition to John Player for £100,000 in 1975.[22] The Croquet Association (CA) established a Sponsorship Committee in 1983 to investigate ways in which the sport could raise income through sponsorship and television coverage. While this early attempt, which suggested televising golf croquet, a scaled-down version of the sport, was rejected by the Association, a second attempt worked in 1986: the Nation's Cup, sponsored by the Royal Bank of Scotland.[23] Sponsors' names as prefixes proliferated in horse-racing in the mid-1980s: as Vamplew points out, by 1984 the racing calendar included the General Accident 1,000 Guineas, the Holsten Pils St Leger, and the Ever Ready Derby.[24] Courage backed rugby union's new club championship for £1.6 million when it was set up in 1987, and cricket continued to bring sponsorship into an increasing number of events, including test matches.

The broader commercial setting of the 1980s, a time when a radical Conservative government was introducing neo-liberal policies and encouraging a free-market economy, made itself felt in other sports, too.

The significance of the early 1980s in this relationship is stressed by the fact that in 1981, the Central Council of Physical Recreation commissioned an inquiry into sponsorship in sport, chaired by former Minister for Sport, Denis Howell.[25] Howell claimed in his memoirs that the investigation came 'not a day too soon – sports sponsorship had been growing at an amazing pace, . . . was totally unregulated, and many governing bodies of sport feared that they would be over-run with commercialism'.[26] This broad survey of some of the developments should be taken merely as illustrative of the range of sports and sponsors involved. In short, sponsorship had pervaded sport by the end of our period. According to the Sports Council, it was an activity worth £2.5 million in 1971, which by 1988 had increased to £200 million. Moreover, by the 1980s it was an industry in its own right, with specialised agencies and consultants working to bring together sports needing money and potential sponsors requiring an appropriate event. These developments require analysis: first, to establish why this has taken place; and second, to examine the effects that this has had on the sports concerned and on sport as a whole.

The reasons behind the growth of sponsorship are complex, and relate both to the state of sports and to the developing role of advertising in the post-war period, particularly after the arrival of commercial television in 1955. One of the significant trends in post-war British sport has been the relative decline of paying spectators at mass sports and the relative increase in individualised sports such as golf, squash, swimming, and out-of-town family-based leisure activities. At the start of the period, the major sports actually experienced spectator booms, influenced by the public interest in a return to normal competitions after the restricted sporting programmes of the war years. In rugby league, record attendances at matches were achieved in the years following the war, such as the 77,605 who watched Bradford Northern beat Leeds in the 1947 Challenge Cup Final at Wembley: the pre-war record gate for this fixture was 55,453 in 1939. This event achieved its record attendance in 1954, when 102,569 officially attended the replayed final between Warrington and Halifax at Odsal. Regular fixtures also attracted larger crowds than before the war, with 1948–9 being the record season when 6.9 million attended games.[27] In county cricket, the late 1940s saw record crowds, including 2.3 million paying spectators in 1947 (excluding subscription-paying members, whose actual attendance rates cannot be calculated);[28] while football, as the largest national sport, drew in 41.2 million paying spectators to the 1948–9 League programme.[29] The fact that both football and rugby league gained their record attendances in the same season is worth stressing. However, by the 1960s the number of paying spectators was falling across the board, a trend that continued in the 1970s and beyond. Staying with the previous examples, we can see dramatic declines. For 1969–70, for example, Football League attendances fell to 29.6 million, a drop of 28 per cent in twenty-one seasons, with the low point coming in 1984–5 when only 17.8 million attended, down 56 per cent from the post-war boom.[30] In county cricket, a decline was evident by the early 1960s with the 'nadir' reached in 1966 'when 513,578 individuals went through the county turnstiles', a mere 22 per cent of the crowds in 1947.[31] The rugby league Challenge Cup Final continued to draw large crowds, reaching capacity crowds at Wembley eleven times between 1966 and 1995, but after the record crowd at Odsal for the 1954 replay, the fixture also failed to fill Wembley on thirty occasions. A more noticeable decline was evident in the league fixtures: by 1968–9, attendances had fallen to 2.7 million, a drop of 60 per cent over twenty-one seasons. Dunning and Sheard's local analysis of Featherstone Rovers' attendances for 1953 and 1973 illustrates the trend graphically: the total crowds of 87,500 in 1953 fell to 66,770 by 1973.[32] This was a time of the game's 'catastrophic decline as a spectator sport'.[33] These examples can be multiplied across the other spectator sports.

The reasons for this decline in attendances were varied. All must be rooted in the general economic context of recession that the UK had entered by the early 1970s, particularly evident in rising unemployment levels and inflation. Some of them were generally noticeable in all sports, such as the shifting patterns of leisure time usage linked to private motoring, television, and family-based activities. Others were sport specific. Football was undoubtedly affected by the emergence of hooliganism as a social problem during the 1960s, a problem which continued to act as a disincentive to many potential spectators, and was reinforced by the tragic events of 1985, when a fire at Bradford City's Valley Parade killed fifty six people, and crowd disorder involving Liverpool supporters at the European Cup Final in Brussels caused the deaths of thirty eight people. However, analysis of the timing of the spectator decline compared with the emergence of anxiety about crowd behaviour shows that hooliganism did not cause the drop, although it may have hastened it. Instead, hooliganism analysts have linked the fall in crowds to the diminishing 'attractiveness' of an expanded Football League to 'an increasingly home-centred, consumption-oriented and discriminating working class faced with an expanded range of leisure choices'.[34] Other sports were affected by the poor facilities they offered to this increasingly discerning paying public, by changes in styles of play that made games less exciting to watch than they were perceived to have been traditionally, and by the increasing amount of televised sport which allowed potential spectators to sample a greater variety of events than they could ever see live without having to pay specific amounts or leave their own homes. A number of governing bodies were genuinely fearful that television coverage of sport was providing a disincentive for the live spectator: this fear had been present as early as 1946 when a number of sports organised themselves into the Association for the Protection of Copyright in Sports, a pressure group which withheld broadcasting rights until it was guaranteed against pirated rediffusion, and which proposed a ban of all live sports coverage in 1949. Televised sport became more competitive when ITV was launched in 1955, with the choice of channels and the opportunities presented by commercial breaks significant here, but some big sports still held out against live coverage: the Football League, for example, turned down ATV's £50,000 offer for live matches in 1955, and held out until 1983 on a package of edited recorded highlights.[35] Some sports clearly welcomed the advent of television, and credited their growth amongst spectators and participants to exposure: for the 1960s and 1970s, Whannel links this to show jumping, darts, and snooker; while for the 1980s, Maguire's analysis of Channel 4's role in launching American football is also relevant here.[36] Wrestling also relied heavily upon television, as has been seen in the sport's decline since ITV dropped it in 1985.[37]

Television, increasing leisure choices, and, from the late 1960s, the recession all played parts in causing something of a rupture in spectator sport in the post-war period. Whatever the exact local and general causes of this trend, the overall result was that gate money receipts, traditionally a staple part of sports clubs' incomes, were declining at a time when costs were rising. Mason links rising costs in football to wage bills in a time of increasing professionalism, the application of VAT to football clubs in 1979, the need for new capital expenditure to meet the safety regulations that arose out of the 1971 Ibrox disaster, and the high cost of policing.[38] Similar pressures were felt elsewhere in sports that relied upon paying spectators coming regularly and fixed assets that were underutilised. Brookes's comment on cricket in the early 1960s in this context has wider application to other sports: 'The simple truth was that tradition was no longer a marketable commodity, and the advent of sponsorship was merely a recognition of this fact.'[39] In this climate, sports were understandably keen to find funding from elsewhere, and commercial sponsorship offered an obvious solution. The way in which many sports embraced sponsorship can thus firmly be linked historically with post-war trends in attendances, and to the rising costs of running sports with industrial origins in the post-industrial 1980s.

It is easy to argue that sports and clubs were motivated in their move to sponsorship predominantly by the need for extra sources of income. While other benefits accrued, such as the product or service being advertised helping to promote a desired image of the sport, and the guarantees of corporate hospitality events that sponsorship would bring, the original push came from financial insecurity. The resistance and antipathy that some followers of individual sports have shown to sponsorship helps to underline this notion that it is often perceived in sport as a necessary evil. This is illustrated neatly by Smith's claims for croquet, where many 'devotees, young and old, are appalled at the thought of money "tainting" their sport. For them sponsorship smacks of "nasty commercialism".'[40] Sponsors, however, have been unlikely to share such idealistic and ahistorical views, and while their motives have been similarly based on financial considerations, they have been rather more complex than the sports' basic need for funds. As Gratton and Taylor have demonstrated, sponsors' motives all link to profit maximisation as part of wider advertising strategies, but with some subtle differences in motivation involved.[41] The promotion of a brand awareness has been central, and explains the reasons for sponsors' policies of getting their name in increasingly noticeable positions during play, particularly televised play: from advertising hoardings at the perimeter of the playing area, to the competitors' clothing, and then onto the playing area itself in some sports. The appendage of the sponsor's name to a competition has additional benefits here, as it brings mentions in media coverage of the event. These related reasons intermesh, as the Howell Committee discovered in its analysis of Cornhill Insurance's backing of test matches in 1981. The sponsorship brought extensive television coverage for Cornhill's name, including '7,459 banner sitings on screen and 234 verbal mentions' in a total of 140 hours of television.[42] This deal is frequently cited as a success story in sponsorship for the increase in brand awareness that it brought:

> Before the deal 2 per cent of the population had heard of Cornhill; by 1985 the 'name awareness level' had risen to 20 per cent. From being relatively unknown in 1980 Cornhill became the second most spontaneously named insurance company after the all-mighty Pru.[43]

As Critcher put it: 'Sports sponsorship reaches the parts of the audience other adverts cannot reach.'[44]

This leads into a second motive: unofficial and relatively cheap television advertising. Sponsorship has grown most notably since commercial television's launch, and advertisers in a range of sectors have been able to buy space in sports broadcasts with identifiable audiences in mind: the glut of commercials with footballing themes during the 1990 and 1994 World Cup broadcasts on ITV suggested that this traditional strategy has become increasingly specialised. However, the sponsorship of sports events and teams has increasingly provided sponsors with access to television coverage outside a specific advertising context. Through sports coverage, names such as Embassy, Coca-Cola, Cornhill, Courage, and Gillette have been made integral to the broadcast, and not been restricted to commercial breaks – or, indeed, even to commercial television. The figures for Cornhill quoted above all relate to BBC coverage which technically excludes advertising, a loophole which sponsors in various competitions have managed to exploit. As the advertising time has not been sold as such by the broadcaster, it has often been cheaper than specialised commercials: Embassy estimated that the television coverage its brand name received during the 1982 World Professional Snooker Championship was worth approximately £68 million in advertising rates, whereas it cost them just 3 per cent of this – £2 million – in a direct sponsorship deal with the sport.[45] When we add to this the fact that cigarette advertising is illegal even on commercial television channels in the UK, the benefits to the sponsor are obvious. Wilson estimated that in 1986, 'about sixteen percent of all televised sport was tobacco sponsored',[46] although subsequent restrictions prevented new tobacco-backed events from gaining airtime. It is largely for this reason, and for the benefit of linking a stigmatised product with a healthy sporting image, that tobacco has consistently been the sector of industry providing the largest sponsorship, as well as the sector that has spent the largest proportion of its advertising budget on sports sponsorship.[47] Manufacturers of alcoholic drinks have similarly been active in sports sponsorship, and while there is a strong historical continuity between brewing and victualling interests and many team sports, the opportunities provided by televised sport have pushed this link to some major sponsorship deals, such as the FA Carling Premiership, Bass Headingley and the Fosters Oval, the Courage Clubs Championship in rugby union, and various events in rugby league backed by Tetley, Stones, and John Smiths. The clashes of interest that can arise here have been pointed out by Cashmore, most notably the shirt-front sponsorship of Liverpool FC by Carlsberg in an event sponsored by market rivals Carling.[48]

Sponsorship, of course, has not been random in its application, and the work of consultants and marketing departments has ensured that sponsors have tended to target their money at sports or events that are perceived to tie in with a desired image of the product in question. In many instances, there has been an emphasis on health and vitality that the sport can maintain, an idea that was present in Oxo's relatively crude sponsorship of the 1908 Olympic Marathon mentioned above. For our period, this has been noticeable at many events. The Milk Marketing Board's deals with cycling from the 1950s and football in the 1980s were parts of wider advertising campaigns that stressed the health benefits of drinking milk. The same has been true of some sponsors of the London Marathon, including Mars Bars which are marketed as energy giving, and, from 1996, Flora margarine, a market leader in low-cholesterol spreads. During 1988, Mars Bars were specially packaged and labelled as the 'official snack food of the British Olympic team' for Seoul. Other sponsorship campaigns have directly linked products that are integral to the sport with the wider public market of the sport's followers in the hope that the name and the sport will be firmly associated. This has been particularly evident in motor racing, through sponsors such as Shell and Duckhams, and in individual participation sports such as golf and tennis, where manufacturers have stressed their products' place in the elite game: the Dunlop Masters Tournament in golf, which ran from 1946 until 1972, was an example of this approach, although it was tellingly subsequently taken over by cigarette companies Silk Cut and, from 1979, Dunhills.[49]

There has also been a more general trend of image by association in sports sponsorship. Here, market research and social trends have helped to bring together products and sports that the sponsors believe to go together, such as Beefeater Gin and the Oxford and Cambridge Boat Race, various financial institutions and rugby union, Sanatogen cod liver oil in bowls, and John Smiths Yorkshire Bitter in rugby league. Changes here are crucial to our appreciation of shifts in popular perceptions of specific sports over time, as illustrated by the growth of financial services sponsorship in football by Endsleigh Insurance and the Nationwide Building Society. It is at this point that, ultimately, complaints about links between sport and tobacco and alcohol become redundant, such as those made by Gate in his history of rugby league when he pointed out that 'all these huge sponsorships emanated from the brewing and tobacco industries and are hardly in keeping with the values the game is supposed to embody'.[50] If sponsorship is about putting a brand name in front of potential customers, then it has been spectators rather than potential players that have been the target of tobacco and drink concerns. While other benefits of sponsorship have clearly mattered to sponsors, such as opportunities for corporate hospitality, the promotion of local goodwill, and even the maintenance of social order, the essential motivation has been commercial.[51]

Sponsorship, in tandem with television, has had an effect upon the way in which sports, and clubs, have been run. The volume of money that has come to be involved, the importance of the money to individual clubs and sports, and the constant need to maximise the potential income have ensured that sports have had to become more business-like. For many sports, this has required a shift from the management cultures which had been inherited from their histories. As Mason put it for football, 'It was not that football and business . . . were expected to inhabit separate spheres. But each was expected to know its place and in sport business was the lesser partner.'[52] The FA's restrictions on dividend payments at just 7.5 per cent from 1914 helped to make sure that football was not a lucrative business for its investors, although involvement in clubs has always brought additional local benefits. For sports such as cricket and rugby union, with much stronger amateur traditions in management, the imperatives of the commercial world were even further removed from clubs' and governing bodies' cultures. However, the loss of staple revenues, the attractions offered by sponsorship and television, and the pressure on clubs to diversify gradually helped to bring about the adoption of a more commercial orientation. Different sports have coped with this shift in different ways, but some general trends have emerged. In many sports, the period from the late 1970s has seen the growth of tiers of management and administration which are connected to commercial and business aspects of the club or sport rather than to the playing side. In 1982, the FA allowed clubs to pay a director for the first time, a move followed by a doubling of the maximum share dividend from 7.5 per cent to 15 per cent. Tottenham Hotspur then broke with the traditional limited-liability status in 1983 by floating on the Stock Exchange, a shift followed by many clubs since.[53] The Football League appointed its first commercial manager in 1987, following the lead from many clubs, and similar trends were evident in cricket, rugby league, and rugby union. This shift represented a gradual erosion of the older habits, based upon poor planning, unprofessional accounting, and *ad hoc* arrangements with commercial interests, and led to a more co-ordinated approach. Unlike the American model, where the way in which elite clubs in the major sports have historically been bought and sold as movable franchises has been linked with far more commercially oriented outlooks from owners and investors, the British experience has tended to downplay this aspect until the competition made it unavoidable.[54] The irony of the lateness of this shift was not lost on Sandiford, who noted the apparent paradox of the voluntary tradition, where 'professional business men serving on MCC as well as various county cricket club committees could reject professional business methods in the running of first-class cricket as late as the 1960s'.[55] Such methods were increasingly embraced in the face of competition, and to attempt to maximise the earning potential of clubs and their resources.

This has had a number of effects. For the paying spectator, the shift in commercial orientation has generally meant an upgrading of amenities. Governing bodies and clubs have attempted to tempt back the more discriminating spectators by providing better facilities, particularly in such areas as food and drink sales, toilets, car parking, and comfort of spectating accommodation. In horse-racing, for example, the closure of seven courses by 1965 in the face of declining attendances and legal off-course cash betting forced the authorities to make some concessions to consumer choice: according to Vamplew, the Jockey Club dropped its old motto 'the public don't count', and replaced it with an official policy 'to promote the attraction of live racing by making the spectator once more the focus of the sport'. Family- and party-oriented improvements in racecourse amenities followed.[56] Gate-taking rugby union clubs had to improve facilities in order to win the crowds and sponsors needed to maintain their assets and growing staff, a process which all elite clubs have had to embrace since the acceptance of professionalism in 1995. Some clubs have moved into ground- and administration-sharing relationships with football clubs, such as Wasps and Queens Park Rangers (QPR). Football itself was forced to address the quality of spectators' amenities from the 1960s onwards. The Chester Report of 1968 criticised clubs for providing poor amenities and unfriendly environments, particularly for family groups, and steps were taken to redress this in an attempt to attract middle-class spectators: not only would such a shift bring in spectators with high levels of disposable income, a shift seen by Critcher as one from 'traditional supporter' to 'modern consumer', it would also help to push out the non-respectable hooligan fans.[57] Clearly, this did not work at once, but the historical development of football architecture and marketing strategies since has built on these ideologies. The process was hastened by the football establishment's reading of the Taylor Report to attempt to continue to win back paying customers. The introduction of administrators from outside the old football establishments often helped to speed this process up. Karren Brady, appointed as Birmingham City's Managing Director in 1993 from a media and advertising background, has left a telling account of this aspect of her arrival at the club, including her general observation on the club's stadium, St Andrews: 'I'd seen better facilities in a Bangkok lavatory.'[58] In a period in which leisure has become increasingly competitive, and spectators' historical links to particular clubs or events have become fractured, an improvement in spectating conditions has been a general trend; and while many, particularly in sports such as rugby league and football with traditions of working-class support, have resisted this process as being unnecessary, expensive, and detrimental to their traditions and interests, it is hard to see the process being reversed.

Another feature of this broad development has been the increasing diversification of sports clubs and agencies. Two particular trends have been discernible: the marketing of franchised and official products; and the rental of clubs' facilities to other users. The franchising and sale of products has been linked to individual clubs in major sports. Replica shirts are the most obvious example, a sector pioneered by football clubs where large numbers of supporters could be relied upon to purchase this kind of artefact. By the late 1980s, the majority of Football League and Scottish League clubs were exploiting the appeal of this item to supporters by changing the design of their strip every two seasons in a market that was then worth £7 million nationally.[59] By the mid-1990s, this had developed so that most clubs changed not just their home and away strips annually, but also had up to four strips on the go at any one time, with replica versions sold through club shops and sports outlets. Rugby league clubs also developed this aspect of their operations, as did county cricket clubs: the adoption of coloured clothing in Sunday cricket, with the county's name across the front of the shirt, was specifically designed to create this kind of market, much to the disgust of many traditionalists. Other club-related products, as diverse as cosmetics, baby clothes, videos, books, mugs, and marmalades, have also been developed, both through shops at clubs' grounds and, for some of the larger football clubs, through club shops and franchises at remote sights. Manchester United have been most prominent in this trend: by 1994, the club had branches in Plymouth, Dublin, and Belfast, and was planning a wider international spread through branches in Tokyo and Sydney, a trend that has made the club 'the footballing equivalent of Marks and Spencer'. As the club's merchandising turnover was £14.2 million in 1993–4, the significance of this sector is clearly crucial.[60]

Some more prestigious sporting institutions have developed another form of franchising, which has left them financially comfortable enough to run their events without affixing sponsors' names or introducing perimeter advertising hoardings. The international model here is the International Olympic Committee (IOC), which set up The Olympic Programme (TOP) in 1985 as a way of generating non-television income without adopting sponsorship. Through TOP, run by the marketing company ISL, the IOC have sold their instantly recognisable symbol of five interlocking rings to selected major companies for use on their products, including Fuji and Coca-Cola.[61] In the UK, a similar pathway was followed by two leading club-run events: the Royal and Ancient Golf Club's British Open; and the Wimbledon Championships for the All England Lawn Tennis and Croquet Club (AELTCC). Their motifs are licensed and franchised for the use of various products: for Wimbledon, these have included tennis rackets, balls, and clothing, as well as towels, foodstuffs, and china. In 1988, the AELTCC's Chairman of the Committee of Management claimed that the Club could make an extra £5 million a year by using a sponsor's name or accepting perimeter advertisements, a significant sum in the context of their 1987 profit of £7 million. However, the more understated form of commercialism involved in franchising was preferred owing to the Club's image.[62] Franchising was also a central part of American football's launch in the UK, with the National Football League extending its indigenous commercial practices by franchising out its logo to manufacturers and retailers of various products, including high-street chains Marks and Spencers and British Home Stores.[63]

The other key form of diversification has been for clubs and sport locations to open their facilities for wider public usage, and so earn more money from the key fixed assets than holding only the regular fixtures there could ever do. In the quest for alternative incomes, some racecourses developed golf driving ranges in their central area and provided exhibition and conference facilities.[64] Some grounds in various sports have been rented out for other large events. From the late 1960s, various football and other clubs rented out their grounds for rock and pop concerts: for example, The Who's venues in the 1970s included The Valley, home of Charlton Athletic FC, and Surrey County Cricket Club's home The Oval, while Wembley Stadium (not owned by any club but designed and primarily run as a sports facility) branched out to welcome Live Aid, The Rolling Stones, Simon and Garfunkel, and others. Religious gatherings in need of large spaces have also been customers of sports clubs, such as Jehovah's Witnesses conventions at Murrayfield and the Rivers of Life 1996 Victory Crusade at Millwall's New Den. Experiments with all-weather pitches, as that pioneered by QPR, were partially designed to facilitate this kind of non-sport use for wider access and rents. Again, as with the more blatant forms of sponsorship, richer clubs have been able to avoid this form of diversification. The AELTCC, for example, has maintained its facilities well below maximum utilisation levels despite its size and location. This decision has been defended in the interests of local relations, the need to protect the grass, and the prestigious image of its major tournament: 'There is a mystique about Wimbledon which might be tarnished if we did things like pop concerts or big fights. To most people, Wimbledon is tennis.'[65] Some clubs have also made their specialised fitness facilities, such as gymnasiums and physiotherapy clinics, commercially available.

As well as bringing in the paying members of the public, concert crowds, and religious conventions, a number of clubs have diversified by renting their facilities to other clubs in the same sport, or to smaller clubs from other sports. Groundsharing became an economic necessity for some south London football clubs in a changing property market in the 1980s, with Crystal Palace renting its Selhurst Park stadium to Charlton Athletic from 1985 to 1991, and Wimbledon since 1991. These deals, while not universally accepted by the moving clubs' supporters, have allowed them to play on paying just 50 per cent of Selhurst Park's running costs per season, plus 10 per cent of the gate money.[66] Some rugby league clubs were forced into renting facilities from established football clubs, including Hunslet's residence at Leeds United's Elland Road from 1982 until 1994. The facilities were not always to the tastes of the rugby league followers: not only was the stadium, 'echoing to the shouts of only a few hundred',[67] far too big for the average gates, but there was an understandable dislike of being 'fenced into penitentiary compounds designed to contain soccer hooligans'.[68] This regular contract led to more lucrative rugby league fixtures for Leeds United, including semi-finals in the Challenge Cup and Regal Trophy Finals.[69] American football's take-off in the UK required clubs to lease facilities before they could make capital outlay on grounds of their own. Tottenham, Millwall, and other clubs have also hosted boxing events. Finally in this context, some football clubs have diversified into other sports, investing money in developing teams to attempt to attract different audiences to their stadia. The biggest development here came in the burst of football clubs fielding rugby league sides in the 1980s, such as Fulham, Cardiff City with the Cardiff City Blue Dragons, Maidstone with Kent Invicta, and Mansfield Town's links with the Mansfield Marksmen. Fulham RLFC enjoyed some early success here when it joined the Second Division in 1980, famously beating Wigan 24–5 in its first match and winning promotion in its first season; and the attendances seemed to justify the football club's diversification, as it averaged a decent 6,096 for a game that had little professional history in London. However, this experiment faltered as uncertainty over Craven Cottage forced the rugby club to move to smaller accommodation at Chiswick's Polytechnic Stadium.[70]

While some of these revenue-raising ventures in diversification have failed, the commercial success of some of the larger football clubs by the 1990s, such as Manchester United and Tottenham Hotspur, has shown that the desperate financial climate of the years from the 1960s to the mid-1980s has been left behind for those which have managed to combine professional management techniques, diversification, and investment from shareholders and wealthy individuals. The model currently emerging around Newcastle United, where successful business man Sir John Hall has invested in various clubs in different sports under the broad heading of Newcastle United Sporting Club, is a mid-1990s development in this sphere that must be seen in the broader context of sport's need for commercial success. From the base of the city's successful football club, Hall brought in Newcastle Gosforth Rugby Club and Durham Wasps ice hockey team in 1994, and planned to develop links with athletics, motor racing, and a regional centre of sporting excellence with commercially run facilities for golf, swimming, and other sports.[71] The scale and ambition of this project, and the resistance it has met from followers of the individual sports for the disruption of tradition that it has brought, are both key elements of the tensions between continuity and change that have characterised sport's relationship with commerce in the post-war period.

As some of the examples cited above have shown commercial diversification and sponsorship have not always been welcomed by sports. The roots of this antipathy are varied, but they have generally been related to the popular notion that sport should be kept separate from aspects of contemporary society that are believed to be external to sport, and whose presence is seen to corrupt sport's ideals and ethical base. Arguments against sponsorship are thus similar to the arguments against political involvement in sport. As with the case of politics, the opposition has been generally ineffective and arguably misguided. To deny links between sport and the society in which it exists is ahistorical, and sport would simply not exist in its present forms were it not for commercial involvement. However, the persistence of opposition in the face of a heavily commercialised sporting scene, and the range of arguments used against it, are crucial to our appreciation of post-war British sport. One trend has been to oppose the presence of advertising on largely aesthetic grounds, based on the way in which sponsors' names are perceived to disrupt the harmonious appearance of sporting action. This has been particularly evident in attacks on cricket's links with sponsors, not just through the heavily criticised introduction of coloured clothing, but also in opposition to the presence of advertising materials in and around the playing area. In 1974, for example, one influential correspondent to *The Times* claimed that 'incongruous and garish' advertising boards were marring his enjoyment of televised cricket;[72] while later, cricket journalist Scyld Berry railed against sponsors' logos painted on pitches, calling them 'a damn eyesore . . . I do wish English tolerance would not extend to letting them get away with it'.[73]

However, as analysts of sport and sponsorship have shown, it is not only in the realm of aesthetics that sport has been adversely affected by the growth of sponsorship as a replacement for gate revenue. What Gratton and Taylor called 'costs . . . to the sponsored sport'[74] have been caused by the loss of independence for clubs and governing bodies that has come with commercial and corporate funding. Just as political controls have given sport both opportunities and constraints, so too have extensive commercial links. The opportunities created by sponsorship at a time when sports needed new sources of income are obvious, but the constraints also need to be stressed. New competitions have been started by sponsors in a number of sports essentially as vehicles for their names. Events of this nature have been blamed for overextending sportsmen and women's programmes, and disrupting their preparations for the more established events at national and international level. In some sports, low levels of public enthusiasm for such events has demonstrated an awareness of their purely commercial nature, as witness the consistently poor attendances in football's newest domestic knock-out competition, the Associate Members Cup, which was first contested in 1983–4, and has been named after successive sponsors Freight Rover, Sherpa Van, Leyland Daf, and Autoglass. While the final brings a glamorous Wembley appearance for clubs who could rarely aspire to success in the FA Cup and the League Cup – winners have included Wigan Athletic, Mansfield Town, and Port Vale – the early rounds have been notoriously poorly attended. Another drawback of sponsorship is that sponsors can disappear as quickly as they appeared, leaving dependent sports suddenly overextended and underfunded. This happened to athletics in 1968,[75] and to women's tennis in 1994, when Autoglass pulled out of its sponsorship deal with the Brighton indoor tournament and the Lawn Tennis Association failed to find a replacement. Unable to cover the costs, including £280,000 in prize money, the event was sold.[76]

Another problem has been that pressure has come through sponsorship and television to change laws and structures of sports themselves in the interests of drama, excitement, and decisiveness. Limited-over cricket has been the most roundly attacked development here, as purists argue that it promotes speed and recklessness over subtlety.[77] John Arlott, in a realistic defence of the concept on commercial grounds, described it as 'the form of the game that spectators like most and the players least'.[78] Golf croquet, which the CA rejected in 1984 as a form of the game suitable for television, was designed to be fast, contained, and easy for spectators to follow: the critics on the CA claimed that it was simply not representative of the real sport.[79] Laws have been changed in all three major football codes to attempt to make play more exciting, such as rugby league's four tackles rule in 1966 (amended to six in 1972), and football's gradual acceptance of the penalty shoot-out and, more recently, sudden-death extra time, in domestic cup competitions and promotional play-offs. In rugby union, law changes introduced since the 1950s were clearly aimed to make the game more attractive, flowing, and attacking, such as increases in the value of the try and the prohibition of kicks into touch from anywhere but players' own twenty-five yard line.[80] The pressures on these changes are not purely commercial: for example, police pressure to reduce the number of replays in the FA Cup helped to introduce the penalty shoot-out in that event. Neither are they purely domestic: the outlawing of the back pass to the goalkeeper in football to prevent time wasting came from the game's international governing body. However, a strong element in the various changes, which have recently included rugby league switching its entire calendar from winter to summer and rugby union accommodating professionalism, has been the desire to increase the various sports' attractiveness to paying spectators, television audiences, and ultimately sponsors. The restructuring of the Football League in 1992, with the former First Division splintering to form the Premier League (later the Premiership), was similarly based on the television and advertising revenue that a trimmed-down elite could attract. The growth of sponsorship has been a driving force in modern British sport, one that has increased significantly in quantity and quality over the post-war period owing to related changes in technology, television, and sport, and as new forms of telecommunications become increasingly available in the home, particularly pay-per-view, this aspect is unlikely to diminish.

Chapter 4

Sport and gender

INTRODUCTION

Gender is an important issue in contemporary sport. The cultural field in general has increasingly become an area for public discussion and negotiation of the roles and identities of men and women, and the relations between them. This has taken place in an increasingly noticeable way because of the major changes that have occurred in gender relations since 1945.[1] While British society is still essentially patriarchal in terms of men dominating economic and political power, there have been a number of notable challenges to this settlement. These include the consolidation of women's presence in the workplace, the coming of age for generations of men and women for whom women's political enfranchisement was assumed, the emergence of feminism and women's liberation as political and cultural movements, the public debate over sexual orientations which has included the limited legalisation of homosexuality, and developments in birth control. These changes have inspired academic and popular debate: first, on the issues of equality between men and women; and latterly, about the way in which masculine and feminine identities are culturally constructed and contested, and the relations between them. While the continuation of an essentially patriarchal power structure has not been prevented by these developments, various common-sense assumptions in everyday discourse suggest that inequalities of opportunity in various fields are no longer acceptable.

For the academic debate on these developments, sport has provided a focus for historical, sociological, cultural studies, and gender studies analyses of gender relations and identities. Sport has been seen so clearly as 'an institution created by and for men'.[2] With its emphasis on public physical performance, it is frequently used as an index of comparative roles, identified as 'an arena of popular culture in which gender representations . . . are played out in potent and powerful ways'.[3] With elite women running marathons faster than all but elite men,[4] older notions of women as the weaker sex are having to be revised, and with women achieving success in team games popularly believed to be traditionally men's sports, notably football and rugby union, a shift in perception of which sports are appropriate for different sexes is taking place. An excellent cameo of this process can be seen in the appearance in the 1980s and 1990s of a number of film and television dramas dealing sympathetically and humorously with women's involvement in football: *Gregory's Girl*, *Those Glory, Glory Days*, and *The Manageress* are examples of this genre which would have been impossible without a shift in public assumptions about sport and gender.

The period has been less easy to label for men's sport. There has been no parallel pattern of films and dramas about men playing netball, a trend which backs up the generally one-way traffic in gendered sport that sees girls and women entering traditionally male sport, but not the other way round, ensuring that 'images of femininity in sport and PE are diversifying more quickly than masculine ones'.[5] However, while men may not have rushed to take up traditionally female sports as a sign of a desire for equality, there have been shifts in perception about how men can behave in sport. Paul Gascoigne's public tears during the 1990 football World Cup semi-final offered an image of change, even if the patriotic meaning of the tears made the act of crying in public 'not wholly unmanly'.[6] The slow but perceptible emergence of openly homosexual sportsmen must also be seen in this context.[7]

In short, British sport by the mid-1990s is the location of changing popular attitudes about acceptable and appropriate behaviour for men and women. As such, it continues to play a part in wider definitions of male and female that have been evident since the emergence of modern sport in the nineteenth century, when most vigorous sports were barred to women on medical and cultural grounds, and sports that rested upon aggression and domination were promoted as worthy pastimes for men.

The academic study of this feature of sport has followed on from the acceptance of sports history and sociology. While the sports history pioneers of the 1960s and 1970s were mainly concerned with filling in the narrative and establishing such crucial themes as the impact of industrialisation on sport and the growth of national sporting cultures, the history of gender issues in sport remained largely unexplored. In part, this was due to the nascent state of women's history itself as a subdiscipline, which had women's leisure activities as a lower priority for research than their political and economic roles. At the same time, the role of men in sport was so fundamental as to go largely unremarked: 'The history of sport in modern Britain is a history of men. . . . Sport has always been a male preserve with its own language, its initiation rites, and models of true masculinity, its clubbable, jokey cosiness',[8] and it was far too early to expect any critical analysis of masculinity to emerge from a predominantly male academic establishment. This absence calls to mind Kidd's claim that 'ideology is like BO: you never smell your own'.[9] Parratt's arguments on the 'traditional periodization' of sports history around the emergence of male sports rather than female sports are useful here, as they suggest another way in which the discipline was, to begin with, uncritically about male sports history.[10] An example of this can be seen in the use of the label 'Golden Age of Cricket', which is generally applied to the men's game before the First World War, without countenancing the 1930s in the women's game as worthy of the title.[11] The sociology of sport was also unable at this point to see beyond what Dunning identified as 'assumptions indicative of an unquestioned male dominance'.[12]

Change in the academic sphere came about gradually, and it made itself felt in relation to women's experiences of sport before it was applied to men's. The emergence of women in higher education was a prerequisite, as was the development of feminism as a theoretical tool for academic analysis.[13] Similarly, the prolific success of elite sportswomen through the 1970s and 1980s made sociological and historical analysis inevitable, and by 1994 gender had become 'the most popular topic in the sociology of sport'.[14] Shoebridge's 1987 bibliography *Women in Sport*, with 1,651 entries covering a wide range of disciplinary approaches and different sports, is a useful indicator of this popularity.[15] Linked to the wider development of women's history as a subdiscipline through the work of such scholars as Lerner, Koonz, and Rowbotham,[16] women's sports history came into focus. It has reached its high point in the British context so far with Jennifer Hargreaves' comprehensive *Sporting Females*.[17]

The historical debate on women's sport has had two major strands. Probably the most obvious and popular has been the move to discover the history of women's success in sport, which not only helps to fill in the gaps in the previously male-centred history, but also serves the contemporary purpose of demonstrating historical legitimacy for women's access to, and success in, sport. This is the kind of women's history that Lerner called compensatory history, stressing 'women of achievement, rather than the mass of women', which Parratt applied to sports history.[18] Blue's *Grace Under Pressure* is an example of this. It includes a list of key dates ('1973 Billie Jean King wins the tennis Battle of the Sexes'), and an appendix covering 'women who surpass men'.[19] Blue's agenda is neatly summarised by a quotation from javelin thrower Fatima Whitbread on the dustjacket: 'When reading this book I discovered for the first time the sacrifices that women have made and their true contribution to sport.'[20] This approach was used more effectively, but from an equally uncritical liberal perspective, by social biologist Dyer in *Catching Up the Men*, a book with the 'underlying messages' that 'women's sporting performances are improving rapidly'.[21] He used statistics to show the catching up process, and often relied upon shock tactics to stress the ignorance and prejudices of historical sports administrations that have failed to provide opportunities for women in sport. While Blue and Dyer have offered accounts of multiple sports, other authors have used this compensatory approach to recover women's histories in individual sports, particularly those which may popularly be seen as male dominated. Mountaineering drew the attention of Birkett and Peascod in 1989 with *Women Climbing*, while different aspects of women's historical involvement with equestrian sports have been covered by Martin and Ramsden.[22] The main achievement of this genre of work has been to rescue women's sporting triumphs from what Thompson, writing in a different context, called the 'enormous condescension of posterity';[23] and it is a useful introduction to critical thinking about the historical roots of the obstacles that exist for women attempting to succeed in sport. However, it has been criticised by sports feminists for being rooted in an uncritical male view of sport. This approach has tended only to foreground those women who have made it in the male sphere and have conformed to masculine values in sport of strength and domination.[24]

An alternative approach has come from sports feminists, such as Parratt, Struna, Dewar, and Jennifer Hargreaves, who have insisted not only upon seeing women's sport as part of women's lived experiences which should not be judged by male criteria, but also upon using gender as a 'fundamental category for analysis' of sport.[25] This work has delved into power relations and the meanings attached to sport, rather than the more positivist tendency to look at the success of elite individuals. Dewar's comment on the relational approach highlights the differences:

The fact . . . that the fastest woman in the world is slower than the fastest man is of no interest in relational analysis. What is important is why this fact is deemed important, what it symbolizes, and how it is implicated in the reproduction of the social relations of gender or male power and privilege in society.[26]

Both approaches are useful for the light they shed on women's attitudes towards, and opportunities in, sport in the post-war period. At present, the critical feminist perspective is proving the most influential in the field. It lends itself to interdisciplinary approaches, particularly in its bid to show how gender relations rather than gender differences are at the root of sports history. An American example is the collection of essays edited in 1994 by Costa and Guthrie, *Women and Sport*, which brought together historians, physical educationalists, political scientists, gynaecologists, and others,[27] and while some of the findings are applicable to the British example, a comparable work from a British perspective is still needed.

Men's sport and the issue of masculinity has not had such a long historiography. This is based on the longevity of common-sense assumptions about sport being a natural domain for men, 'one of the few privileged areas where we seem to be dealing with unmediated "reality", where we know "what's what" . . . . Running faster, jumping higher, throwing further can be *seen* – not interpreted.'[28] This has had the effect of placing it beyond critical analysis from a largely male academic establishment. Wider than this, it is linked to the absence of masculinity as a research topic in mainstream academic enquiry before the mid- to late 1980s. Roper and Tosh helped to draw attention to the developing debate on the interdisciplinary academic analysis of masculinity in their 1991 collection *Manful Assertions*, where they defined their main aim as being making 'men visible as gendered subjects' in history.[29] This kind of approach has been attractive for those working on sport because of sport's obvious role in defining masculinity and manliness: we need only cite footballer Trevor Ford's observation that football 'is not a woman's game, it's not a pastime for milksops or sissies, it's a man's game',[30] or wrestling promoter Max Crabtree's view of his sport as 'strictly a man's game',[31] to see the centrality of common-sense masculinity in popular perceptions of sport. Dunning's 1986 essay on masculine identity helped to identify the huge gaps that existed in the analysis of sport and gender. This has been developed since the 1980s, in particular in a British context by the work of Dunning and his colleagues on masculinity and football hooliganism,[32] and by Mangan on Victorian constructions of manliness, which has heavily focused upon sporting culture.[33] The collection of essays he co-edited with

Walvin, *Manliness and Morality*, offers crucial insights for the sports histo-rian,[34] as does the pioneering work on rugby and masculinity collected by Nauright and Chandler in 1996, introduced as an attempt to focus attention on 'the effect that gendered identities, created and perpetuated over time, have had on sports, the men and women who play them . . . and . . . on the place and values of sport in society generally'.[35]

This strand of critical historiography has been supplemented by work in sociology, cultural studies, and gender studies which has offered feminist and gay critiques of men's sport.[36] The insights of the work in this field are only tentatively being applied to the history of men in sport. Whereas the aims of early women's sport historiography were to uncover a hidden history, the work on men has had to explore the reasons for a dominant, common-sense history, and fill in the silences and blind spots that common sense has allowed to develop. It has had critically to look at the ways in which values linked to dominant forms of masculinity have been built into all the major sports, with emphasis on aggression, speed, and domination: as Coakley has wryly pointed out, 'if sports had been created by and for women, the Olympic Games motto would not be *Citius, Altius, Fortius* (faster, higher, stronger); instead it might be "balance, flexibility, and ultraendurance"!'[37] It has also explored the ways in which sport has been used to reflect and confirm patriarchal society by marginalising femininity and homosexuality. This work has emphasised the semiotics of dominant masculinity and its alternatives: Pronger's work on the ambivalence between heterosexual display and homosexual aesthetics in North American sport which he labels 'Jocks and paradox' and traces through sporting themes in gay pornographic films such as *Basket Practice* and *Pumping*, is an example of this.[38] This awaits a British application, although Simpson's essay on homoeroticism in football sets up leads that historians could follow.[39]

With these historiographical observations in place, this chapter will explore the issue of gender in sport in the UK since 1945. Earlier surveys, such as those by Holt, Mason, and Brailsford, tended to deal only with women under the category of gender, thus reproducing the common-sense silence on men. Even Cashmore, with his interdisci-plinary approach, has not included a discussion of masculinity as a gender problem in the second edition of his key text, preferring instead to keep his gender focus on 'why women are devalued by sports'.[40] With the insights provided by Dunning, and Roper and Tosh, as well as that of the sports feminists, this study will consider the experiences of both sexes, looking at the related issues of what kinds of sport and sporting behaviour have been practised by men and women, and how assumptions about men's and women's sports have been reproduced and negotiated. In doing so, it is acknowledged that it is reductionist and somewhat artificial to treat the issue of gender separately. To discuss only the gender of somebody involved in sport as if it were separable from other parts of his or her make-up – age, ethnicity, class, religion, and health, for example – is misleading. However, gender has historically been treated as a powerful determinant, of even greater importance than class: Jennifer Hargreaves claims with justification that 'the whole of the history of modern sports has been based on gender divisions'.[41] These divisions are manifested in various ways: in the differentials in prize money and media coverage that gives women's events less prestige than men's; in the small number of sports played by men and women as equals; in the dominance of the sporting establishment and media by men; in the media coverage that presents sportsmen and women as gendered subjects; in the marketing of different sports at different sexes; and in the simple structural constraints in changing facilities that assume not only differences between the sexes but also heterosexuality. Clearly, these divisions are still assumed and deeply embedded in the ways in which sport is played, watched, and organised.

WOMEN AND SPORT IN POST-WAR BRITAIN

Over the course of our period, there have been some notable changes in the whole issue of women and sport. In the mid-1990s, women generally have greater opportunities for access to participation and spectating, thanks to such developments as childcare facilities at sports amenities, than was possible in the mid-1940s. Moreover, elite sportswomen have a far higher profile than their forebears did, and women have increasing access to sports that were previously defined and guarded as male preserves: both rugby codes and football are the obvious examples. However, these changes have been paralleled by a number of continuities. The popular notion of female-appropriate sports, those that emphasise grace, agility, flexibility, and aesthetic performance, is still as strong as ever. Arguably, it has even been strengthened by the public emergence of rhythmic gymnastics and synchronised swimming, both added to the Olympic programme and thus given international mass media attention in 1984. Moreover, popular cultural portrayals of sportswomen still rely heavily upon uncritical traditional perceptions of femininity and its opposites, exemplified in an extreme form by Auberon Waugh's provocative comments in *The Spectator* on the differences between the 'extremely ugly . . . self-proclaimed lesbian' Martina

Navratilova, and the 'deliciously pretty' Gabriela Sabatini.[42] A similar kind of ideology is visible in some popular sports history, exemplified by May's coverage of leading golfer Jan Stephenson, whose action picture's caption begins 'Blessed with great good looks and a beautiful golf swing'.[43] With such ambivalence still evident in the discourse on women and sport, it is the purpose of this section to explore women's experiences in sport since 1945.

Coming out of the Second World War, women's sporting roles were heavily constrained by norms that had been established during the nineteenth-century debates over medicine and anatomy. These had limited women in a number of ways. First, women were pushed into certain sports deemed appropriately feminine, essentially those emphasising aesthetics and grace over strength and speed. Second, team games developed in a limited way in parallel to rugby and football at boys' schools, but these typically involved less direct physical contact between players than the male team games: netball, hockey, and lacrosse were the main sports here, and attempts to establish women's football and rugby teams were resisted from the male authorities in those sports. For example, the FA withdrew its brief support of women's football in 1921.[44] Third, some sports were deemed appropriate for both sexes, but were generally diluted to accommodate women's perceived weaknesses: lawn tennis, with its three-set matches for women and five for men, with mixed doubles being played to the women's standard of three sets; women's hockey, with matches lasting for sixty minutes, men's for seventy; and athletics, with its limited range of events for women keeping female athletes out of longer distances and the heaviest throwing events, are examples. Dyer suggests that this differentiation has been based on the assumption that men's sports are the norm, with sportswomen seen as 'immature or truncated men'.[45] As well as these respectable sports, Hargreaves has shown an underside to women's sports in the '"low-life" sports' of boxing, wrestling, mud wrestling, and weight-lifting, often linked to fairgrounds and circuses.[46] Their existence cannot be ignored, but they need to be seen as marginal. It was out of this sporting inheritance that women entered the post-war world. The difference, of course, was that the economic and social impact of the war had caused some re-evaluation of women's roles, and increasing opportunities for sport and leisure gradually became part of the wider debate on gender relations.

In the immediate post-war period, mainstream sport and sports coverage remained generally entrenched in a separate spheres ideology. Underpinned by physical education ideologies that separated the sexes and taught them different physical activities based on cultural models, women's access to sport remained relatively limited. The attitude of the time has often been summarised with reference to newspaper coverage of the star of the 1948 Olympic Games, held in London. The Dutch athlete Fanny Blankers-Koen, who won four gold medals at Wembley, was written up in the *Daily Graphic* in terms that defined her traditional role as wife and mother alongside her impressive athletic achievements: 'Fastest woman in the world is an expert cook'.[47] However, such press attitudes do not disguise the achievement. In addition to the Olympic Games, at which fifty one of the British team were women (14 per cent),[48] women's representative sport continued to grow in this period. In the winter of 1947–8, for example, the Women's Cricket Association (WCA) organised its second tour of Australasia,[49] and similar patterns were followed in other sports. However, these events were given marginal treatment by the media, and were underfunded by governing bodies, with players largely having to fund their own travel expenses.

It was from the mid-1960s that a whole range of events took place that helped to challenge the idea of separate development. These can be broadly linked to the politics and cultural politics of feminism which were emerging in the public sphere. In various walks of life, the issue of equality of access and opportunity between men and women was aired. Sport was a significant forum for this debate, alongside the workplace and the educational system, for the same reasons that sport had been a significant forum in the nineteenth century: it is based upon the public and symbolic usage of the body. There were diverse developments in this period from the mid-1960s onwards that allow us to see the trend of women's sport emerging as a feminist issue.

The most obvious trend has been the increasing provision of sportive leisure activities for mass participation by women. Since the 1970s, various events based on principles of individual health and fitness have developed, often under American commercial influences. Jogging is a classic example. This emerged as a non-competitive, relatively cheap sport that did not require purpose-built amenities, and was promoted as beneficial to both sexes for cardiovascular health and weight loss. It became particularly attractive to women as a friendly, sociable sport that tested and developed the participant in a non-aggressive way. A guide to women's running, written by Alison Turnbull, the founder of the Sisters Project to encourage more women to take up running, claimed this aspect as a central part of the sport's appeal: 'It is much easier for a woman to find the support and encouragement she needs when taking those first steps if she is running with other women who understand the sort of problems she is likely to have.'[50] Her guide, designed to encourage women of all ages to take up running, included endorsements from a number of women that stress this theme of friendship, support, and self-enhancement, including the 18-year-old student who claimed that running had 'greatly increased my confidence', and the 47-year-old solicitor who, thanks to the benefits accrued from running, had 'a new lover and my sex life is marvellous'.[51] The competitive side of the sport has grown remarkably over the period, particularly through such high-profile events as the London Marathon. However, the sport has retained, for all but the elite, an air of fun and self-improvement that is absent from many competitive sports. Aerobics and all its variants – boxercise, slide, step, pop mobility and so on – has been the other major development in this context. This is heavily based upon previous models of women's exercise from nineteenth-century gymnastics onwards, emphasising rhythmic movement to train and develop flexibility, suppleness, and agility. As with jogging, it has also been linked to weight loss and cardiovascular improvement, while boxercise has also provided transferable self-defence benefits. Again, aerobics has developed a competitive side, but as a mass participant sport it has played a significant role in mobilising women since the late 1970s.

These developments have been criticised.[52] While it has been easy to concentrate on the numbers of women involved in these sports and view this as a triumph for women appropriating leisure time and improving their health, this has obscured the fact that not all women have had equal access. Fees for private and municipal aerobics sessions, particularly under the influence of Conservative local government policy (see Chapter 1), have tended to keep the sport in the middle class, and while concessionary prices and subsidised childcare facilities have helped to bring more women in, the sport is still dependent upon wider economics of time and transport which are not always available for working-class women. The sport has also come in for criticism for promoting itself as liberating for women whilst being structurally involved with an international leisure industry of equipment, clothing, and magazines, all of which have tapped a fruitful market through women's sporting activity. The images used in advertising and videos have been attacked for promoting ideal body types that are unattainable, and thus for reproducing inequalities and inadequacies amongst participants: with increases in eating disorders linked to these images, the emancipation value of such activities is debatable. A final critique has been that by concentrating on grace, agility, and rhythmic movement, aerobics is simply reproducing the traditional norms of women's exercise cultures: far from being a feminist activity, it is distinctly patriarchal. While similar work needs to be done in a British context, MacNeill's work on television coverage of aerobics in North America, which she has characterised as 'sexually oriented (some would say pornographic)', has some useful insights on this aspect of the sport.[53]

Alongside this boom in women's sport has been another crucial aspect, the spread of women playing sports traditionally defined as men's. These have included combat sports such as wrestling and boxing; team sports such as football, cricket, and both rugby codes; pub- and club-based sports such as snooker, billiards, and darts; and body cult sports such as body-building and weight-lifting. All of these examples have historically developed in specifically masculine environments, ranging from public schools to public houses, and the development of women's interests as players rather than just in supporting or servicing roles has been contested. In particular, the physical activity involved in these sports challenged predominant views of women as passive creatures. The development of these events was strongly linked to a broad feminist agenda, which critics have noted has included liberal strands calling for equality of opportunity, and more radical strands which have sought to undermine existing gender relations and stereotypes and construct new identities: this is most obviously seen in body-building and weight-lifting, where the muscular aesthetic undermines traditional notions of femininity. The seriousness of these sports can be gauged by the fact that they have developed their own administrations and bureaucracies, following the pre-war pattern of the WCA, formed in 1926.[54] The Women's Football Association (WFA) was set up in 1969, followed by the Ladies' Jockey Association in 1972, the Women's Billiards and Snooker Association in 1976, the Women's Rugby Football Union in 1983, the Women's Amateur Rugby League Association in 1985, and the British Ladies' Boxing Association (BLBA) in 1993. In all of these sports, British sportswomen have been involved in promoting national and international competition, and have often proved successful. In cricket, the WCA and the International Women's Cricket Council organised the inaugural World Cup in 1973. Contested by seven teams (England, Young England, Australia, New Zealand, Jamaica, Trinidad and Tobago, and an International XI) on a league basis, this event was staged in England over a five-week period: England won the event after a final match against Australia at the Oval.[55] England also won this event in 1993. In football in 1988, England won the women's World Cup, *Munialito*, beating the hosts Italy 2–1 in the final, a feat which earned them the Sports Team of the Year award from the *Sunday Times*.[56] The year 1991 saw Wales host the inaugural women's rugby union World Cup, with twelve national teams taking part (including England and Wales). England lost the final to the USA. Also in 1991, the national three-division league for women's football was established. These trends towards separate organisation have been complemented by the establishment of the Women's Sports Foundation (WSF) in 1984 as an umbrella organisation to promote women in sport. Based on North American models – the WSF was set up in the USA in 1974, and the Canadian Association for the Advancement of Women and Sport in 1981 – this body has received Sports Council and commercial funding to help it publish the magazine *Women and Sport* and to organise an awards scheme.[57]

The general trend towards women's sport has been facilitated by the growth of an equal opportunities culture which has actively promoted the idea that women should have the same access as men to political, economic, social, and cultural activities. While this was established – albeit incompletely – in law by the Sex Discrimination Act of 1975 (SDA), developments in some sports predated this. A classic example comes from horse racing in the mid-1960s. A number of women had trained horses in the past, but owing to Jockey Club rules barring this activity, they had registered in the names of their senior stable lads: 'the most farcical and frustrating situation ever to exist in British racing'.[58] In the 1930s, Norah Wilmot repeatedly applied for a licence in her own name, and was repeatedly refused, a pattern also followed by Florence Nagle from the late 1940s, who later claimed of this period, 'The only real qualification for getting a training license seems to have been a pair of trousers'.[59] When she asked for a reason, the Jockey Club replied that 'It would not be in the best interests of racing, for women to be granted trainer's licences'.[60] In 1965, Nagle made this matter public by suing two members of the Jockey Club. Her High Court victory in February 1966 forced the Jockey Club not only to grant licences to herself and Wilmot, but also to any 'suitable women'.[61] Women riders were also accommodated shortly after this. Before 1972, only one race under Jockey Club rules, the Newmarket Town Plate, was open to jockeys of either sex, and this was only through a historical anomaly discovered by women riders in 1923. However, the Jockey Club remained opposed to women riding in their races, and women had to content themselves with less prestigious races organised by the Pony Turf Club and the Pony Racing Society. In 1972, however, following on from the legal defeat over women trainers, the Jockey Club staged its

Croquet, a slightly older Victorian lawn game that temporarily declined when lawn tennis emerged, has also historically been run with mixed competition alongside single-sex tournaments, and while men have dominated the Croquet Association's British Open Championships which have run, with stoppages for both world wars, annually since 1896, it has been won by women on six occasions. Only one of these has been in our period – Mrs Hope Rotherham in 1960. No post-war women have come close to the legendary success of Dorothy Steel, who won the Open Championships four times in the interwar period.[67] The apparent decline in the standards of women has been linked by some apologists to the decline of domestic help for the players, an observation that tells us a lot about the sport's class basis. Smith, a player and one of the sport's historians, is more realistic with her assertion that links the trend to wider structures of gender relations: 'Croquet is a highly competitive sport and with the present domination by men, it takes a tough personality to challenge them on equal terms.'[68] However, the point remains that despite the obvious imbalances, Association Croquet is played on an equal basis at the highest national level. Below this, garden croquet – like much club and informal tennis – is perennially structured around mixed-sex play.

Other sports have also developed either without regard of the player's gender, or with certain competitions and events based on equal access. For example, equestrianism has developed internationally as a mixed-sex sport since the war, with the International Olympic Committee allowing women into the dressage classes in 1952 and the show jumping classes in 1956, and British women have often proved successful both in individual and mixed-team events at the Olympic Games. In the individual three-day event at Los Angeles in 1984, for example, Virginia Holgate won bronze on Priceless; while at Munich in 1972, Ann Moore won silver in the individual jumping on Psalm, and the British team that took gold in the team three-day event was made up of Richard Meade, Mary Gordon-Watson, and Bridget Parker.[69] Road running and cross-country events are often staged simultaneously for both sexes (and increasingly for wheelchair competitors of both sexes), with segregation in the results but not in the event: this has certainly added to its appeal as a sociable and, at mass level, non-aggressive sport over the past two decades. Another crucial development in this context was the start of graded mixed-sex track races under British Athletics Federation rules in 1993. A final development worth noting here is the example of korfball, a sport invented by a Dutch schoolmaster between 1900 and 1902 specifically to incorporate both sexes and to counter the division of labour and specialisation of other team sports. This was introduced to the UK in 1946 after a demonstration by Dutch players in Willesden. It never became a major sport, and has remained geographically limited to London and the south-east of England. But the foundation of the British Korfball Association in July 1946 signified an acceptance of sporting forms that did not segregate the sexes and give women inferior roles or reduced games. However, Summerfield and White's research of the sport in 1989 suggested that it was still structured around physical and traditional gender roles, with men not only taking the central playing roles, but also the most important roles in administration, coaching, and refereeing. They concluded that far from being a 'model of egalitarianism', the sport allowed 'the a priori gender structures of the wider society' to 'reemerge in clearly defined microcosm'.[70]

A number of the major developments highlighted so far suggest that the structure of women's sport is changing in line with a liberal, equal opportunities culture, and that the barriers that prevented women in the pre-war and immediate post-war period from participating in sport have been either demolished or at least dented. The fact that the sporting establishment is taking women's sport seriously – witness the FA's absorption of the WFA in 1993, or the work of the Sports Council in promoting women's sport[71] – is easily read as an optimistic sign. However, it is clear from the evidence and the academic analysis that the situation is far from this simple. The situation has not altered radically since 1983, when Whannel claimed that authentic equality of opportunity for women in sport would come only with

> a genuinely non-sexist educational system, an undermining of domi-
> nant attitudes about the inferior physical abilities of women, a
> greater responsibility taken by men for domestic labour, more social
> provision of childcare and more women in positions of influence in
> sport organisation.[72]

There is still a strong ideological assumption underlining popular discourse that women involved in sport are breaking their natural gender roles, and that by being active and dynamic rather than passive, they are compromising or even destroying their femininity. Houlihan described the perceptions within both sport and society in general that 'to be a woman is to be an inadequate athlete and to be a successful woman athlete is to be an inadequate woman'.[73] This situation in the world of elite sport was corroborated at a grassroots level by a Sports-Council-funded survey in 1985–6 of young people's decisions about participation in sport, where youths of both sexes tended to rehearse their reasons for interest or lack of it on strongly gendered lines: for example, many of the young women interviewed had rejected sport because they did not associate it with womanhood, whereas the young men saw sport as an integral part of adult masculinity.[74] These perceptions are linked to the presentation of sport by various agencies, including the family, the education system, sports clubs and governing bodies, and the media. It is worth closing this analysis of women in post-war sport by considering the role of the media in perpetuating stereotypes and negotiating new identities.

Women's sport has consistently received less coverage than men's sport in all form of news media: as late as 1993, despite the growth of women's sport and the equal opportunities culture in general, a Sports Council survey found that women's sport received, on average, between 0.5 and 5 per cent of the newspaper space of men's sport. Moreover, the stories often tended to highlight women as challengers in traditionally male sports, such as football and long-distance yachting, rather than on everyday women's events in hockey, netball, and gymnastics.[75] These findings are not always applicable during major events, such as the Wimbledon lawn tennis championships or Olympic athletics, where women get more normative coverage, but even here, research has shown the inequalities of coverage between men's and women's events, and how even exciting and record-breaking women's events are not given the priority of more standard men's ones.[76]

Within this environment, then, women's sport has frequently been presented in ways which have attempted to reinforce the notion of natural roles whilst reporting sportswomen's successes. It is a process that Mary Dunne claims starts with girls' comics and teenage magazines, where sports (mainly in school contexts) are presented as normal for pre-pubescent girls, but as secondary to an interest in boys and fashion for adolescents.[77] In the adult world of press and broadcasting, such norms have been maintained through codings that stress the basic natural womanliness of these extraordinary women in sport. The unconscious agenda has been to confirm that they are heterosexual, home-loving, child-bearing females despite their success in the competitive, aggressive world of sport. A few examples from across the period can illustrate this. When the MCC allowed the England women's cricket team to practise in the nets at Lord's in preparation for the 1951 visit by the Australians, the London *Evening News* headlined the story 'Grace returned to Lord's to-day'.[78] BBC television coverage of a Wightman Cup match in November 1979 claimed that 'Since Chris [Evert] married, tennis hasn't been quite at the top of her priorities – which is quite natural';[79] and, when Alex

Greaves became the first woman to ride in the Derby, the *Mail on Sunday*'s feature on her 'ride into history' described her as 'mother-of-two Alex Greaves', and noted that she had taken three years out of racing 'to take a course in catering management'.[80] There has also been a tendency to emphasise conventional female beauty in sports coverage, which has served the purpose of reinforcing wider assumptions about singular femininity. The tabloid press in particular has traditionally used flattering and eroticised photographs of certain sportswomen, such as Sabatini – 'known more for her face and figure than for her forehand'[81] – who was frequently pictured in the press with her underwear showing; or athlete Tessa Sanderson, described by a BBC television commentator in 1980 as 'another of the beauties in Britain's team'.[82] This treatment has clearly helped to reinforce stereotypes. It was explicitly condemned by the Sports Council's 1993 call for newspaper editors to '[e]liminate sexist references and photographs in the coverage of women's sport'.[83] However, it is difficult to see the media offering any major alternatives, when even some supporters of women's sport have played this issue as a joke: as Brian Johnston put it in a call for more media coverage of women's cricket,

> I can see one or two pitfalls for commentators: what girl would enjoy hearing that she has got two short legs – one of them square! On the other hand she would not, I'm sure, complain if she heard that she had a very fine leg![84]

The other aspect of this has been the tendency for the media to provide more negative portrayals of sportswomen who do not fit the preferred stereotype. Across the period, and with increasing bluntness in keeping with shifts in the discussion of sexual issues, the subtext for athletic women who do not obviously fit has been one that has challenged their femininity. England footballer Marieanne Spacey has been forthright in her claim that the game has had an image problem of being 'just a bunch of dykes running about a football field',[85] and this image problem is clearly rooted not just in educational experiences that have separated the sexes in sport, but also in the way in which the patriarchal media have presented women in aggressive and contact sport. Stereotypically masculine traits have been overemphasised, such as an ITV commentator's remarks at the 1980 Olympics that a woman swimmer 'almost swims like a man – she's certainly got a man's physique'.[86] With coverage like this, it is hardly surprising that some sportswomen have striven to stress their heterosexuality, sometimes in a manner very hostile to lesbianism. This is exemplified in Rachael

Heyhoe Flint and Netta Rheinberg's comments on sponsorship opportunities for women's cricket: 'it would be wrong to become associated with products which are essentially masculine; women cricketers have had enough trouble in the past to convince people that they are normal!'[87]

One crucial media development that may have an impact upon this kind of predominant treatment is the presence of women sports journalists and commentators. Traditionally, a female presence in the commentary box or studio was limited to retired players offering expert analysis, and was thus restricted to women's sports: lawn tennis, gymnastics, and ice dance are the key examples, although even there the women were clearly supplementary to the professional male commentators and anchormen. Similarly, in the printed media, women journalists were restricted to women's sport. A change became evident from the late 1970s, with a number of professional women journalists emerging, including *The Guardian*'s football reporter Cynthia Bateman, and Helen Rollason on television. Since then, other women have increasingly taken on traditionally male roles. Shelley Webb co-hosted the BBC's football magazine programme *Standing Room Only*, while Helen Rollason presents magazine programmes covering a range of sports. A good example of a sportswoman making the shift from player to pundit to presenter has been Sue Barker, whose media career began with expert analysis on tennis, then shifted to aesthetic sports such as ice dance with her coverage of Torville and Dean at the 1994 Winter Olympics, and has, at the time of writing, made it to the position of anchor: not just for coverage of Wimbledon, where she has shared the role with Des Lynam; but also for *Grandstand* as a whole, including a key role in BBC television's coverage of the 1996 Olympic Games. It is too early to tell if these changes will fundamentally alter sports coverage, and if there will eventually be no female-free areas of sports journalism, such as boxing. Just as in any other male domain, women have had difficulty in establishing their credibility, a situation illustrated by Michele Savidge of the *London Evening Standard*'s sports desk. A cricket enthusiast and journalist, she described meeting John Stephenson of the MCC at a cricketing lunch in 1991: Stephenson's opening gambit in conversation was 'Are you something to do with the catering?'[88] Magazines marketed at women interested in sport have also developed, aimed at a discerning and critical market and not reliant upon gendered assumptions on sport: *Born Kicking*, the fanzine on women's football, is an example of this.

Overall, then, the post-war period has seen both continuity and change for women in sport. Predominant assumptions about certain sports being appropriate and others being inappropriate have survived, and while there have been numerous challenges to them, they remain intact in the mid-1990s in media portrayals and popular discourse. Women's sport is still very much the poorer sphere. However, there has also been a great deal of change, in line with wider changes in the politics and economics of gender relations, where sport has offered a public forum for debate because of its inherent focus upon the body and its public display. By the end of our period, women are openly and approvingly competing in events previously suppressed or marginalised, including long-distance running, football, and both rugby codes. The approval has come through increasingly sympathetic media coverage, as well as through private and public sponsorship of women's sport initiatives: the WSF, for example, has received not only Sports Council funding, but also sponsorship from sanitary product manufacturers Tambrands.[89] It has also been negotiated and legitimated in the media of film and television. *Gregory's Girl*, *The Manageress*, and *Born Kicking* all challenged and undermined notions that women cannot play football with and against men. Advertising has also played a role here. Across the period, various anti-perspirant products have used women's sport settings as the narrative for the television commercials, including such extreme activities as women's boxing and endurance running: the former was sanitised – the boxers are seen only training – but the text here goes in the face of tradition that women should not sweat. Campaigns for sanitary products have also used images of active women in traditionally masculine sports, including parachute jumping and football. The images portrayed in all of these examples of dynamic, active, post-modern women playing what they like must be read as a sign that popular discourse on sport has been influenced by feminism. As such, it is a perfect example of how the sport played and watched in post-war society is part of that society.

MEN AND SPORT

As yet, there is no critical historiography of men and sport comparable with that of women and sport for our period. The bulk of the work that has been done on British sport as a male preserve, or on how sport has helped to define masculinity at given moments in history, has concentrated on the nineteenth century; and while sociological and gender studies work has helped to establish masculinity and men's part in gender relations as crucial research topics, our period has not been fully explored. Partially, this must be seen as a general problem of contemporary history: it is, in some ways, easier to apply new historical theories to periods with apparently clear end dates, rather than to the more immediate past. This was illustrated by the arrangement of Messner and Sabo's collection of essays. Here, one section covers 'Theoretical and Historical Foundations', including material on the development of early modern sport, baseball from 1880 to 1920, and rugby in nineteenth-century public schools, but everything after 1920 is covered either as a contemporary issue, or as a piece on challenge and alternatives.[90] Dunning's 'Sport as a male preserve', which demonstrated a broad historical overview, explored masculinity issues from the nineteenth-century development of team sports through to contemporary football hooliganism. However, despite his assertion that sport has historically been 'one of the major male preserves and hence of potential significance for the functioning of patriarchal structures', the gaps in the analysis he identified have not yet all been filled.[91] Nauright and Chandler's collection of essays on rugby and masculinity, for example, does not include any British case studies beyond 1915.[92] So, in a work of this nature, we are starting with much less work to synthesise than for women. However, it is still possible to examine the major issues relating to men and sport since 1945: the continued predominance of men's sport; and the role of sport as an area for the public display and popular discussion of masculinity and effeminacy in men.

The main theme in the post-war period has been a strong continuity whereby sport has been defined and defended as a masculine sphere. The continuity was from pre-industrial and nineteenth-century sport, where the aggression, strength, and speed that came to be important parts of various sports made sport as a whole emerge as an area in which orthodox masculine identities were displayed and reproduced. This role has continued since 1945, despite the challenges of feminism and sexual politics, and sport is still frequently perceived as male unless otherwise stated. This can be seen most simply in the way in which labels denoting male involvement have been rare compared with labels denoting female involvement. Football, both rugby codes, cricket, and golf as proper names have invariably meant men's football, men's rugby, and so on, and this position is very difficult to shift. In other sports where there has been a publicly acknowledged tradition of female competition, such as athletics or lawn tennis, the appropriate sex is denoted, but the superiority of the male event is highlighted by its timing as well as its prize money and coverage. The men's singles final at Wimbledon, for example, has traditionally been played at the end of the fortnight as the climax of the whole tournament, and, since going open in 1968, has always had a significantly larger prize attached. The differential has changed over the period – in 1968, Billie Jean King's £750 was only 37 per cent of Rod Laver's £2,000, whereas in 1990 Martina Navratilova's £207,000 was 90 per cent of Stefan Edberg's £230,000 – and it is defended as reflecting the different length of matches.[93] It is through these features of sport's everyday organisational realities that sport remains an area primarily defined as one where men naturally exert their superiority. This has been reflected and confirmed by the way in which the media has not drawn overt attention to men's everyday family lives in its coverage in the way that has been illustrated above for women. The Sports Council has reproduced this assumption: for example, its review of *Women and Sport* did not show any evidence that media coverage of sportsmen could be seen as sexist and stereotypical in the way that media coverage of sportswomen could be. Overall, it is difficult to see any evidence of men's sport being problematised from within sport: it has taken history, sociology, and cultural studies to point out the unspoken ideologies involved. To apply Roper and Tosh to sports history, it has taken academic discourse to make 'men visible as gendered subjects . . . to demonstrate that masculinity has a history: that it is subject to change and varied in its forms'.[94]

This visibility needs to be established for any understanding of how sport has become a public forum for celebrating, displaying, and reproducing masculinity. The sports defined as male during the industrial revolution have continued in that role in the post-war period, and the educational system and media have continued to equate success in sport with orthodox masculine qualities. It has been set up as natural at the crucial level of children's comics and literature. Boys' comics have traditionally combined staple stories on war and sport, with the narratives between these equally masculine settings frequently interchangeable. The presentation of real sport at a juvenile level has also frequently stressed a separate and natural sphere for males, as exemplified by the *News Chronicle*'s annual *Boys' Book of All Sports*. The 1953 edition, for example, carries features on such sports as football, rugby union, cycling, boxing, long-distance swimming, cricket, and athletics. There is little room for ambiguity here: from Bill Hicks' editorial that begins 'Hullo boys!' through Ross McWhirter's promotion of rugby union as 'a medium for good fellowship' and the tips for young sportsmen from Billy Wright and Len Hutton, these sports are confirmed and reconstructed as being for boys and men.[95] Throughout our period, this kind of material has played an important role in naturalising sport to boys, and in setting it up as something of a rite of passage into manhood.

In the mass media, sportsmen have subsequently been confirmed as ideal men. Just as sportswomen have had their elegance and beauty praised, so have sportsmen had their aggression and courage emphasised, frequently in language that stresses violence and martial qualities. This is standard in the hand-to-hand combat sports of boxing and wrestling, where strength is combined with skill and wits to assert physical superiority over an opponent, and in the body culture sports of weight-lifting and body-building, where the display of strength and musculature are the only ends. That these events have become increasingly made into spectacles, both through body-building events and through sportised television competitions between the world's strongest men, suggests that there is a public appetite for such displays: the development of women's body-building, and the popular revulsion it has frequently received, can be read as an inversion and corruption of the rampant masculinity in the orthodox version. It is also evident in both rugby codes, and in football, and can also be seen in non-contact sports: for example, a BBC radio commentary on Jimmy Connors at Wimbledon in 1978 used the extraordinary language of violence and masculinity for a sport in which no physical contact between players is involved, claiming that 'Connors today became a man if I may say so. He got his opponent down on the ground and tore him to pieces.'[96] Men have also been idealised for being able to take physical pain in sport, as this is a key signifier of orthodox masculinity. Wrestlers' memories of 1970s star Les Kellett, for example, included his ability to continue training with a plaster collar on for a neck injury, and his demand of a fellow professional to stamp on his hand to remove the poison from an infected bite prior to a bout, are extreme examples of this.[97] These displays of masculinity are also evident in various films with sporting themes, evidence of their centrality to sports culture due to the marketing needs of the film industry. The best example is *Chariots of Fire*, a fictionalised account of two British athletes at the 1924 Olympic Games, which glorifies the runners' manliness not just in their characterisation – they are both determined, dedicated, honourable, courageous, and strong – but also in the way in which they are filmed in training and in competition. Just as sportswomen have been portrayed in the media in ways that have eroticised them, so too have sportsmen's bodies been emphasised as male bodies: muscular, tough, and capable of aggression. Virility has also been a frequent subtext of sports coverage: the advertised promiscuous lifestyle of George Best was the best example of this, although the element of self-publicity was crucial here. As he put it in one of his autobiographies, 'It's not good for an athlete to spend every afternoon fucking, every evening drinking and every morning thinking about fucking and drinking.'[98]

Attendant sporting cultures have also continued, in many sports, to offer a haven for celebrations of masculinity, often in a way that has excluded and derided women. Post-match cultures in rugby and, to a lesser extent, football, with obscene songs, ritualised drinking, and stripping, have continued to show these traits.[99] The exclusion of women from clubhouses and key areas at Lord's and the Royal and Ancient at St Andrew's must also be seen as examples of this tradition. Football hooliganism has also been read as a phenomenon of aggressive masculinity allied to a sense of place and nation. The large body of work on hooliganism by Dunning, Murphy, and Williams has frequently stressed this linkage, with adolescents and young men using ritualised violence at and around football as a way of stating their male identities.[100] By the end of our period, there is evidence that some of these rituals and traditions are at least being challenged. Sport's male 'language, . . . initiation rites, and models of true masculinity' and 'clubbable, jokey cosiness'[101] are showing some signs of strain under the influence of feminism, an equal opportunities culture, and marketing, particularly in the establishment of a family culture of football spectating as a means of diluting the rampant masculine image of supporters. It does, however, remain, and is a clear continuity in the post-war period.

Alongside this traditional emphasis on orthodox masculinity has been an ambivalent relationship between sport and homosexuality and homoeroticism. The mainstream media coverage and popular discourse on sport throughout the period has denigrated and denied homosexuality and effeminacy (generally equated in the popular mind). This is evident in countless examples of popular discourse about 'real men' in most sports. The depth of feeling on this theme can perhaps be seen by the fact that even football fanzines, which emerged in the 1980s as vehicles for a progressive statement of fans' interests and have generally been liberal on racial and gender equality, have frequently continued to vilify and denigrate homosexuality. The jokes about Justin Fashanu when he came out are testament to this: for example, a Brentford fanzine speculated that the club was about to buy Fashanu, as the manager 'needs him to stiffen up his back four'.[102] Dunning, and White and Vagi, have explored anti-gay sentiments in rugby culture, expressed for example in the ironic singing of 'For we're all queers together,

Excuse us while we go upstairs' identified by Dunning as an attempt to 'counter the charge [of homosexuality] before it is made'.[103] The theme has been present in other songs, such as 'Little boys are cheap today/Cheaper than yesterday./Small ones are half a crown/Standing up or lying down./Big ones are four and six/'Cause they've got bigger dicks.'[104] The ideologies that such songs express are clearly based on strong antipathy towards homosexuality, although the overt denial has been seen by some commentators as evidence of suppression. Simpson's observations on both football and body-building, for example, and Pronger's on sport in general shed light on the paradoxes of male sexuality beneath the orthodoxies of assumed heterosexuality.[105] This phenomenon can be illustrated by various practices in sport that break taboos on orthodox behaviour between men, including excessive physical contact, kissing and hugging in moments of triumph, and open admiration of each others' physiques.[106] Impressionistic research on body-building cultures has reinforced this aspect of sport, as reported in the *Independent on Sunday*'s lifestyle section in August 1995: 'women who work out tend to ogle the bodies of men, while male gym junkies can't take their eyes off the bodies of . . . other men'.[107] While solid work needs to be done on the historical development of this phenomenon, the examples cited and the analysis emerging from gender studies and cultural studies point the way towards a greater understanding of this crucial part of men's experiences in sport. The public acceptance by some sportsmen of roles that mitigate their traditional masculinity, such as Gascoigne's tears or Will Carling being shown cooking for his partner in television advertisements, may have blurred the edges of sport's relationship with masculinity, but there is still much cultural significance invested in the sporting male body as an idealised, orthodox, heterosexual sign.

The post-war period, then, has seen sport continue to act as a location for the display and negotiation of gender politics. In line with changes in the political and economic spheres, sport as a physical activity has provided women in search of equality and recognition a cultural sphere in which to test traditional assumptions based on physiological difference, and the popularity by the end of our period of women's rugby, football, cricket, athletics, and even boxing demonstrates a change in the wider discourse of gender relations. Similarly, the fact that, by the end of the period, some sportsmen are able to go against tradition and acknowledge emotions out of keeping with mainstream manliness shows that changes in acceptable behaviour in sport have not been restricted to women. However, all other evidence shows that sport is still heavily based on gender differences, and that popular notions of physical strength, courage, speed, and stamina still dictate that men's sports get the bulk of the attention and the funding. While there is still a great deal of historical research to be done on this theme for the post-war period, we can conclude by noting that while academic analysis can highlight gender relations as the crucial factor, popular common sense still holds firmly to the notion of difference.

Chapter 5

Sport, social class, and professional status

INTRODUCTION

One of the most obvious ways in which sport is seen to connect with its setting is through its links with class stratification. Without being overly deterministic, it is clear that access to leisure in general, and sport in particular, has historically been constrained by time, space, and disposable income, all of which are variable across class lines. Organised sports have thus historically developed with class characters, so that sports themselves have become associated with certain groups. Hopcraft's claim that football spectators 'are never going to sound or look like the hat parade on the club lawns of Cheltenham racecourse' and 'are always going to have more vinegar than Chanel'[1] may well have been a generalisation, but its use of popularly recognisable stereotypes helps to stress the common-sense notion of sport's social segregation. Moreover, John Hargreaves' analysis of modern sport, which stresses the continuity from pre-industrial models of class display in leisure – the 'theatre of the great' – has given the simplistic view in Hopcraft's piece more depth. It has shown how different classes have assumed specific roles within individual sports, based upon wider divisions of labour and wealth, with sports serving to mirror and reproduce wider social relations.[2] The classic example is the trophy-giving ritual at the end of the FA Cup Final, where royal patrons surrounded by a bourgeoisie of administrators reward the players of predominantly working-class backgrounds. The class character of sport is emphasised not just by intrinsic aspects based on rules and assumptions governing conduct during play, but also in the attendant cultures of sports' social and organisational features. It is also a feature of sport of which advertisers and sponsors have been aware. Products and services aimed at target groups through sport demonstrate market researchers' links between, for example, the polo followers from social groups 1 and 2 who might drink Pimm's and the group 3 and 4 rugby league supporters who might drink Stone's bitter.

This preliminary observation can form the basis of a historical enquiry into class and sport for the post-war period in the UK. The period has witnessed an extended discourse on class, both in political and academic settings. The welfarism of the post-war Labour governments, pursued by their Conservative successors, gave a high profile to the issue of equalising opportunity and access to services across class lines: education, health, and social security were to be available to all. Despite the flaws in this settlement, it was seen to be addressing inherited class-based inequalities. The shift towards a less equitable culture popularly associated with the radical conservatism of the Thatcher administrations, in which merit and achievement were prioritised over equality of access, similarly kept social stratification in the public eye. In different ways, these ideologies have aspired towards a mythical state of classlessness, thereby acknowledging the centrality of class in social structure and popular consciousness.[3] Academics in a range of disciplines have also helped to entrench class as a recognised and recognisable feature of post-war society, with sociology, economics, history, cultural studies, and other specialisms freely using class as an area of analysis. Increasingly, as Reid points out, 'other forms of social stratification – mainly sex and ethnicity'[4] have been taken into account, forming a complex set of interrelations in these disciplines. However, despite this widespread discussion, class has remained difficult to define to everybody's satisfaction, and models using occupation, wealth and income, education, family background, geographical positioning, lifestyle, and accent have been applied to the period.[5] However, this lack of consensus cannot detract from class's viability and significance as a category for enquiry.

Sports historians have frequently used class in such a way, allowing us to see at the academic level a strong association between social status and sport that confirms the more impressionistic links evident in Hopcraft's piece. As sports history developed in part out of history from below, which prioritised the rediscovery of mass experiences, this should not surprise us. Mason, Vamplew, and Bailey all highlighted the different roles that different social groups had in the historical sports and leisure practices they uncovered in the 1970s, which cleared the way for some more specific class-based analyses, such as those conducted by John Hargreaves, Jones, and Lowerson.[6] The major works of synthesis – notably Holt's emphasis on the contrasts and connections between public school, middle-class, and working-class sport – have consolidated its significance.[7] However, as Holt subsequently stressed, working-class sport has had a smaller historiography than the sports of 'the gentleman amateur and public-school athleticism': it was one of the 'areas of patchy coverage and unexplored topics'.[8] His collection of essays has helped to redress the balance, but there is still much to be done here. In particular, the post-war years have not had as much coverage as previous periods. However, the literature has ensured that class has never been invisible in academic sports historiography, in the way that some other aspects, notably masculinity, have been until recently. Its continued presence, now complemented in sports research by a growing awareness of Reid's 'other forms of social stratification', has made it a major part of the discipline.

Used critically and flexibly, and assuming that class as a label is meaningful without being deterministic, a consideration of social class and the related issues of status and professional cultures can lead us into some key features of post-war British sport. The commercialisation of sport across this period discussed in Chapter 3, which has brought higher financial rewards for elite performers than at any previous point in history, has enabled professional sports to act as channels for social mobility, providing the most successful sportsmen and women in certain sports from lower-class backgrounds access to the lifestyles and living standards of the upper middle class. The professionalisation of the occupational cultures of many sports that took place from the 1960s helped this process, consolidating the historical trend whereby sport was

> one of the few paths of upward mobility open to the children of the dominated class; . . . the working-class cult of sportsmen of working-class origin is doubtless explained in part by the fact that these 'success stories' symbolize the only recognized route to wealth and fame.[9]

At a more general social level, sports have increasingly come to be seen as signifiers of lifestyle linked strongly to class and status. Participation in certain sports is popularly held as a mark of belonging within the social structure. What has been particularly noteworthy for the post-war period, as participation in sport has generally shifted from the industrial to post-industrial setting, has been the fluidity of this process, linked to disposable income, private transport, and the growth of the white-collar workforce. Here, previously restricted sports have become more mixed, and the ownership and control of certain sports has been contested in class terms. These themes will provide the focus for our analysis of class in post-war sport.

SPORT, MOBILITY, AND PROFESSIONAL CULTURES

The payment of individuals for their performance in sport has been a continuous feature of many British sports, from the hired pedestrians and prize-fighters of the pre-industrial period through to the full-time waged footballers and cricketers of the late nineteenth century and beyond. The financial rewards of sporting achievement for the elite few have allowed access to enhanced social status. In the post-war period, commercial and media investment in a number of sports, combined with shifts in sportsmen and women's economic and social self-perception, has facilitated a growth of professional cultures strongly linked to social mobility through increased wealth and status. As a result, the pre-industrial and industrial settings for sports professionals, linked to land ownership and patronage in cricket, horse-racing, and pedestrianism, and commercial and manufacturing interests in football and rugby league, have gradually been modified by the development of paid sportsmen and women into actual professionals: specialists and careerists rather than merely paid athletes. Here, the post-industrial economic setting of the emergent leisure industry is heavily involved, through such areas as golf and tennis clubs using professionals, and television, advertising, and media opportunities for elite sportsmen and women as personalities. And, as with sponsorship of sport, it is a trend that has been linked to the increasing internationalisation of sport, and the global commercial context in which it now operates. From this history, two related themes emerge which can be analysed separately: first, the growth of professional identities and assertiveness amongst sports professionals; and second, the acceptance of professionalism in a number of sports that had traditions of hostility towards the notion of pay for play. Both of these developments have been strongly linked with class and status issues in sport.

While professionals in a number of sports had historically estab-lished notions of collective identity and power, contractual restrictions and the uncertainties involved in playing professional sport helped to minimise the assertion of rights until the post-war period. Professional footballers' early attempts at strike action help to illustrate this.[10] However, economic changes in sport in the post-war period helped to establish a climate in which the most organised professionals were able gradually to win concessions from clubs and authorities, providing a setting in which the most successful could earn significantly more than average wages and adopt lifestyles associated with higher social groups. The notion that all sports professionals have thus become bourgeois is, however, simplistic on two counts. First, the vast majority of professionals in all sports have continued to draw average wages during inherently short careers; and second, there is also debate over whether the bourgeois lifestyles associated with successful sportsmen and women are matched by any shift in class values. However, it is beyond doubt that social, economic, and cultural changes in the professional sport settings from the 1960s onwards established a new phase of industrial relations. In this phase, more professionals became organised; more benefits were gained to provide protection and security; and more opportunities were established for the most successful to move into superstar lifestyles. This can be seen through a number of case studies, of which football has attracted most historical attention, although the trends can also be seen in other sports.

Challenges to the existing labour relations in football emerged forcefully in the late 1950s and early 1960s, challenges which helped to focus attention on the rights and professional status of sportsmen and women which continued throughout the decade and beyond. Wagg and Redhead[11] have explored these events, which Wagg locates in the setting of post-war rises in wage levels outside football and a growing perception within football that players' occupational culture was closer to that of entertainers than to the skilled working class from which they predominantly and traditionally came. In this context, the restrictive features of professionals' contracts came under increasing attack. The two main problems were the maximum wage, maintained by the Football League ostensibly as a means of preventing the richest clubs from monopolising the talent; and the retain and transfer system, which restricted players' ability to initiate transfers, and allowed clubs to keep players on their books who were not playing and not being paid. Philip Goodhart, a Conservative MP who supported the battle against these restrictions, called the professional footballer's contract 'something a fifteenth century apprentice might view with suspicion'.[12] Some outspoken players had also drawn attention to their antipathy towards their contractual situation: Len Shackleton, for example, had referred in his 1955 autobiography to the contract as 'an evil document' and a 'canker' that caused 'unrest and dissatisfaction to spread through soccer, season after season'.[13] As well as limiting the opportunities and freedoms of players, these contractual restrictions encouraged a number of talented British players to move to overseas clubs where they could earn more and pursue lifestyle choices more strongly linked with entertainers than with sportsmen. Italy was a popular location, favoured by Charlton Athletic's Eddie Firmani in 1955 and Leeds United's John Charles in 1957 in their moves to Sampdoria and Juventus respectively, although the controversial move of Manchester United's Charlie Mitten and Stoke City's Neil Franklin and George Mountford to the Colombian club Sante Fe in 1950 had brought this issue to light at the start of the decade. Mitten recalled telling his manager Matt Busby of the move by linking it to the maximum wage:

> 'I'm 29 now, and I've got £300 in the bank and I'm living in a club house and I'm supposed to be one of the best wingers in the game.' . . . '[W]e've won the Cup and we've won the League three times for you, we've won everything except the Boat Race for you and we've got nothing.' He said, 'I understand, laddie, but that's the rules'.[14]

The players' union (the Association Footballers' and Trainers' Union to 1958, then the Professional Footballers Association (PFA)[15]) began earnestly to attack these issues in the mid-1950s. A public scandal over illegal payments at Sunderland helped to polarise the situation: when the union's Chairman, Fulham's Jimmy Hill, collected the signatures of 250 professionals who had received illegal payments, the whole structure of wages was brought under public scrutiny. Backed by the Ministry of Labour, negotiations between the players and the Football League brought no solution, and the situation was brought to a climax by the vote in favour of strike action at the 1960 AGM, causing the Football League to back down in 1961 and remove the maximum wage.[16] The players had a great deal of public sympathy for their cause, and were able to argue effectively for change on the obvious inequalities of the system: as Hill later summarised it, 'No other profession in this country . . . had a restriction on the top, and it was even more unfair in that a professional footballer's life is a very short one.'[17] While the long-term effect of this abolition may have been the concentration of talent into a small number of clubs, its significance for the players at the time was crucial: not only were large wages suddenly possible for the elite – England captain Johnny Haynes, coincidentally a team mate of Hill's at Fulham, became the first £100 per week player immediately after the abolition – but there was also a general sense of elevated status for players. As George Eastham put it, 'what was once a job has become a profession'.[18]

It was Eastham who helped to challenge the second major restriction on players' career development, the retain and transfer clause. In 1959 he asked his club, Newcastle United, for a transfer: they not only refused, but also dropped him and stopped paying him. Ironically, his manager was Charlie Mitten, who had flouted the employment structures in football himself in 1950. Coming roughly parallel with the developing battle over the maximum wage, Eastham issued a writ against the club for restraint of trade in June 1959, which set off a long legal process that finally reached the High Court in 1963. By then, not only had Eastham managed to move to Arsenal after five months out of the game, but the Football League had agreed to abolish the retain and transfer system; Eastham thus became a test case, funded as such by £15,000 from the PFA to cover the legal costs in a court case that Eastham claimed to have found 'a more gruelling ordeal than a dozen cup-ties'.[19] The court found in Eastham's favour, and thus established that the rules of the Football Association (FA) and the Football League illegally restrained individual players' trade, although Eastham did not win the damages he had claimed for lost earnings. Wagg has argued that the Eastham case did not enjoy the same kind of attention as the dispute over the maximum wage, because of the loss of Hill to management and a wider complacency amongst players after their basic success. However, the victory did not lead to freedom of contract or, indeed, to an end to the transfer system: 'All the PFA gained . . . was to make the retain-and-transfer system less objectionable, without confronting the issue of labour market controls *per se*.'[20] Redhead has argued that the two victories must be seen as 'symbolic breakthroughs rather than fundamental changes in the legal and social status of professional footballers', as the employment structure that survived them still relied upon enormous inequalities in wage distribution, and restrictions on the employees' freedoms that would be unacceptable in other professions (such as disciplinary regimes related to training).[21]

However, these two cases clearly helped to establish footballers on a more professional footing in the early 1960s, and helped to clarify to the most successful players that they were marketable careerists with greater opportunities for earning than the previous generations of players had been. These changes set the context for the shift in occupational culture of the most successful footballers in the 1960s, epitomised by the heavily publicised pop star lifestyle of Manchester United's George Best. These changes were also linked to the rise in transfer fees during this period, in which players were able increasingly to negotiate personal terms and signing-on fees, rather than accept a League maximum. Through the 1960s and 1970s, transfer fees grew at an enormous rate. By the end of the decade, the pre-abolition record of £55,000, paid by Manchester City to Huddersfield for Denis Law in 1960, had been replaced by the £200,000 paid by Tottenham to West Ham for Martin Peters in 1970. In the inflationary 1970s, Nottingham Forest broke the £1,000,000 barrier by paying Birmingham City £1,180,000 for Trevor Francis in 1979. At the time of writing, the record has risen to £15,000,000, paid by Newcastle United for Blackburn Rovers' Alan Shearer in 1996. While it took fifty-seven years (1905–62) for the record to rise from £1,000 to £100,000, a 10,000 per cent increase, the increased freedoms and influx of income from the early 1960s have set the context for a 15,000 per cent increase from Greaves to Shearer in thirty-five years.[22] Earnings for the most successful players have risen disproportionately to those of skilled workers, illustrating Wagg's point about entertainers becoming foot-ballers' 'new reference group' on wages.[23] Between 1955 and 1964, average earnings for Football League players rose by 148 per cent, compared with 62 per cent for average industrial wages. Since then, a minority of players have earned extremely high salaries. Mason's figures for the 1985–6 season show that eighty-seven registered players in the Football League earned over £50,000 a year, but, as he emphasises, this represents just 4.4 per cent of the 1,950 players, whereas 40 per cent of them earned less than £10,000.[24] Contractual conditions have continued to alter across the period. Threatened strike action in 1977–8 led to a greater freedom of contract, with players able to move when their existing contracts expired in return for compensation from the new club.[25] The domestic implications of the 1995 European ruling on Marc Bosman have extended these freedoms by allowing players at the end of their contract to move clubs without requiring transfer fees or negotia-tions. While many involved with smaller clubs have bemoaned this development, it has enhanced professional footballers' control over their own careers.

This changing social and economic setting led many commentators to see footballers in the 1960s and 1970s as increasingly bourgeois. From a sociological perspective, Critcher's 1979 analysis of the 'severe repercussions' that such changes had on the 'cultural significance' of players' contacts with their working-class roots modelled four stages of transition in professionals' lifestyle and status. From the 'traditional/located' of Stanley Matthews to the 'superstar/dislocated' of George Best, via the 'transitional/mobile' of Bobby Charlton and the 'incorporated/embourgeoised' of Alan Ball, Critcher exemplified changes in the value structure and class identity of top players.[26] He ended by looking beyond the crisis of the footballer as pop star to the post-Best generation of Kevin Keegan and Trevor Francis, who 'avoided London clubs, married and "settled down", took proper economic advice, [and] learnt how to handle interviews'.[27] This academic discussion of the changes in status associated with the changes of the 1960s was complemented by more popular and journalistic discussion. Hunter Davies spent the 1971–2 season with Tottenham Hotspur, and wrote it up to try and 'illuminate the lives of the people taking part' in football.[28] This included discussion of the players' social and political attitudes, as well as their attitudes towards football itself, and the findings were widely interpreted as evidence of the bourgeois culture that footballers were moving into. From his observation that most of the players were 'apathetic Tories'[29] to his analysis of such personal status indicators as holiday destinations, newspapers, cars, and homes, Davies drew a vivid picture of a group of men with working-class roots dealing – or failing to deal – with the opportunities and advantages that the professional game in the early 1970s could offer. These views were, to a degree, endorsed by Douglas in 1974, particularly in his analysis of Martin Peters, 'classless in his accent and attitude, though he says he votes Conservative. . . . His politics might shock his father, a Thames lighterman, and his neighbours from his native Plaistow.'[30] However, by looking at lower-division players as well as stars, he stressed that 'the new deal' of the post-maximum wage period had not effected any real shift in values, only one in appearances. He claimed that footballers 'tend to display some of the flashier trappings of their new-found wealth: smart cars, new clothes, trim houses', but this did not equate to becoming bourgeois: 'They may wear their hired tails and toppers in the best traditions of the society wedding, but they are still tied to their class.'[31] The assumptions about mobility that underpinned this reading of the game were attacked by Redhead. He argued that it fostered a mythical version of the legal victories of the early 1960s leading to all professional footballers becoming bourgeois virtually overnight, an assumption he classes as 'highly dubious'.[32] Not only did it ignore the mass of professionals in lower divisions who did not directly benefit from the changes in wage structure, it also made reductionist assumptions about the rigidity of income and class: 'there is *no necessary* correlation between the increasing affluence of the player and any particular social and political attitudes'.[33] The debate illustrates the contested nature of class-based analyses of sport, and, even accepting Redhead's critique, it has shown how social and cultural changes in footballers' lives were both real and aspired to from the 1960s onwards.

While no other sports had such dramatic and public discussions of the rights and roles of professionals in the 1960s, cricket and tennis both significantly shifted their restrictions on professionals in the 1960s, allowing top players increased access to earnings commensurate with their entertainment appeal. Cricket, often seen as a truly national sport because of the way in which players from different social classes traditionally played together, retained distinctions between amateurs and professionals until 1963. The historical roots of the distinctions were semantically underlined by the terminology of 'gentlemen' and 'players' respectively. The alleged on-pitch equalities were subject to fairly specific protocols and practices, including the use of a player as a captain only if no gentlemen were available, and the positioning of initials either before or after the surname on the scorecard to signify status. In the immediate post-war period, however, county and national managements began increasingly to recognise players more. Locally, wages were increased and counties began to appoint professionals as team captains. The Marylebone Cricket Club (MCC) increased fees for test matches, and, in 1949, awarded honorary life memberships to a number of players. The MCC also recognised professionals' leadership abilities by appointing Len Hutton as England captain in 1953. Interestingly, his county club, Yorkshire, did not use him in a similar role, and only 'succumbed to reality' in 1960, when Victor Wilson became the county's first professional captain.[34] However, part of cricket's crisis in the 1950s, influenced by dramatically falling gates, was also caused by changing patterns of recruitment into the first-class game. The number of gentlemen able to devote themselves to the game was reduced by a 'combination of higher taxation and more rigorous academic standards', as was clarified by the fact that in 1949, 38 per cent of county cricketers had been amateurs, compared with 19 per cent in 1961.[35] Similarly, the quality of professionals was perceived to be declining owing to the disincentives of relatively low wages and the uncertainties of seasonal employment. As Bowen put it, 'No one of intelligence, nor even anyone possessed merely of quick reflexes will go into cricket as a career if he can get better pay elsewhere';[36] or, in Brookes's phrase, 'Small wonder . . . that parents, schoolmasters and career advisers began to think twice before recommending a cricket career.'[37] In 1963, in the face of these problems, the MCC formally abolished the distinction between gentlemen and players, and established the single term of 'cricketer', allowing individuals to negotiate for wages with their counties if they so wished.[38]

As with the changes in football contracts at the time, this helped to improve the standing of professional cricketers, with enough collective interests being apparent by November 1967 to allow for the formation of the Cricketers' Association as a professional organisation. The idea of a union for cricketers was developed by Somerset's Fred Rumsey, and despite a rather indifferent response at first, the Association was soon able to negotiate successfully on a number of issues, including the establishment of an industrial tribunal in 1973, a minimum wage in 1979, and a limited freedom of contract in the 1980s, allowing players to reject their county's offer of a new contract and discuss terms with other counties. As Marqusee points out, this is 'anomalous in the modern labour market, even compared with other sports',[39] but it was an improvement on the constraints on mobility that existed before. John Arlott, himself involved with the organisation, was more sanguine, claiming in 1979 that the Cricketers' Association had 'freed [cricketers] from feudalism'.[40] As in football, the growth of top individuals' earnings, and the general rise in status for professionals, can be linked both to the increasingly commercial context and the collective work of the trade association. For cricketers, another symbolic moment came in the late 1970s when a number of leading players were poached by Australian television channel owner Kerry Packer for his alternative World Series Cricket (WSC). The players, including England captain Tony Greig, defended the move: they broke no contracts, and were simply attempting to maximise their earning potential by ensuring well-paid play during the English close season. The MCC and the Test and County Cricket Board took the matter to law to attempt to prevent Packer's moves on the players, and their portrayal as mercenaries, pirates, and circus employees showed the way in which they were being attacked for breaking cricket's traditions as much as its contemporary arrangements. However, just as the High Court had found against the football authorities in 1963 for illegally restraining players' trade, so too did cricket find itself operating outside the law in 1979. Although Packer's WSC was quickly accommodated with the Australian cricket and broadcasting bodies, this incident stressed that professional cricketers had rights over their own careers that their employers had not been allowing them.[41]

While football and cricket have been explored most fully, thanks to the existing literature, similar associations and unions have developed in other sports during this period, including the Flat-Race Jockeys' Association, formed in 1966, the Association of Lawn Tennis Professionals in 1972, and the Rugby League Professional Players' Association, formed in 1981, which lasted only until 1987 but was influential in achieving a number of advances for players, including an improvement in insurance coverage and the replacement of the retain and transfer system with a fixed contract scheme.[42] So, while the late industrial period was clearly a time in which professionalism emerged in sport in that individuals were paid for their playing services, it has been the commercial setting of the post-war period that has seen a fuller culture of professionalism emerge in sport. The social mobility that these changes can afford to elite individuals has become part of the popular discourse of sport, suggesting a consensual acceptance of the notion that success in sport can elevate individuals, often from working-class and lower- middle-class backgrounds, out of their family social setting and into a new band. For the majority, however, it must be stressed that these organisations offer mutual protection for careers that are uncertain and pay only average wages.

Another part of the shift in status for elite sportsmen and women can be seen in the way that many individuals have diversified their own careers through advertising, endorsements, and media work. As with so many other features of the commercial face of post-war sport, there is a great deal of continuity here from the earlier years of organised sport. W. G. Grace, for example, endorsed a variety of products for money, some related to cricket, others with no connection, such as Coleman's Mustard. Interwar footballers, tennis players, and golfers had also exploited this form of revenue: Fred Perry, for example, the leading British tennis player of the 1930s, was employed by Slazenger to promote its equipment, with a contract that formally employed him in Australia to allow him to keep his amateur status in the UK.[43] As with the sponsorship of sporting events, however, this was another area of commerce which experienced qualitative and quantitative changes in our period. The increase of this kind of work was firmly linked to the growth of commercial television and the gradual shift of sportsmen and women into the entertainment sector, and it can be seen as part of their growing self-perception of professionalised status. Jimmy Hill put the case firmly for footballers as part of his wider argument on their short and unpredictable careers and their role in bringing spectators into the game: 'I uphold the professional's prerogative of squeezing every penny out of his situation.'[44] What Wagg, writing of football, called the game's 'growing rapprochement with the world of advertising and public relations ... the élites and ethos of impression management'[45] began to be experienced in all sports across the period: one of the effects was for sportsmen and women to take Hill's advice and market themselves. The post-maximum-wage occupational culture of elite footballers was perhaps the most obvious feature of this. Mason explores how the 1970s Liverpool, Bayern Munich, and England star Kevin Keegan became a commodity himself through his advertising work for diverse products, including some that were related to the sport (Mitre sportswear and Patrick boots) and others that were not (including Fabergé cosmetics, and Nabisco and Heinz foods), a history that led Wagg to call him 'English football's first clone – a persona consciously fashioned with a huge audience of consumers in mind'.[46] Many other leading footballers appeared in television and other advertising media from the 1960s onwards giving their particular images and names to, amongst others, sausages (George Best), Bisto gravy (Alan Ball), Shredded Wheat (Brian Clough and Jack Charlton), Lucozade (John Barnes), and Walkers Crisps (Gary Lineker). While elite footballers led the way as the highest-paid and most well-known sports stars, they were not alone. Boxer Henry Cooper became well known to a generation too young to have seen him knock Cassius Clay down in 1963 for his 'Splash it all over' catchphrase in Brut aftershave commercials in the 1970s; while athletes Daley Thompson (Lucozade) and Steve Elliot (milk), snooker's Steve Davis (Heinz foods), cricketer Ian Botham (Heinz foods), and rugby union footballer Will Carling (Quorn) have also advanced their careers through this kind of work.

Also in this context, we need to see television work taken on by sportsmen and women alongside and after their playing careers, which has provided them with further opportunities to exploit the earning potential of their fame. They have been helped by the expansion of televised sport, particularly when they have been employed to offer expert analysis on events in which they are not participating. This approach was developed by ITV's employment of an expert panel for the 1970 football World Cup, and has since become a permanent feature of sports broadcasts. In cricket, players and ex-players including Geoff Boycott, Tony Lewis, and David Gower have made successful transitions to commentary and analysis positions, as did Eddie Waring in rugby league, Sue Barker in tennis, Daley Thompson in athletics, and Bob Wilson, Jimmy Hill, Trevor Brooking, and Alan Hansen in football. Opportunities, however, have not been limited to actual sports coverage. Sports-related game shows have been another opening since *Quiz Ball* in the 1960s, which pitted representatives of different football teams against each other. The staple feature here has been BBC's *A Question of Sport*, launched in 1970 with a format of two regular captains joined by four guests each week. The original captains were Henry Cooper and rugby union's Cliff Morgan, whose successors have included jockey Willie Carson, footballers Emlyn Hughes and Ally McCoist, Ian

Botham, and rugby union player Bill Beaumont, and the show has consistently managed to attract big-name guests. Its format and appeal has given rise to a deconstructionist imitator in *They Think It's All Over*, launched in 1995 with Gary Lineker and David Gower as captains joined not just by sportsmen and women, but also by comedians.[47] Such shows, as well as the more active 1970s children's show *Superstars*, have all provided opportunities for leading performers to extend their celebrity, to reach new audiences, and to earn money from their potentially ephemeral sporting fame.

As well as these changes in culture in cricket, football, rugby league, and racing, all of which had histories of play for pay that pre-dated our period, the post-war years have seen the growth of professionalism in other sports, including some that had traditionally been hostile to the idea of payment. Again, this contestation of the traditional organisational structure was based largely on players' demands for remuneration commensurate with their appeal and their self-perception as professionals. Rugby union and athletics are the best examples.

Rugby had split into two codes in 1895 over the issue of payment, and continued to maintain throughout most of the twentieth century that players should not make a profit from their play. The resistance to professionalism was firmly rooted in the sport's historical circumstances as a game for the recreation and diversion of the professional classes, and the Rugby Football Union's (RFU's) strict rules on payment ensured that no players could make their living from the game. Allegations of illegal payments persisted, particularly in the working-class cultures of rugby union in South Wales, but the national governing bodies continually refused to countenance waged players. Pressure on this historical settlement emerged with increasing force from the 1950s. Dunning and Sheard's exploration of the forces at work here has shown the influence of class, as the sport's diffusion downwards in the educational system brought in grammar schools and their former pupils alongside the more elitist public schools. Alongside this, the unavoidable demands for cup and championship competitions (met in 1971 and 1976 respectively), the growing dependency of clubs and the RFU on gate money and broadcasting fees, and the game's appeal relative to other team sports set up a climate for change.[48] Moreover, the occupational backgrounds of rugby union players had changed, setting up a more financially aware body of men: by the 1970s and 1980s, they were 'no longer the teachers and sales representatives of the 1950s . . . they were increasingly the financial advisers, building society managers and business executives of a commercial world in which rugby personalities were now marketable assets'.[49] In Wales, similar shifts were discernible: players 'ceased being the miners, steelworkers and policemen of yesterday to become the sons of those who so worked' as educational opportunities and economic diversification from coal and steel to services brought in players from the commercial, financial, and educational sectors.[50]

Players also had opportunities for earning money from their skills elsewhere. The main alternative was the switch from union to league, a move that was attractive enough for many to be worth the lifetime ban from union that it incurred (although the 1995 restructuring of rugby union included an amnesty). Another outlet was to switch to playing or coaching rugby union in France, where the rules on amateurism were increasingly flouted by clubs and the governing body to try and undermine the league game there. In 1989, for example, Neil Back of Nottingham was offered £200 per match to play in France.[51] In this changing climate, where as early as 1979 analysts had claimed that 'top-class Rugby Union has become virtually indistinguishable from a professional sport',[52] a number of leading players began to agitate for changes in the laws to allow payment. This was publicly aired in May 1995, when England captain Will Carling said in a television interview, 'If the game is run properly as a professional game, you do not need 57 old farts running rugby.'[53] When he was stripped of his captaincy as a punishment, a press, public, and player revolt forced the RFU to back down. In 1995, a century after the original split in rugby over the issue of payment, the International Rugby Football Board accepted professionalism, and allowed clubs to pay players. This immediately created a body of new professionals in the sport, with clubs entering into transfer deals on similar lines to those in football and rugby league: Newcastle and Richmond, both in the Courage League Second Division, were notable examples of high-spending clubs, with the former breaking all records in 1997 by paying Wigan £1 million in fees and compensation for Va'aiga Tuigamala. The restrictions also allowed a more consistent practice on players involved in advertising and endorsements. What Sandiford claimed for cricket in the 1960s – that 'it had finally become clear that Victorian forms of amateurism made little sense in modern cricket'[54] – could be applied to rugby union in the 1990s. We can expect to see a professionalised elite of rugby union players emerging, with economic and cultural advantages over footballers and rugby league players to allow them more quickly to exploit their situations.

Like rugby union, athletics also remained hostile to professionalism beyond many other sports. Crump claims that it was 'one of the last major sports whose governing bodies sought to isolate the sport from the commercial pressures which surrounded it'.[55] Again, there were strong historical reasons relating to the timing and context of athletics' emergence that helped to maintain this ideology, and as British athletics has been structurally tied to the Olympic Games as one of its major showcases, notions of amateurism were allowed to thrive long after other sports had rejected them. As in rugby union, however, pressure for change was developing through the 1970s. Successful athletes, such as Daley Thompson, Sebastian Coe, and Steve Ovett, were becoming increasingly aware of their earning potential, and their training needs necessitated full-time commitment for them to compete in an increasingly professionalised world arena, where the USA made use of college scholarships and the USSR exploited conscription to maintain effectively full-time athletes. In the light of this, and the money that was coming into the sport through sponsors and advertisers for appearances by leading athletes, the governing bodies were eventually persuaded to operate various co-ordinated funding schemes. In 1976, the Sports Aid Foundation had been set up by the Sports Council to attract money from industry, government agencies, and individual donors to help fund sportsmen and women in training for major events, and athletics was a leading beneficiary of this. Television fees to meeting organisers also helped to bring money in, with athletes' appearances being increasingly well-paid: Linford Christie, for example, began to receive £5,000 per race after breaking the European 100 metres record in 1986.[56] During the 1980s, the authorities also set up the system of trust funds as a means of controlling payments: athletes' earnings for advertising, media work, and appearances would be held in trust until their retirement from the sport, with only expenses drawn out during their careers. This was rather cosmetic, as expenses were allowed to cover mortgages and car prices as well as training and travel costs. Through schemes such as these, and in an international setting where the notion of amateurism in athletics was becoming increasingly redundant, British athletes achieved a limited form of professional status in the 1980s, legitimising and permitting enhanced social standings for the elite individuals concerned.

The social mobility for an elite that these changes have permitted is just one aspect of sport's links with social class. However, owing to its links with wider notions of meritocracy and rewards for achievement and effort, it has been a particularly important part of sport's appeal to performers from low social backgrounds. As John Hargreaves argued, sport's emphasis on meritocratic mobility gives convincing substance to the ideology that the ambitious, hard working, talented individual, no matter what his social origin, may achieve high status and rewards, and so it reproduces the belief among subordinate groups . . . that the social formation is more open and amenable to change than it really is.[57]

Sport has played a key role in maintaining social stratification for this period through promoting aspiration and desire of enhanced lifestyles and social mobility. For most, the rewards and benefits enjoyed by George Best, Ian Botham, and Frank Bruno remain fantasies, but the public attention on those rewards and lifestyles has helped to maintain sport as an activity based on aspiration within the wider structures of class and status. However, this has not been sport's only linkage with class. At the levels of mass spectating and amateur participation – the recruiting ground for the elite, as well as a self-contained sport setting in its own right – sport has also been strongly linked with maintaining and reproducing both the image and the reality of social differences.

SPORT AS A SIGNIFIER OF STATUS

Veblen's *The Theory of the Leisure Class*, first published in 1899, offered an influential critique of the connections between social status and leisure choices,[58] and while his arguments have been superseded by Marxist, feminist, and post-colonial insights, his work has formed a crucial strand in sociological and historical analysis of class and sport.[59] The emphasis of this strand, which can also be seen in Bourdieu's work on sport and class, is that different social groups use their sporting and leisure practices as a forum for public display of their status and identity.[60] Assuming that different groups have 'differential resources that [they] can bring to bear' in their play,[61] and that these resources do not just consist of the basic determinants of disposable income and spare time but also of 'cultural capital' and the 'meaning and function given to the various practices by the various classes',[62] these insights have allowed a subtle and flexible approach to class and sport emerge. This has gone beyond the vulgar Marxism of Brohm, who viewed sport in reductionist class terms as a new opiate,[63] without losing sight of the many ways in which sport is, and has been, influenced by class formation. For the British example, it has allowed historians to see certain sports as being linked to certain groups. Most obviously, sports involving the highest investment of time, money, and 'cultural capital', such as hunting, shooting, and equestrian sports, have been linked to the aristocracy, the landowning classes, and mobile urban professionals, while those involving mass spectating in low-prestige locations, such as rugby league and football, have been pegged in working-class culture. The groups richest in these resources have been able to maintain the exclusivity of their sports through legal protection, such as laws on trespass, and through institutional structures, such as club rules that allow for 'closure',[64] a practice also followed by upper middle-class sports wishing to maintain their exclusivity. The working classes have had restricted choices based on commercial, voluntary, and state provision in predominantly urban environments. The most basic observation of the social and cultural variations between darts and carriage driving, or between polo and rugby league, demonstrates these points, and, as we shall see, the post-war period in the UK has experienced an element of continuity in this aspect of sport's identity.

Meanwhile, many sports have remained stratified themselves, with different social groups having different roles within them. The best example is probably horse-racing, which has always 'appealed . . . to the upper-class owner, the middle-class trainer, and the working-class *habitué* of the betting shop'.[65] The special role played by members of the royal family in this traditional 'sport of kings', most popularly symbolised at present by Queen Elizabeth the Queen Mother, is also notable. This hegemonic aspect of British sport, where example and coercion are demonstrated through the cultural practice with room for compromise in the face of resistance, has also offered an element of continuity.[66] However, British sport in this period has also seen fluidity in this realm, in keeping with the broader context of blurring class distinctions. Participation patterns have shifted as part of the wider social and economic changes linked to the rise of the white-collar workforce with spare time and disposable income, and the later growth of an underclass linked to long-term structural unemployment and inadequate training opportunities. In this setting, upper working-class options have relatively expanded, while others from the traditional working class have virtually disappeared from the formal sport scene because of an absence of resources. Throughout the post-war period, then, sport's class basis has seen both continuity and change from its pre-industrial and industrial inheritance. While attempting to avoid simplistic labelling that does not allow for movement and fluidity, it is possible to analyse this through surveys of the sporting choices of upper, middle-, and working-class groups.

In his analysis of sport and class, Bourdieu asked a fundamental critical question: 'according to what principles do agents choose between different sports activities or entertainments which, at a given moment, are offered to them as possible?'[67] For the upper classes in the post-war period, as before, these choices have been based upon elitism, difference, exclusivity, and closure. Sports involving the hunting of animals, particularly foxes and stags, have remained an important part of the culture of the landowning classes throughout this period, stressing the role that tradition plays in sporting choices. However, these sports have found themselves under pressure from various directions. The landed exclusivity was effectively lost in the nineteenth century owing to economic changes in agriculture. Hunts had to open themselves up to subscription-paying members, and this element has hastened in the post-war period in keeping with the decline of servant keeping, the rising costs of hunting, and the impact of transport and urban growth on hunting land. As a result, the social profile of the hunt has become increasingly diverse, with landed and titled hunters being joined by city-based commuters from the professional classes, and by pedestrian or car-based supporters from lower-middle- and working-class backgrounds.[68] Some of the anti-hunting discourse of the post-war period has been based on class issues as well as on humanitarian and animal welfare issues. An extreme example of this appeared in the anarchist magazine *Class War* in 1985: 'The rich scum will again be out hunting the small foxes. . . . Of course they'd really like to be hunting you and me. The fuckers think they still live in the feudal days.'[69] In the face of this criticism, pro-hunt writers have often stressed the sport's social mix, claiming it as a sign of its distance from elitism. As Carroll points out, supporters' clubs are a 'tangible force that has lowered some of the sport's social barriers and is a formidable defence against its critics',[70] while the British Field Sports Society's attempts from the 1960s fully to involve anglers and gun club members in its work shows a related concern to stress the cross-class nature of field sports.[71] However, in terms of ownership and control, fox- and stag-hunting have remained socially exclusive, tied to the broader culture of land and its rituals, and the class backgrounds of different functionaries within hunting are fairly specific: the Master of Foxhounds and the professional huntsmen are strongly linked to class relations. Field shooting has managed to remain more exclusive in this period. Being based on estates rather than across countryside, it has been able to remain relatively untouched by car and foot followers of hunting, and its rarity and costs have kept it limited to upper-class and professional circles. While clubs and syndicates have broadened the access, the need to obtain authority from the landowner and to maintain particular forms of conduct have maintained a strong element of closure.[72]

Other sports that have retained strong links with land and profes-sional circles have included carriage driving and, with historical links to the officer class in the army, show jumping. The team game of polo has also played a role here, with royal patronage, high costs, and strong military links maintaining its elitist nature as it survived the Second World War and then grew in the 1980s and 1990s. By 1990, however, it still boasted only 1,200 players based in 30 clubs nationwide.[73] All of these sports have been open to limited entry by groups from outside the traditional ownership groups, a fact that stresses the fluidity of the class/sport relationship, and of the social structure in general. However, it is important to note that what has continued to make them attractive to the upwardly mobile has been their traditional image, and the oppor-tunities that they offer for the display of wealth. Along with other sports based on high capital investment in equipment and high maintenance costs, such as power boat racing and ballooning, these sports have remained focused on possession. They have also remained, to a degree, pre-industrial in that (with the exception of polo) they take place across unenclosed land or waterways and without the same regard for time that less expensive sports have had to develop. Social mobility based on wealth and time has brought new money into these sports, thus providing essential funds for pastimes rooted in a declining agricultural economy, but the trappings involved in absorbing the new entrants have helped these sports to retain a sense of difference and elitism. These sports have continued to act as outward signifiers of wealth and status, whilst also offering opportunities for socialisation and contact.

The sports pursued by middle-class groups and individuals have also seen both continuity and change in the period. While the upper sections have been able to enjoy increasing upward mobility in their sport, the established sports of golf, lawn tennis, squash, and croquet have all flourished as part of middle-class culture since 1945. Largely based on participation through membership, and with a strong element of social-isation as well as play, these sports have offered continuity from the Victorian period for suburban dwellers. Their club settings have offered, as Stoddart put it on American golf courses, 'a social oasis' where 'exclusiveness and real estate value physically separate them from the rest of the community'.[74] They have also grown, under the influ-ence of rises in disposable income, leisure time, private car ownership, and the awareness of the role of active sport in personal good health. Squash provides an excellent example of this. This individual sport with club basis and relatively high costs in terms of membership, space, equipment, and time, boomed in the 1970s and 1980s: where the

Squash Rackets Association had had 425 clubs and 1,380 individual members in 1965, it had 1,650 and 7,848 respectively by 1989, figures which do not cover the unquantifiable number of casual players in school, college, workplace, and municipal facilities. Its social positioning is stressed by the 1987 General Household Survey (GHS) finding that 72 per cent of players were from non-manual groups, and by the domination of club-based facilities: in 1990, 40 per cent of the courts in England were provided by commercial or private clubs, compared with 22 per cent by local authorities.[75] Similar findings relating to provision and membership profiles have been evident across the period in a number of other sports, and the 1987 GHS showed that golf, lawn tennis, and rugby union among others were all dominated by players from non-manual occupational groups.

Dunning and Sheard's analysis of the social background of rugby union players stressed the sport's middle-class basis. At the elite level of the English game, no England internationals in the period 1942–71 had come from the Registrar General's groups 4 or 5, and only 5 per cent from 3 (manual) and 8 per cent from 3 (non-manual). The vast majority – 66 per cent – were from group 2, while group 1 had provided the rest. This was backed up by their contemporary survey of a sample of non-international players, where 1 and 2 provided 34 per cent and 58 per cent respectively. They concluded that while the post-war spread of the sport to grammar schools had facilitated a diffusion within the middle class, the 'diffusion came to a virtual standstill at the boundary between the middle and working class'.[76] For the post-war period, such sports have continued to offer the attractions so ably expressed by Holt for the interwar period, where 'Tennis and golf clubs were worlds within worlds, business contacts and mutual reassurance for the reasonably well-off, islands of sociability within the unfathomable seas of domestic privacy.'[77] Their class basis for our period can also be stressed by the kind of sponsorship they have drawn since the boom in advertising that sport has experienced since the 1960s. Companies wishing to target more affluent and discerning audiences have chosen sports which they perceive to be followed or played by them, which has led to insurance companies, finance houses, and specifically upmarket alcohol and tobacco products being sold through these sports. AXA Equity and Law in cricket, Dunhill in golf, and Stella Artois in tennis are examples of this trend.

For the working class, the staple spectator sports of the inner city and industrial areas, most notably football and greyhound-racing across most of the UK, rugby union in South Wales, and rugby league in northern England, have shown remarkable resilience in spite of the multiplying alternative attractions of the period. Although live attendances in these sports declined, particularly from the mid-1950s to the early 1990s, interest in the team sports continued through television coverage and for participants. These sports had strong historical links with notions of representation of towns, cities, and areas of cities,[78] and their relative cheapness and the low level of 'cultural capital' involved in following them helped this linkage to survive the changes in working-class community culture that followed the Second World War.

Football's historical ties with the working classes have provided the focus for a great deal of analysis, particularly in relation to the debate over hooliganism. As violence around football became increasingly perceived as a problem from the 1960s, so theories to explain it proliferated. The focus of one particular strand has been on how changes in football's culture served to alienate it from its historical heartlands of male, working-class support. In this view, diversification, the elevation of top players from Critcher's 'located' working-class heroes to 'dislocated' superstars, and the sport's attempt to appeal to a more affluent, bourgeois audience all fitted in with a time of fracture within working-class culture itself. The result of this mix of an upwardly mobile sport and a class fractured by economic, demographic, and familial changes was an attempt by young male supporters to reappropriate their game: 'Hooliganism comes out of the way in which the *traditional* forms of football watching encounter the *professionalisation* and *spectacularisation* of the game. It is one of the consequences of the changing relationship of the audience to the game.'[79] Dunning *et al.* criticised this view from their developmental perspective for being too 'present-centred' and not historical enough,[80] but praised its emphasis on social relations as a context for hooliganism. Working-class cultures, notably those associated with masculinity and local and national identity, have remained at the centre of their analyses of the issue.[81] They have shown, for example, that despite the great publicity given to the tiny number of convicted hooligans who have come from professional backgrounds, the bulk of recorded hooligans (in this case, those convicted of offences or recorded through academic surveys) have come from social groups 3, 4, and 5: of the 519 employed hooligans covered in their analysis, 91.5 per cent were from these groups.[82] Obviously, hooligans cannot be taken as typical of football supporters for the post-war period, nor can they be seen as typical of the working class as a whole, and there is a consensus in the analysis on how the emergence of a violent minority group acted, along with the existence of rival leisure options, as a disincentive for more respectable working-class supporters to stop attending. But the debate over hooliganism and social relations has demonstrated some of the ways in which football has maintained its traditional association with the working class in the post-war period. Despite the sport's attempts to reach new audiences through ground improvements and corporate strategies from the 1960s onwards, the sport's links with local identification and class-specific forms of masculine behaviour have not fully dissolved this partnership. Moreover, it is not only hooligans who have contested this apparent upward shift in the game's profile: the more respectable voice of young, predominantly male, and (by their own admission) traditional supporters, the fanzine movement, has also had an anti-middle-class slant. However, the long-term effects of the changes in the game since the disasters of 1985 – one of which, the Bradford fire, was described by Taylor as essentially 'a class issue' due to its cause in stadium infrastructure failure[83] – remain to be seen. The increasing influence of satellite television on spectating habits, and the current legal requirement towards all-seater stadiums after the Hillsborough disaster of 1989, can be seen to be causing repercussions in the class basis of support more far reaching than the changes in the 1960s and 1970s.

As with the targeted sponsorship of golf and tennis, marketing decisions over football and rugby league have also helped to demonstrate the assumed basis of their following in social groups 3 and 4, as with Tetley Bitter and Carling lager in rugby league and football respectively. In addition, the emergence of pub- and social club-based sports into the elite fold has been strongly connected with working-class followings and participants, with darts and snooker in particular being taken up more widely and attracting television audiences without losing their roots. Interestingly, the Sports Council withdrew its recognition of darts as a sport in 1996 on the grounds that it was not physical enough. The British Darts Organisation perceived this as really about image and lifestyle: 'They're really saying that they don't want to be associated with fat blokes with fags in their mouth.'[84] Boxing has continued to attract participants and followers from the skilled, semi-skilled, and unemployed working class, with its strong links with violent masculinity, community-based gymnasiums, and the prospect of a fortune for those who can succeed in the sport. A study of boxing culture in 1990s Sheffield, Beattie's *On The Ropes*, offered a sympathetic account of the place of the sport in a world of pawnshops, nightclub bouncers, debt collectors, and pit bull terrier owners. Here, self-made scrap-metal millionaires and the occasional successful boxers – in this case, Naseem

Hamed and Herol Graham – were hailed as local heroes who had managed to rise above the material deprivation.[85] Similarly, a recurrent theme in Garfield's oral history of wrestling is its appeal to working-class sensibilities and tastes.[86]

The publicity and self-publicity surrounding the elite from such backgrounds has helped to keep this sport located within a working-class culture with aspiration and social mobility in-built. As such, it provides an excellent example of the complex ways in which sport can be seen to be part of class relations rather than simply class stratification. Sport has offered mobility and improvement for an elite, and has also been a key location for grassroots and amateur participants to make public statements about their status. Here, the fluidity of class relations in post-war Britain is crucial, with sport as one of the cultural spheres where taste, attitude, and command of resources can be demonstrated, and where upward mobility can be displayed through the acquisition of new sporting interests deemed appropriate. However, as the case of football has shown, those who feel themselves as traditional or rightful owners of the sport have contested social change. It is essentially a contest for meanings, a struggle over 'why some people's "accounts" count'.[87] Beyond the football crowd, this can be traced in different modes of watching the same sport: for example, between a traditionalist emphasis on quiet contemplation at live cricket that has been challenged by the recent importation of the Barmy Army's noisier approach,[88] or between polite applause and the Mexican wave at Wimbledon. It is also present, as suggested by Bourdieu, in the different ways that people from different classes approach their physical culture, from the 'working-class demand' for 'the outward signs of strength' versus the middle-class emphasis on good health and hygiene.[89] The obvious placing of wrestling and boxing as working-class sports, emphasising violence and physicality, can be compared here with the more prestigious forms of exercise and display, such as aerobics and cardio-vascular workouts at health clubs. The survival of such differences, and the public way in which they are contested, helps to stress the continued importance of class issues in British sport as it enters the twenty-first century. Class and status are not the only issues here, of course, and they cannot be seen in isolation from age, gender, ethnicity, ability, and other factors, but the ways in which the resources needed for sport are strongly linked to income, time, and status have kept class as a major issue throughout the post-war period.

Chapter 6

Sport and ethnicity

INTRODUCTION

In 1988, after Liverpool FC had bought John Barnes from Watford FC, manager Kenny Dalglish attempted to stem the controversy that the transfer had aroused: 'He's not a black player – he's a player'. Defending the signing on terms of Barnes's quality, Dalglish claimed that the issue of Barnes being the club's first major black signing 'was something that had not crossed my mind until it was pointed out to me'.[1] The controversy – including the racist chants, the bananas thrown at Barnes during matches, the labelling of Liverpool as 'Niggerpool' by some supporters of local rivals Everton – and Dalglish's diplomatic response offer useful insights into the issue of race and ethnicity in sport in the UK since 1945. As a public arena for physical display and interaction, sport has proved to be a significant location for the playing out of discourses over racial stereotypes, prejudices, politics, and integration. As with gender, the inherent use of the body in sport has meant that popular questions have been asked and answered over physiological differences between sportsmen and women from different ethnic groups.[2] Moreover, the twinned issues of constraints and opportunities for non-whites in post-war Britain have been acted out publicly through sports clubs, school sports, and national teams. Time and again, sporting examples have been used by non-sporting agencies and individuals to illustrate integration or difference. From the mass media's 'paternalistic infantilization of Frank Bruno and Daley Thompson to the status of national mascots and adopted pets',[3] through to Norman Tebbit's notorious claims that the patriotism of second- and third-generation black and Asian Britons could be assessed by seeing who they supported in test matches,[4] sport's popular and readily accessible position has ensured that it has played a role in defining issues of ethnicity and race for a wider context.

However, before this aspect of post-war sport can be explored, it is worth thinking critically about the terminology and ideology involved. As Cashmore has concisely shown, academic discourse from the 1930s has moved away from the notion of 'race' as a meaningful category: the purity of genetics and biology that is needed to classify humans as belonging to one racial group or another is simply unrealistic, and it is impossible to set up dividing lines between racial groups that would be meaningful or satisfactory to all analysts.[5] Instead, race has come to be seen as 'essentially a social construction and not a natural division',[6] in much the same way as gender has come to be viewed. Various theories have been explored as to what informs the construction in any given society, but the variations discovered, based on gender, class, and economic variables, suggest the notion of race to be cultural and environmental, rather than natural. In place of race as a meaningful label, social science discourse now prefers 'ethnicity', which stresses the 'cultural heritage' of any given group seen to have features in common, rather than biological features. Thus, cultural markers such as language, family structure, and religion are seen to be more significant than physiological markers such as skin colour and hair type.[7] However, the terminology and ideology of race has retained its popular currency, and can be experienced on a daily basis in the media, the workplace, schools, and conversation. As the outward physical signs of difference – most crucially, skin colour – are more immediately discernible than cultural heritage, so race remains a part of everyday common-sense ideology in a multi-ethnic but predominantly white society. As sport plays such an important role in contemporary common sense, it is crucial to explore the ways in which ethnicity has been played out in this public, popular, and physical domain, where 'White men can't jump' and, as a Luton Town FC coach claimed, Asians cannot play football because 'they don't like the physical element [and] . . . their eating habits are a problem'.[8] These developments tell us that ethnicity is not just a minority issue: it is something possessed by everyone. However, the main analysis and debate for our period has concentrated on minority ethnicities; this chapter will explore the impact of non-white immigration and settlement on sport in the UK, and the roles which sport has assumed in relations between different ethnic groups.

To understand this area of British sport in the post-war period, the context of non-white immigration and settlement has to be taken into account. Fryer has painstakingly uncovered a black presence in Britain dating back to the Roman invasion, and dates the first British-born blacks to the start of the sixteenth century, but the growth of a numerically significant non-white population has come about since 1945.[9] We also need to bear in mind the much wider history of immigration and settlement as a whole, which, as Holmes reminds us, has involved a greater ethnic diversity than simply Asian and Afro-Caribbean.[10] However, for our purposes the main centre of attention is the growth of a black population in the UK since the Second World War, and the issues of accommodation, assimilation, discrimination, and hostility.[11] This is because it has been the emergence of black sportsmen and women, their successes and failures in a white sports structure, and the way in which this development has fed into wider thought about sport and ethnicity that has, to borrow Cashmore's phrase, 'been the subject of bar-room discussion and academic controversy'.[12] The meanings attached to the presence of other significant immigrant and settler groups, such as Poles, Irish, Chinese, and Ukrainians, have not been played out in sport in the same way as those related to blacks have, and there is no major historical research on how individuals from these ethnic groups have fared in sport. Moreover, the sporting history of South Asian immigrants and their children has not been explored in depth, a gap that helps to reinforce the popular stereotype that Asians are more interested in studies than in sport. Sociological and ethnographic work in this area that has been forthcoming since the mid-1980s has helped to challenge this assumption, and to show the ways in which sports have been approached by Britons of Indian, Pakistani, Bangladeshi, and Sri Lankan origin.[13] Some journalistic work has also uncovered for otherwise ignorant white audiences the extent of Asian involvement in football at local league levels, although at the time of writing a significant breakthrough into the professional game is still not apparent: the lack of role models in comparison with black players, and coaches' stereotypes of Asians as passive, weak, and overcommitted to religious observance, are blamed for this absence.[14] However, the small amount of historical material on sport and Asian Britons has unfortunately meant that the experience cannot be properly explored in a work of this nature. It is to be hoped that this situation will soon be rectified.

For Afro-Caribbeans, however, the research has been fairly wide ranging. Ethnicity did not emerge as an area for analysis by British sports academics until the late 1970s. Earlier work from the USA came out of the civil rights and Black Power movements of the 1960s, whilst also being influenced by the contemporary debates over sporting contacts with South Africa due to its segregation of sport. Edwards' work with black athletes, written up in *The Revolt of the Black Athlete* in

1969, and Scott's wider-ranging *The Athletic Revolution* helped to clarify the debates over representation, stereotyping, and the politics of sport for ethnic minorities. The connections were clarified when Tommie Smith and John Carlos gave Black Power salutes on the medal rostrum of the 1968 Olympic Games in Mexico City.[15] From here, a great deal of work was carried out on key questions about the overrepresentation of blacks in some sports, notably athletics, football, and basketball, and their absence from others, such as golf, lawn tennis, and swimming. Stacking – the division of labour in a sports team in accordance with racial stereotypes – has also been analysed in many settings. This research suggests that in basketball, football, and baseball, black players have consistently been deployed in positions that require speed and agility but not decision-making abilities (although Birrell, in her call for more sophisticated analysis, argued that stacking was overstudied 'simply because the data is there'[16]). Some of the analysis of racial issues in sport was covertly racist: Kane's notorious 1971 piece, 'An assessment of black is best', for example, relied upon mytholigised readings of ideal physiological differences and claimed that blacks had genetic advantages over whites in sport.[17] However, the social science and cultural studies approaches established economic, social, and cultural reasons for the ethnic situation in contemporary and historical American sport.[18]

These insights were brought into British sports analysis in the late 1970s and early 1980s. Just as civil rights and Black Power formed a context for the American work, so too can this research be seen as part of a wider investigation of ethnicity. This was a time of realignment in the politics of race and ethnicity: the 1976 Race Relations Act, the adoption of multiracial teaching strategies by some education authorities, the limited electoral successes and street presence of the National Front (NF), the Brixton riots of 1981, Rock Against Racism, and Margaret Thatcher's 1978 claim that the UK was being 'swamped' by blacks were diverse expressions of this process as the polity and society tried to come to terms with the fact that roughly 3 per cent of the UK's population was, by the early 1980s, not white. The situation had changed radically from 1945 when, according to Holmes, blacks and Asians 'were statistically insignificant and their representatives were widely regarded as anthropological curiosities'.[19] The specific sporting context for the research is also clear. In British sport, the 1970s and early 1980s were a time when a significant number of black British sportsmen and women were achieving elite success nationally and internationally, including Viv Anderson and Cyrille Regis in football, boxers

Tom Conteh, Maurice Hope, and Cornelius Boza-Edwards, athletes Tessa Sanderson, Daley Thompson, and Sonia Lannaman, and Clive Sullivan in rugby league. This 'rise to prominence . . . of black sportsmen and women in British society'[20] helped to focus academic attention on this issue in the UK.

Cashmore made a significant breakthrough in 1982 with *Black Sportsmen*. He has continued to deal with this issue in his other writings on race and sport, with *Making Sense of Sports* including a chapter on it.[21] Since *Black Sportsmen*, which surveyed a number of individuals about their experiences and gave an overview of the history of blacks in British sport, other writers have approached the issue. Some have picked up on the American examples on stacking, and explored the phenomenon in a British setting: Maguire has covered this in football and rugby union, for example, and Melnick has also looked at football.[22] Its relevance to historical enquiry was stressed by Mason, who devoted some space to stacking in his survey *Sport in Britain*.[23] The terms of debate have been broadened since the early 1990s with the application of the notion of ethnicity to sport: Jarvie's 1991 collection, which covered a range of British and non-British subjects, shows some of the scope here.[24] Other historians have gone further back to explore the presence of black sportsmen in the interwar period: Jeff Hill's work on overseas cricketers in the professional leagues is significant here, as is Vasali's research on black footballers before the 1960s.[25] Outside the academic context, there has been a move towards reclaiming earlier black sporting heroes which must also be seen in this context. For example, South African footballer Albert Johanneson, who had been one of the few black players in the Football League in the 1960s when he played for Leeds United, was revisited in this way after his death in 1995, recalled by one obituarist as 'an exciting and intelligent player in an era of famous cloggers'.[26] The Commission for Racial Equality (CRE) mobilised history as part of its campaign against racism in football by funding a new memorial on the grave of Arthur Wharton, the Jamaican-born sprinter who was also the first black player in the Football League, playing for Preston North End from 1886. This trend has much in common with the women's sport historiography aimed at reclaiming past heroines for the pedigree and legitimacy.

Sport has also been taken seriously by some analysts from history, sociology, and cultural studies who are interested in the wider experience of immigration and settlement. Here, sport has acted as an index for studies of integration, exclusion, and cultural identity. Holmes, for example, referred to the 'continuing visibility' of blacks in sport as one of the reasons for their extensive presence in writing on immigration.[27] Geographers Hudson and Williams cited boxers Frank Bruno and Lennox Lewis as highly visible individuals who had 'achieved great success' despite obstacles in the UK, although as their other examples – Lenny Henry and Joan Armatrading – were also drawn from the broad field of entertainment, the authors' scope seems rather narrow: why not Diane Abbot, Stuart Hall, or Bill Morris?[28] Fryer included detailed coverage of the careers of black prize-fighters as an appendix in *Staying Power*, and Gilroy has drawn attention to the need for cultural critics to take account of black sports icons as well as intellectuals in his challenging 'Frank Bruno or Salman Rushdie'.[29] This wide range of material has been paralleled by strategic research into ethnic minority participation in sport for various official organisations, such as local authorities and the Sports Council. Here, literature reviews and qualitative and quantitative research helped to highlight some of the constraints that were related to ethnicity, and set up strategies to combat them: Parry's literature survey for the London Council for Sport and Recreation offers summaries of many such projects, and the review itself is an example of policy-driven research.[30] Thus, in various research settings, race and ethnicity were accepted as problematic issues in sport by the mid-1990s, while sport was also seen as capable of shedding light on black culture and history more widely.

As with gender, it is easy to fall into the trap of reductionism when dealing with ethnicity, and to treat a sportsman or woman's colour and cultural heritage as if they are the only things that matter about them. This can be exemplified by a *Guardian* interview with Viv Anderson printed the day after he became the first black football player to represent England: 'Anderson's look of mild amusement said it all: why is this reporter going on about Martin Luther King, Muhammad Ali, Pele, ethnic groups and racial prejudice when I'd rather stick to talking about football?'[31] It is clearly a view that has been influential in sports coaching, management, and media coverage, with blackness and supposedly related natural physical attributes being readily emphasised in discourse. However, it is important to stress as a caveat that, as with gender, separate coverage of ethnicity here is not meant to obscure the fact that no participant or spectator in sport can be broken down into individual factors or aspects. It is discussed separately precisely because of the popular assumptions that have historically prioritised ethnicity in any discussion of non-white sportsmen and women. The theme can now be explored through a historical survey of the post-war period, which will show the ways in which sport has acted as a public forum for debates on ethnicity in a multi-ethnic society. This issue will be studied through the related themes of accommodation and assimilation, and discrimination and prejudice. While the thematic structure must be seen as problematic in so far as it may disguise the chronology, it has been chosen here to allow our attention to focus on trends rather than lists. Moreover, a concise narrative of the events up until the early 1980s is available in Cashmore's *Black Sportsmen*, and it would be inappropriate merely to offer an update. Instead, the thematic approach helps us to keep British society as the focus of attention, and to see the continuities and changes around the history of ethnicity that have developed in sport.

Before the mass immigration of the post-war period, and the subsequent settlement and regeneration of non-white communities in the UK, there had been black sportsmen in the UK since the late eighteenth century, when the freed slave Bill Richmond was brought to England as a prize-fighter. Imperial connections ensured a presence of blacks in British sport in its more modern phase from the late nineteenth century up until the Second World War. As well as Wharton, they included the welterweight boxer Andrew Jeptha from Cape Town, who won the British title in 1907, and sprinter Jack London from British Guyana, who was Great Britain's first black Olympic medal winner with his silver in the 100 metres at the 1928 Olympic Games in Amsterdam.[32] English cricket also attracted black players from the West Indies, the most famous being Learie Constantine of Trinidad, who played league cricket for Nelson and Rochdale in the interwar period.[33] On the whole, however, these men were exceptions, and their presence was generally seen as unproblematic due to their individuality, without a larger non-white community to be seen as a threat by whites. Constantine's friend James recalled of their days in Lancashire that they were 'the only coloured men in Colne' apart from 'someone who went round collecting refuse in an old pushcart', and confirms Holmes's claim about non-whites being regarded as 'anthropological curiosities': 'We could not get rid of the feeling that whatever we did would be judged as representative of the habits and standards of millions of people at home (and goodness knows where else).'[34] Larry Gains, the Canadian-born black heavyweight boxer, recorded similar perceptions of his career in the UK in the interwar period: 'There wasn't prejudice amongst the public then 'cause there was only a handful of coloureds here, anyway.'[35] However, all this was to change after the Second World War, when the black and Asian servicemen who remained in the UK were soon joined by significant numbers of immigrants. It was in this environment, with frequent public hostility being expressed towards black workers and settlers, that sport gradually began to play its part in shaping the multicultural society that emerged in the UK over the next half century.

ASSIMILATION AND ACCOMMODATION

One of the aims of policy and discourse over ethnicity in post-war Britain has been to achieve a smooth transition into a multi-ethnic, multiracial society. While the UK has historically always been some-thing of a meeting point for various cultures and ethnic groups, owing to its imperial role and its role as a place of refuge, the challenges thrown up by post-war Commonwealth immigration have been particu-larly acute because of the significant cultural and ethnic differences between the Afro-Caribbeans and South Asians and the predominantly white population. It was clear from the start of the immigration in the late 1940s that assimilation and accommodation were going to be more difficult than for white European migrants, a fact made very clear in 1948 when white merchant seamen refused to work with black colleagues, which helped fuel racist attacks on workers' hostels in Liverpool.[36] Despite subsequent legal restrictions on non-white immi-gration in 1962, 1968, 1971, 1981, and 1987, it was clear from the mid-1960s that racial prejudice and discrimination were being suffered by immigrants and their British-born children. This was driven home by a widely publicised investigation by Political and Economic Planning, *Racial Discrimination in England*, released in 1967 and rewritten as a Penguin Special the following year, which concluded that in employ-ment, housing, and public services, 'there is racial discrimination varying in extent from the massive to the substantial'.[37] This realisation gave rise to various strategies to promote better relations and outlaw overt inequalities: the Race Relations acts of 1965, 1968, and 1976 all aimed at this liberal solution.[38]

Sport, as a popular public phenomenon, has had a significant role to play in this gradual process of allowing black immigrants and their chil-dren to earn some form of respect and acceptance from white society. The assumptions underlining this position are optimistically functional. Sport is held as a means of meritocratic social mobility, as well as a way in which national unity can be redefined and promoted in a multicul-tural setting: this was the meaning of the 'Tebbit test' for cricket supporters. It also assumes an objectivity and neutrality in sport due to its emphasis on physical tests, summed up in Cashmore's ironical ques-tion: 'How can you discriminate in an area where success or failure is determined by a stopwatch or a measuring tape?'[39] Clearly, it is a view that fails sufficiently to ask enough awkward questions about the lived experience of all people in sport, about the structural and institutional racism in sporting organisations, and about media coverage and stereotypical assumptions. However, it must be dealt with as it is a view that has a lot of common-sense credibility, and many black sportsmen and women have declared their belief in it. From Frank Bruno's pride in the fact that boxing has allowed him to pay for his daughters' private education, to Linford Christie's belief that 'by representing my country, I'm trying to show that there is really no need for the problems we have. . . . [B]lack sportsmen are uniting the country', this popular notion of sport promoting harmony and accommodation is persuasive.[40] There are a number of areas in which we can see this throughout our period, including the public debate over racism and racial segregation that has been played out in some sporting settings; the emergence of black sportsmen and women in a number of sports that has provided individual mobility and a disproportionate representation at elite level; and the accommodation of some black sports stars by the media and other areas of society. In these, it is possible to read a colour-blind history of post-war British sport.

A major sign that sport was prepared to change in line with the needs of post-war society came, significantly, in 1948. In the year of the first major arrivals of West Indian immigrants, and the British Nationality Act, the British Boxing Board of Control (BBBC) removed its colour bar that had prevented non-white boxers from challenging for its titles. This bar had been justified in the pre-war period in the interests of keeping British titles in British hands, rather than in those of imperial and Commonwealth boxers, but its application to British-born blacks, such as welterweight Len Johnson of Manchester who won 86 of his 116 professional fights between 1921 and 1933 but was never allowed to fight for a national title, suggests that the issue was ethnicity rather than nationality.[41] Larry Gains campaigned against the bar in the 1930s. The BBBC finally modified it in 1948 to allow for boxers who were 'normally resident and domiciled' in the UK, and had lived in the UK for at least ten years.[42] According to Cashmore, the change was made in order to accommodate Dick Turpin, a successful professional middleweight from Leamington Spa, the eldest son of a white woman and a British Guianese father who had settled in the Midlands after service in the First World War. Turpin duly won the BBBC's middleweight title in 1948. He was followed by his younger brother Randolph, who not only won the British middleweight title in 1950, but went on to beat Luc Van Dam of Holland and Sugar Ray Robinson of the USA for the European and World titles respectively in 1951 (although he lost the World title back to Robinson after just two months). Turpin's tragic demise has been well documented as a cautionary tale on the fickleness of the social mobility that sport can bring: his earnings were mishandled, and his sporting career ended in what Cashmore called the 'humiliating depths' of fairground bouts against wrestlers, before his bankruptcy in 1962 and his suicide in 1966.[43] Despite this ending, his short-term fame as a black national sporting hero was an early sign of some of the changes that the presence of black Britons was going to have on sport as a public arena, and it is significant here as it came about after a British governing body dismantled its segregationist policy. However, it is worth noting that the BBBC's rule on residence 'effectively barred a generation of young men from competing for titles'.[44] It has continued to be perceived by some black boxers as racially motivated: Bunny Johnson, who was one of the leading British heavyweights by 1971 but was denied a title fight until his ten-year residency was complete in 1973, claimed 'For nationality you can read "racialism" '.[45]

This particular example of a policy change by a sport in recognition of the changing wider environment may have been pragmatic and opportunist rather than principled, but the strand of sport being used publicly to promote equality of opportunity has surfaced at other points since the 1940s. The struggle against apartheid by British opponents and South Africans in exile focused heavily on sport specifically because of its public nature and popularity, and while the main focus of opposition was the treatment of blacks in South Africa, the timing of the various campaigns from the 1960s onwards tied in with a growing awareness of race relations in the UK. As we have seen in Chapter 1, a number of opponents of the abortive 1970 South African cricket tour drew attention to the damage that the tour would have on the domestic situation. Stop The Seventy Tour (STST) campaign organiser Peter Hain was convinced that the attention the movement drew to racism was crucial in mobilising anti-racist opinion in general, and in bringing the 'comparatively watered-down British form' of racism into the open: 'STST quite unconsciously became not merely a focus for anti-apartheid feeling, but a focus for anti-racialist feeling as well. Some saw in us the only real alternative that was being put to Powellism'.[46] Although this example differs drastically from the BBBC's end to the colour bar, in that this pressure against racism in sport came from agencies outside sport, the impact was in some ways similar: inequalities between ethnic groups that were being reproduced and maintained through sport were becoming increasingly offensive and obsolete in post-war British society. The Anti-Apartheid Movement's continued opposition to sporting contacts with South Africa, including opposition to Zola Budd's flag of convenience and various rebel English cricket tours to South Africa, helped to keep this aspect in the public eye until South Africa's reforms in the early 1990s.

A final example of sport being used as a public forum for discussing racism and discrimination came in 1993, when the CRE and the Professional Footballers Association (PFA) launched the 'Let's Kick Racism out of Football' campaign, with the post-Heysel fans' pressure group the Football Supporters Association joining in 1994.[47] Many felt that this action by the CRE came too late, as certain aspects of foot-balling culture had been conducive to racism since the emergence of significant numbers of black players in the late 1970s, and many independent fan groups had already run local campaigns, such as Leeds Fans United Against Racism and Fascism which started in 1987, and the fanzine movement had, in general, taken an anti-racist stance since the mid-1980s.[48] The vast majority of Football League clubs backed the scheme. It aimed, through community schemes, fanzines, and educational material, to discourage racist activity around football, including the shouting of abuse and the recruiting activities of right-wing groups, and to make football grounds more pleasant environments for spectators of all ethnic groups. Although the campaign did come rather late, it was indicative of the way in which a shifting public discourse on ethnic relations – in this case, the equal opportunities culture of the 1990s – was aired in a sporting setting. While the FA, the Football League, and the clubs were criticised for not taking the initiative themselves, the fact that the PFA helped to start the campaign suggests that sportsmen were aware of the problem, and were prepared to act on it despite the sport's traditional 'denial of racism, backed up by the fallacious claim that talking about it would make it worse'.[49]

These three examples, while standing only as case studies, can help us to see how sport has been involved in broader contestations of racism in British society and beyond. They serve to illustrate ways in which sport's public nature has made it an appropriate setting for positive action against aspects of race relations that have lost currency in a multicultural society. A more direct way in which sport can be perceived to have ameliorated ethnic differences in a multi-ethnic society has been in the opportunities it has offered to sportsmen and women from Afro-Caribbean backgrounds. As in the USA, where a number of blacks have achieved social mobility through their success in boxing, athletics, basketball, football, and baseball, and as in the UK from the early twentieth century where working-class Jews such as Ted 'Kid' Lewis and Jack 'Kid' Berg achieved success in boxing,[50] a number of sports have drawn heavily upon black talent. The main sports involved have been athletics, boxing, and football, with both rugby codes following behind.

In the immediate post-war period, before mass Afro-Caribbean immigration and the growth of a black population, this trend showed a great deal of continuity with the interwar model of black sportsmen using imperial and Commonwealth connections to settle in the UK and practise their sports there, either as professionals or alongside studies and other careers. A boost to this was given by the structures of armed service during the Second World War, which ensured that many West Indians, Africans, and Asians experienced life in the UK, and some chose to stay. The most illustrious examples from this period were the athletes Arthur Wint of Jamaica and McDonald Bailey of Trinidad. Both served in the RAF during the war – Wint as a Flying Officer, Bailey as an Aircraftsman – and both enjoyed great track success after the war. Their national fame was secured at the Amateur Athletic Association (AAA) championship in 1946, where Bailey won the 100 yards and 220 yards double, and Wint the 440 yards and 880 yards double. They competed in the 1948 Olympic Games in London, Bailey for Great Britain, and Wint for Jamaica: the latter took gold in the 400 metres and silver in the 800 metres. Bailey also competed at the Helsinki Olympics in 1952, winning the 100 metre bronze, and won a record sixteen AAA titles, including the 100 yards and 220 yards double seven times between 1946 and 1953. Their success helped to make them enormously popular with white audiences – athletics historian Mel Watman placed them with Roger Bannister as 'the Holy Trinity' of post-war British athletes[51] – at a time when their ethnicity was not only valued because of the war effort, but only just becoming the source of friction that immigration precipitated.[52] However, it was not until the late 1970s that a number of specific events in British athletics, especially the 100 metres, 200 metres, and the long jump, became dominated by black athletes. In both men's and women's events, a stream of Afro-Caribbeans emerged at the elite level. Some were the children of original immigrants; others, like sprinter Linford Christie, had been born in the West Indies and had come to the UK in their childhood. Decathlete Daley Thompson, the son of a black Nigerian father and a white Scottish mother, was one of the first to gain international recognition, winning the 1978 Commonwealth and 1980 and 1984 Olympic events. However, he famously played down his ethnicity: when Cashmore approached him for his research on *Black Sportsmen*, Thompson replied 'I don't know what you want to talk to me for, I'm not black.'[53] However, while his own perceptions are crucial, public perceptions of the changing face of British athletics meant that, by the end of our period, athletics was heavily identified as one in which black men and women were able to excel. International success for, amongst others, sprinters Linford Christie and John Regis, Tessa Sanderson in the javelin, and hurdler Colin Jackson, drew attention to the fact that black athletes were disproportionately overrepresented in the sport in relation to the size of the UK's black population. Moreover, the role that many of them have taken in promoting an image of ethnic harmony in the name of national unity has helped the sport's image as colour blind and unified. Christie's overt use of the Union flag during his post-victory celebrations, and his published claims that teaching young black children a sense of national pride through the singing of the national anthem and a taught respect for the royal family would alleviate problems in British society, exemplify this.[54]

This popular notion of overachievement, often taken at face value to mean that sport has helped to accommodate black Britons and has offered them means of advancement, has also been marked in boxing. Again, with the Turpin brothers as notable exceptions, the early figures here were predominantly Commonwealth nationals who moved to the UK to fight. The Nigerian featherweight Hogan Bassey, who settled in Liverpool in 1952 and won the Empire title in 1955 and the World title in 1957, was an example. Others included light-heavyweight Yolande Pompey from Trinidad, who was unsuccessful in his world title bid in 1956, and Nigerian middleweight Dick Tiger, who also settled in Liverpool in 1955 and went on to win the World title twice, in 1962 and 1965, before moving up to the light-heavyweight division, where he also won the World title in 1966.[55] By the 1970s, an increasing number of black boxers were emerging who helped to reorient the sport nationally as being, like athletics was to become, disproportionately contested by Britons of Afro-Caribbean background. Boxing historian Harding has described this as a 'revolution' in the sport.[56] Some had moved to the UK themselves in the 1950s and early 1960s, and thus qualified as British under BBBC rules: for example, the Jamaican-born middleweight Bunny Sterling, who won the BBBC title in 1970, had moved to England in 1954. Others were the children of earlier immigrants, and had been born in the UK: among the most successful in this category have been a number of world champions, including welterweight Lloyd Honeyghan, light-middleweight Maurice Hope, light-heavyweight John Conteh, and heavyweight Frank Bruno. Black domination in this sport at the professional level is obviously not restricted to the UK: in 1995, 90 per cent of the world champions in all weight classes were black.[57] However, as with athletics, the public identification of boxing as a sport where blacks face opportunity and mobility has helped to maintain the commonsense notion of sport as an area free from racism. This notion was summed up by Des Morrison, the Jamaican-born light-welterweight who won the BBBC title in 1973 by beating Ghanaian-born Joe Tettah, the first national title fight between two Afro-Caribbean immigrants: 'If you're good enough and you've got a great manager . . . , you'll make it in the end, whatever your colour.'[58]

Football has also seen an overrepresentation of black players in relation to the black population, particularly since the late 1970s. After the war, a handful of black players from Commonwealth countries played in the Football League and the Scottish League with varying degrees of success. From the West Indies, Jamaican Lindy Delaphenha played for Portsmouth and, most successfully, for Middlesbrough, where he scored ninety goals between 1950 and 1957, and Giles Heron, also of Jamaica, played for Celtic in 1951. A number of black Africans also played in the UK from the late 1940s onwards, in the wake of the visit to England of a Nigerian representative team in 1948: two of the tourists went on to play for British clubs, including Tesilimi Balogun, who played for Queens Park Rangers in the 1950s.[59] Others who bridged the gap between Commonwealth migrants and black British players included South African Albert Johanneson at Leeds United and York City, famously celebrated as the first black footballer to play in a Wembley cup final, and Bermudan Clyde Best at West Ham United. It was in the mid- to late 1970s that the number of black players in the professional game started to become significant. Popular attention particularly focused on three black players at West Bromwich Albion who emerged during the 1977–8 season: Cyrille Regis, Laurie Cunningham, and Brendon Batson, nicknamed the Three Degrees after the American soul group.[60] A major breakthrough was made in November 1978, when Nottingham Forest's Viv Anderson, born in Nottingham two years after his parents' 1954 arrival from Jamaica, made his England debut against Czechoslovakia at Wembley, the first black player to represent the country.[61] The pace was hastened by the selection policy of Bobby Robson as England manager from 1982 to 1990: publicly claiming 'if the best eleven players in the country were black they would all be selected for the national side', his first two senior and under-21 squads included thirteen black players.[62] By 1985–6, when Maguire surveyed all ninety-two Football League clubs for his study of race and position assignment, 7.7 per cent of the players who had made first-team appearances were black. The proportion had risen to 11.5 per cent when he revisited the subject for the 1989–90 season.[63] In this period, black players have also achieved successes in Scotland, and the England national team has drawn regularly on black players since Anderson's debut in 1978, with Paul Ince becoming the first black captain in 1993. The popular acceptance of these individuals unquestioningly as national heroes suggests a unifying role for sport as well as its alleged colour blindness.

Although athletics, boxing, and football have been the main sports in which blacks have overachieved, other sports have, to varying degrees, proved open to black performers at elite levels. The first black sportsman or woman to captain a national side was Clive Sullivan, who led the Great Britain rugby league team to victory in the 1972 World Cup in France. Sullivan had played rugby union in his native Wales, and became a rugby league professional with Hull whilst in the army in 1961. Despite a number of serious injuries, he went on to represent both Great Britain and Wales, and captained the former to victory in the 1972 World Cup. His heroic status in Hull, where he also played for Hull Kingston Rovers, was confirmed after his early death when a major new road was named the Clive Sullivan Way in his honour.[64] Since Sullivan, both rugby codes have seen the emergence of black players at club and representative level, including Jeremy Guscott and Martin Offiah. English cricket has continued to be an attractive option for migrant professional Asians and West Indians as well as white Australians, New Zealanders, and South Africans: Bishan Bedi at Northamptonshire in the 1970s, Clive Lloyd at Lancashire from 1968 to 1986, and Viv Richards and Joel Garner at Somerset in the 1970s and 1980s are a few post-war examples of cricket's imperial and Commonwealth history that has always brought overseas players in.[65] However, cricket has been relatively slow in accommodating immigrants and British-born black players at the international level: the first West-Indian-born player to represent England was Roland Butcher, who took part in the 1980–1 tour of the West Indies, and David Lawrence became the first black player born in England to make the national team as late as 1988.[66] While other sports with specific class bases, such as polo and croquet, have remained virtually impervious to the existence of a black population, the public face of the most popular spectator and television sports is, by the mid-1990s, more ethnically mixed than many other parts of society. Sport's reliance upon physical excellence and achievement has ensured that the popular view of advancement on merit still has some credence, a view that is bolstered by pronouncements on sport being colour blind. One of the best declarations of this was made by Ron Greenwood, the England football manager who first selected Viv Anderson: 'Yellow, purple or black – if they're good enough, I'll pick them.'[67]

The wider issue of how black sportsmen and women are accepted and treated by the media and other areas of society is also telling in this context. Since the mid-1980s, a number of elite performers have managed to make crucial inroads into the careers that can go alongside actual playing, including advertising, endorsements, and media work. Frank Bruno is an excellent example. The London-born heavyweight boxer, whose parents were immigrants in the 1950s, has paralleled his sporting career with media and charity work, acting in pantomimes, and product endorsements. He has even earned an honour from the establishment in the form of an MBE. Gilroy has analysed Bruno's appeal to white society as lying in his 'sincere patriotism and cultural authenticity',[68] and Bruno himself has been candid about the mobility and acceptance that his sport has brought him. He has defended it against the anti-boxing lobby in terms of the

> good the sport does by helping people – the boxers and their families – to escape the poverty trap. Thanks to the rewards from boxing I am able to offer my wife and daughters a far better future than they could ever have hoped for had I still been stuck as a labourer on the building site.[69]

Bruno is probably the most successful example of a black sportsperson who has achieved so much in other fields, but there are many others. Footballers John Barnes and Ian Wright have both had side-careers in advertising and endorsements, Barnes promoting goods including Lucozade drinks and Diadora sportswear and Wright using what Majors analysed in an American context as 'cool pose' in his promotion of Nike footwear.[70] Athletes Daley Thompson (who also advertised Lucozade) and footballer Garth Crooks have both crossed over into media work, presenting sports items not only on their own sports, but, particularly in the BBC's coverage of the 1996 Olympic Games, on sport in general. Crooks and Brendon Batson also both took on high-profile representative work with the PFA. Footballer John Fashanu has made one of the biggest breaks from his field, co-presenting the television programme *Gladiators*.

These are avenues that have gradually been carved out for sportsmen and women throughout the post-war period, as greater professionalisation, the growth of commercial television, and the continuing growth of the media expert have all provided extended options for those successful in sport. It can be seen as a mark of black sportsmen and women's mobility and credibility in the eyes of predominantly white planners and controllers that these avenues have not been barred to them.

DISCRIMINATION AND STEREOTYPING

Despite these optimistic signs, it would be naïve and misleading to rely on such a harmonious image. Immigration and settlement have given rise to overt racism in politics, both at the levels of street violence and legislative control, and to various forms of institutionalised racism in employment, housing, education, and other agencies. These have been under attack in public discourse since the 1960s, through such agencies as the Race Relations Board and later the CRE, and through the adoption of multi-ethnic teaching and employment policies and the growth of an equal opportunities culture. However, racial stereotyping and abuse remains a feature of British life in the 1990s. With this more critical view of the post-war period, it is crucial to investigate the ways in which sport has been a focus for perpetuating ethnic differences and a vehicle for wider racism. While the functionalist reading of sport as a unifying agent and a means of mobility may work for an elite of black sportsmen and women, it has less relevance to the majority. We need to take a more critical stance that sees sport as a contested realm. This means adopting Small's view that 'Black people are not supreme in sport, we are simply the best in a tiny selection of sports, and our success can only be explained by a complex combination of opportunities, motivation, economics and role models'.[71] Colour-blindness becomes irrelevant here, and is replaced by colour stereotyping; and the notion of ethnicity is replaced by the less satisfactory but more popular notion of race.

The fact that the overrepresentation of black sportsmen and women has occurred only in certain sports should be the first area of analysis. Athletics, boxing, and football have many features in common that have made them attractive options to black youths concentrating on sports, and have thus drawn most heavily on Afro-Caribbean talent. They are all relatively cheap; they can be played at playground and scratch level with a minimum of equipment; and they are relatively accessible through school, youth club, and sports club settings in working-class urban environments where most black Britons have primarily lived. Moreover, they are sports that had pre-war traditions of recruitment amongst disadvantaged urban groups due to the rewards on offer for the elite. Working-class men in football and boxing in particular, and immigrants in boxing – such as European Jews in London and Irish in Scotland – were role models for the Afro-Caribbean entry into sport. Of course, the limited career prospects and the risks of injury have been factors here: as Holt put it, 'Black immigration, recession, and the enormous purses which television can provide have meant there remain a ready supply of men willing to risk brain damage in the ring.'[72] By the same token, a number of sports that have economically and spatially been connected historically with the middle and upper classes have failed to attract black sportsmen and women in significant numbers. Golf, lawn tennis, and equestrian sports, for example, have remained predominantly white in the post-war period. Coakley has argued that the reasons for this continued segregation in some sports are linked not just to class, space, and cost, but also to the dynamics of the sports themselves. The sports in which blacks have achieved overrepresentation – in the USA, these are basketball, football, track and field events, and baseball – are those that do not contain the same kind of off-pitch social obligations as lawn tennis, golf, bowling, and other middle-class sports.[73] According to this view, a black presence is tolerated by white sports establishments only in so far as it does not involve too much mixing. These insights are useful, although the socialising that is important in athletics needs to be considered here, and empirical research applying them to the British context would be welcome. What the imbalance between the levels of ethnic mixing in different sports does show up is that black successes in key sports owe a great deal to social class as well as to ethnicity: clearly, football and boxing have historically been the great sporting ladders out of the ghetto for working-class men, and their appeal to working-class black youths must be seen in this context.[74] There have been exceptions. Black players have made inroads in rugby union in England, traditionally perceived as a relatively exclusive sport, and the presence of Oliver Skeete in equestrianism has challenged public perceptions of the sport. However, the absences from elite levels in British swimming, lawn tennis, golf, motor racing, and other sports need to be seen alongside the overrepresentation in football, athletics, and boxing before sport can be seen as having ameliorated ethnic differences in post-war Britain.

Moreover, even within the sports in which blacks have overachieved, there is evidence that our period has seen practices in coaching, management, and administration that have rested upon whites' stereotyped views of blacks' physical attributes. The notion of blacks possessing natural aptitudes for certain physical activities has a long pedigree, linked, as Coakley has shown, to the 'race logic' borne out of and used to justify imperialism.[75] By typifying Afro-Caribbeans as less developed than whites, and as animalistic, white hegemony could be assured. These ideas have obviously survived their original settings, which included slavery in the USA and colonialism for the British, and have continued to be applied to blacks in other contexts. Sport has been an obvious one, owing again to its physical nature, and the success of black sportsmen and women has frequently been explained in terms of genetic superiority and a range of assumed physical attributes, including agility, speed, strength, and reflexes, but excluding stamina, courage, and intellectual abilities. These views were given credibility and approval by American coaches and commentators in the 1930s and 1940s, at a time when black athletes and boxers were beginning to dominate their sports. For example, Dean Cromwell, a successful track coach at the University of Southern California, claimed that

> the Negro excels in the events he does because he is closer to the primitive than the white man. It was not long ago that his ability to sprint and jump was a life-and-death matter to him in the jungle.[76]

This common-sense racist notion of difference as applied to sport was popularised by Kane in 1971, and has frequently resurfaced in our period, not just in popular sports discourse but also in scientific settings. It was given a controversial airing by Sir Roger Bannister in 1995, when he asserted that the superiority of black runners must depend upon 'something rather special about their anatomy or physiology'.[77]

These beliefs have been linked not just to the sports which black youths have most access to (which, as we have seen, are also connected to class and economics), but also to the roles within those sports that blacks have assumed. Boxing, as an individual sport, is not open to this kind of analysis. While athletics is also heavily individual, the general pattern from Wharton onwards, through Jack London, and into the post-war era has been for Afro-Caribbean athletes to concentrate on sprints and the long jump, events clearly linked to the assumed physical attributes listed above. There have been exceptions: Arthur Wint ran middle distances at 800 metres and 880 yards in the 1940s, in the 1970s and 1980s Kriss Akabusi specialised in 400 metres and 400 metres hurdles, and Daley Thompson confounded all stereotypes by becoming one of the most successful decathletes in history, a gruelling ten-discipline track and field event. Denise Lewis has continued to break the pattern with her success in the heptathlon. However, the majority of the black athletes who have excelled in the UK from the late 1970s have been concentrated in the shorter, more explosive events, while middle- and long-distance races and the throwing events have continued to be dominated by white athletes.

The phenomenon of role assignment has been most debated in relation to football and, to a lesser extent, both rugby codes. This has built on American work on the notions of stacking and centrality, which has claimed that coaches' perceptions of blacks' 'natural' abilities have led to black players being pushed into peripheral roles that require speed but little intelligence, while whites have been overrepresented in central, decision-making positions. Melnick and Maguire have explored position assignment on ethnic lines in British team games. Maguire's work is the most convincing, in so far as he is far more familiar with the sports' cultures than Melnick. However, their findings show many similarities with the American research, despite the relative fluidity of positions in football and, to a lesser extent, both rugby codes compared with American football. Melnick, analysing the First Division for the 1985–6 season, found that 11 per cent of the total number of players were black, but that this proportion was not represented randomly or evenly across different positions: 20 per cent of forwards were black, compared with 6 per cent of midfielders and 2 per cent of goalkeepers. Looked at another way, the figures showed that twenty seven of the fifty-two black players, or 52 per cent, were forwards, while only seven of them (13.5 per cent) played in midfield. Assuming that the midfield positions involve most centrality, in terms of creating play and linking defence and attack, he concluded that this distribution suggested that the 'black athlete stereotype' was being drawn upon and reproduced in the Football League.[78] Maguire, particularly in his 1991 study, went further than Melnick, and provided a more balanced argument that drew upon qualitative as well as quantitative material. He was also able to draw upon new research in this growing area of sports studies carried out by undergraduate and postgraduate students at Loughborough University. He set his stacking analysis in the wider context of overt racism in football, such as racist acts from supporters, and also drew attention to the different rates of black representation between First Division and lower division clubs, which he linked to degrees of cosmopolitanism.[79] Revisiting his earlier work on the 1985–6 season,[80] he found that in 1989–90, black players were still overrepresented in peripheral and stereotypical positions, and underrepresented in the centre: 11.5 per cent of players were black, with 21 per cent of forwards but only 5 per cent of midfielders coming from Afro-Caribbean backgrounds. For his study, there were no black goalkeepers, and only one black captain in the entire Football League. His findings for both rugby codes suggested similar notions at play there, although the small number of black players made statistical analysis difficult. In the 1988–9 rugby union season, thirteen black players played in the Courage Club Championships, making up just 2.4 per cent of the total: eight of them were wingers, a peripheral position prioritising, yet again, speed and agility over decision-making ability. Similar patterns were evident in rugby league, with black players 'again over-represented in the wing position'.[81] As we have seen, the whole approach of analysing stacking has been criticised by Birrell, and it is significant that Cashmore rejected it in favour of qualitative work in his major 1982 survey of race and sport. Clearly, as Maguire has shown, we need to take the statistics together with other evidence, including analysis of players' motivations and aspirations, and coaches' assumptions: 'the concept of "stacking" is, in itself, of limited value and has been used here only to serve as a preliminary tool to tackle the subtle social processes at work'.[82]

However, taken in connection with the statistical evidence on blacks' overrepresentation in boxing, athletics, and football and their underrepresentation in other sports, the figures do suggest that far from promoting positive images of black men and women and notions of equality, sport actually reproduces crude racial stereotypes for society at large. When the statistics are read in conjunction with some coaches' comments about black players, then we can clearly link this process of position assignment to stereotyping. Jim Smith of Queens Park Rangers can be used to illustrate this with his claim that black players 'seem to use very little intelligence; they get by on sheer natural talent most of the time'.[83] These notions can also be linked to the low number of retired black sportsmen and women to have taken up coaching and management positions. Cashmore has linked the athletics establishment's lack of support for John Isaacs at Haringey to this stereotypical view of blacks' lack of intelligence,[84] and a number of footballers who have attempted to go into coaching have met resistance from clubs. Ricky Hill, for example, took up a coaching position in the USA because he felt that in the UK, 'the view that black people are not capable of management still persists'.[85] While the first black League manager was actually Tony Collins at Rochdale in the early 1960s, it is only from the mid-1990s that a few ex-players are beginning to make an impact in this sphere, including Keith Alexander at Lincoln, Viv

Anderson at Barnsley and Middlesbrough, and Luther Blissett at Watford.[86]

The idea that blacks' 'position as outsiders in soccer and rugby union may also reflect their status in British society in general'[87] can be more humanly rooted when we look at the ways in which black sportsmen and women across our period have been or felt themselves targets of racial abuse and stereotyping. This has taken various forms. One of the most common has been the paradoxical situation whereby successful black sportsmen and women, who have been praised publicly for their achievements in sport, have remained victims of everyday racism in society at large. This is the kind of situation that Edwards summed up with his observation on sporting success giving blacks only temporary fame and recognition, 'the only difference between the black man shining shoes in the ghetto and the champion black sprinter is that the shoe shine man is a nigger, while the sprinter is a fast nigger'.[88] It is an experience that many black sportsmen and women in the UK have recorded. The most famous example, which resulted in a successful legal action, occurred in 1943, when cricketer Learie Constantine and his family were turned away from the Imperial Hotel in London owing to complaints from another customer and fears that their presence might upset Americans staying in the hotel. He was evidently told that the hotel 'did not want niggers'. Constantine made an example of this act by taking the hotel owners to court in order 'to draw the particular nature of the affront before the wider judgement of the British public in the hope that its sense of fair play might help to protect people of my colour in England in future'.[89] This was a high-profile event involving a famous and well-respected Trinidadian, and it occurred before the mass immigration of the post-war period which gave rise to a more normalised everyday racism. This is the kind experienced by so many black sportsmen and women as children, recalled in their interviews with Cashmore and their memoirs. For example, Ainsley Bennett recalled his reception at school in Birmingham at the age of 12 as 'another black monkey for our school',[90] a type of experience shared by Linford Christie, rejected from a playground game as a 7 year old in West London on the grounds that 'My mummy said I shouldn't play with blackies'.[91] As with Constantine, it is a feature of British society that has remained with many of the individuals, despite their successes. Christie again reported frequent police harassment when driving new cars, and Frank Bruno claims to have received 'quite a bit of hassle from extremists on both sides – black and white' related to his marriage to a white woman.[92] These kinds of experiences outside the sporting setting have obviously had different personal meanings for the individuals concerned, and many claim that white racism actually pushed them into sport in order to counter their attackers. However, they stand as a counterbalance to the comfortable view that the achievement of fame through sport has automatically led to universal acceptance.

These incidents that take place outside sport have been supplemented by overt racism within sporting settings, thus further denting the naïve view of sport as a field of equal opportunity and treatment. Most obviously, it has taken the form of racist chants, shouts, and acts from football supporters directed at black players. While both Johanneson and Clyde Best were taunted by spectators in the 1960s,[93] this developed mainly in the late 1970s, as part of the emergence of large numbers of black players. It included – and still includes – monkey noises when black players had the ball, as well as the throwing of bananas at the players and individual barracking, the 'obscene descant' of football crowds.[94] Another method of abuse was the anonymous threatening letter: according to Batson, Regis even received a bullet through the post when he was first named in the England squad.[95] Culturally and politically, it was linked both to the wider setting of football hooliganism at the time, and to the presence of fascist groups such as the NF and the British Movement which were active at certain clubs, notably Chelsea and Leeds United.[96] Fascist involvement in organised football violence soon became widely believed, particularly when the media publicised *Bulldog*'s league table of 'patriotic' supporters, and when fascist leaflets were found at Heysel. However, no solid evidence of planning was found: in Dunning *et al.*'s view, marginal political groups' roles in orchestrating violence is a comforting explanation as it gives the sometimes incomprehensible violence a name.[97] Different players dealt with the abuse in different ways: some chose to ignore it; others quietly but firmly displayed their contempt, for example by kicking the thrown bananas off the pitch; and some have attempted to turn the abuse into humour to be turned back at the perpetrators, notably Batson who once put a thrown banana down his shorts in mock imitation of the stereotypically well-endowed black man, and at other times ate pieces of the thrown fruit.[98] The shouting of racial abuse at football matches was outlawed on the recommendation of the Taylor Report after the Hillsborough disaster, an official recognition of the problem. It has, however, been notoriously underenforced by police and stewards. This abusive practice has also been witnessed in rugby union, where Gerald Cordle of Gloucester physically assaulted an abusive spectator at Cardiff in 1987,[99] and at cricket, where

Gloucestershire's David Lawrence recalled the notoriety of some Yorkshire supporters: 'They called me nigger, black bastard, sambo, monkey, gorilla; they threw bananas and I had to take these insults.'[100] This kind of behaviour from spectators was one of the targets of the CRE's campaign against racism in football, and in the mid-1990s it is less prevalent than in previous years. However, it is an aspect of racism that has characterised post-war British sport, and must be seen as another way in which the equality assumed in functionalist readings of sport is mythical. That the sports media have frequently failed to comment on or condemn this kind of behaviour, when television audiences can hear and see what has occurred, can be seen as helping to reinforce the common-sense separation of sport from the rest of society, and reproduce wider notions of neutrality.[101]

These are just a few of the ways in which blacks involved in sport have been victimised on racial grounds in post-war Britain. In an area of public life that concentrates so fully on the physical, it would be naïve not to expect common-sense notions of difference and stereotyping to be played out in sport by various agencies: spectators, the media, coaches, owners, and players themselves. Sport has undoubtedly been a means of mobility and acceptance for an elite of black sportsmen and women, but it has also been the location for the less harmonious aspects of race relations that have been discussed here. For black Britons, sport has remained a double-edged sword in post-war society, offering both advancement and obstacle, acceptance and crude stereotype. That many individuals have excelled must be read both as a sign of a growing tolerance – particularly when national representation is at stake – and as a sign of perceived limited opportunities in other walks of life that encourage many Afro-Caribbean youths to concentrate on sport rather than on academic work. At the time of writing, there are some trends visible in sports discourse that suggest a mellowing of some of the forms of racism and stereotype that have been evident throughout the period. The 'cool pose' of individuals such as Ian Wright and Linford Christie, with an emphasis on a distinctly black style of masculinity, has become increasingly popularised and imitated, as have hairstyles based on dreadlocks for sportsmen and women after the international success of Dutch footballer Ruud Gullit from the late 1980s. Gullit's own emergence in the UK in the summer of 1996, as an articulate and imaginative BBC expert for the European Championships and as Chelsea's manager, helped publicly to dent many stereotypical views of blacks. However, while it is easy to read these developments as grounds for hope in a global sporting world that can celebrate diversity without denigrating difference, they must be seen against the persistence of stereotype and abuse. While Gullit has offered intelligence, style, and cosmopolitanism to the English game, he has still been a target of racial abuse from rival supporters making monkey noises. The public testing ground for physicality that sport remains has ensured that it can always be used as a channel for such attitudes.

Conclusion

These six thematic chapters have demonstrated ways in which sport has been part of the post-war British historical experience. Beyond reflecting social, cultural, economic, and political trends, the heterogeneous world of competitive and recreative physical games has been part of those trends. They have literally given physical form to the wider debates being played out about gender, class, and ethnic relations, and have been part of the growth of the state, the contested notion of national identity, and the commercial setting of post-industrial society. While sport may have been neglected by historians until recently, its role in these processes demonstrates that it was not neglected at the time, and by recovering the history of those relations, we have gone some way towards establishing a fuller picture of the period as a whole. While total history, like total football, may be a practical impossibility, there is no doubt that the endeavour – in both cases – is worth the effort.

The studies in this book have demonstrated that sport in this period has experienced both continuity and change. If we are to understand sport in our historical period, we need to see both ways in which it has changed and ways in which it has remained the same. These issues, however, are more problematic than they may at first seem, because continuity and change are not notions that all parties concerned will necessarily agree upon. Change in a sport may be seen by one interest group as a positive force, while another group will condemn it as ruinous. This contestation was evident in the debate over changes in the structure of rugby league in 1995–6, where individuals and agencies differed in their interpretation of the shift to a summer season, the institution of the Super League, and the mergers of some clubs. For example, novelist and former player David Storey and Rugby Football League president Kath Hetherington were referring to the same changes when the former said 'I mourn the transformation of rugby league from a community-based sport to another branch of the entertainment industry' and the latter claimed 'There was no question that we had to accept the money. . . . We need to look to a new market, to spread the game nationally, and this deal gives us the chance to do just that.'[1] However, while continuity and change may be relative concepts, they are broadly identifiable, and it is one of the challenges and duties of history to chart and analyse them.

As we have established, it is impossible to understand sport without looking to history. Such intrinsic and extrinsic features of organised sports as their rules and rituals, the time and place at which they are played, and the social, ethnic, and gender profile of the players, spectators, administrators, and patrons are not recreated on a daily basis: they are inherited from the past, including the immediate past. When sudden change does come, it is frequently contested by various agencies and individuals precisely because it goes against tradition: in other words, because change fractures comfortable and familiar personal, communal, and national histories. This can be seen in such diverse areas as the relocation of football clubs, golf clubs admitting women as equal members, the sanctioned growth of professionalism in rugby union, and the debate over the social and ethical acceptability of boxing.

Such localised changes need to be seen in a wider context of the themes explored in this study. Writing in the mid-1990s, we can see numerous specific ways in which sport is now different – in some ways, almost unrecognisable – from its condition in the mid-1940s. The state has a more structured relationship with sport than it did, providing funds and communication networks. British sport has become less insular, embracing full membership of international organisations and participation in international and continental competitions. Older assumptions about British superiority have been, to a degree, replaced by a recognition of the need to compete on equal terms, evident in the emergence of training and an excellence culture, and in the shift from amateur to professional management structures. Sport has become far more commercially oriented than it was, as traditional forms of funding declined and the new patrons of television and advertising became permanent fixtures in the sporting structure. Women now have more access to more sports than they had at the start of the period, and are increasingly taken seriously in the previously male-dominated spheres of performance, journalism, and administration, while men have more opportunities to use sport as a way of questioning rigid definitions of masculinity. Professionalisation and social mobility have both altered the class appearance of sport, while the development of communities based on Commonwealth immigrants and their children has brought a greater ethnic diversity to sport in the UK.

Moreover, we can identify a number of characteristics of contemporary sport that can be labelled post-modern or post-industrial which were not evident in 1945. There is a greater diversity of sport available for people to participate in and watch, with a notable emergence of wider access to such individual sports as squash, tennis, and golf, and a relative decline in mass spectator sports. Many sports have reversed the trends of the urbanisation period and gone out of the cities, with mountain biking, running, mountaineering, and off-road motor events reclaiming the countryside for popular play. There is a greater globalisation of sport, with transnational media coverage and a greater mobility of the labour market in sport. These and other features suggest a period of radical change, and can lead us to believe that we are now in a third age of sport: after the traditional and the industrial comes the post-industrial, characterised by demands for access to an increasingly fragmentary sporting life.[2]

However, it is also clear that there has been a great deal of continuity in our period, and while the appearance of sport is different, it is arguably only a quantitative difference rather than a qualitative difference. While Holt and others have shown the continuities between pre-industrial and industrial sport, it is clear that there were many structural changes that, by the late nineteenth century, gave sport a distinctively different character from what had gone before: most obviously, we can see this in such areas as the emergence of governing bodies, the enforcement of standardised rules and regulations, and the development of regular organised competition.[3] If we project these characteristics forward to our own time, we can see that they are still essentially in place. There has been a proliferation of governing bodies and competitions as more and more activities become sportised, which is where the post-modern notion of diversity and cosmopolitanism comes in, but the fundamental model of regulation and competition has not yet been undermined. Mountain biking, for example, may well be a post-industrial activity, but its inclusion in the Olympic Games from 1996 and its emphasis on regulated and enforced codes and practices suggests that it still aspires to the predominant norms of sport, which are still based on the industrial phase. More specifically, we can see continuities in a number of our chosen areas. Voluntarism and amateurism have survived the period, and continue to form the framework within which the mass of sport is administered and played.

League and knock-out structures may have been tampered with in all sports, but they remain the basis for the competitive testing of teams by merit over an agreed annual time span: non-competitive sport, at elite level, has not become a viability. The maintenance of club names, colours, and cultures reinforces the notion of continuity. Gender relations may have increased opportunities, but there is still a residual common-sense perception of what is a 'man's game' and what is not, while economic and cultural constraints survive to limit any idealised classless sports.

One crucial overarching feature of the history of sport in the post-war period that can be stressed here is the way in which sport has been part of the debate over equality and inequality of opportunity. Starting with the growth of state welfarism after the Second World War, and continuing through the establishment of equality of opportunity as an orthodoxy by the late 1980s, we can see that the period has been characterised by a recognition of gender, social, ethnic, and other inequalities, and the desire – or pretence – to manipulate them out of existence. Hence a comprehensive welfare system, legislation on racial discrimination, the outlawing of sex discrimination, the provision of facilities for the disabled in various public settings, and so on. The reality has not always lived up to the rhetoric, and a cynical reading of this trend as a specific form of hegemony would point out the structural inequalities that remain untouched beneath this cosmetic programme. This feature was highlighted from a sporting context in England basketball player Ian Day's perceptive 1982 comment on business methods in his sport: 'Are we not falling into the same trap as our social system where we create opportunities for all, but restrict them to a few?'[4] With this basic critique in place, the debate over equality of opportunity can be seen to have been a central one to this period. This discourse forms a backdrop for any cultural practice for the post-war period, and it would be possible to write histories of opera, fine art, television, cinema, literature, popular music, and any other form that shows its influence. Sport, as a cultural practice, has provided us with our chosen case study. A historical survey of how sport has been influenced by this discourse provides a contextual analysis of sport in society, with its municipal swimming sessions for women only through to the Commission for Racial Equality's attempt to 'Kick Racism out of Football'.

However, this survey of sport has not been just a random case study designed to illustrate wider historical trends. As we have seen, individual sports, and sport as what Briggs called a 'conglomerate' term,[5] have been specifically significant for a number of reasons. First, they take place in public, thus offering a highly visible forum for the playing out of trends, and the debate between tradition and change. Their public nature has meant that, to apply Jarvie's observation of Scottish football more widely, sport has 'dramatized and defined expressions of class, gender, religion and nationality'.[6] Second, they have enormous popular appeal, particularly when television, radio, and newspaper coverage are taken into account. While television audiences of over 20 million may be rare, they have been reached in the UK by a number of sporting events, including the 1990 football World Cup semi-final between England and West Germany. As such, sport as a whole can be said to be a truly national popular cultural form, which gives its history a particular significance. Linked to these general but still tangible contexts, sport is significant because it inherently involves struggle and contestation over the use of, and access to, people's resources. Land, time, wealth, as well as the cultural resources linked to the individual's gender, ethnicity, age, level of ability, and class, are all key factors in people's choices, opportunities, and limitations in sport. Sport is thus a crucial part of the debate on equality and inequality. These themes have shed light on how groups and individuals holding different resources have coped in their play during a period in which such differentials were under attack. The sports most closely tied to those groups and individuals with the most resources – such as polo, hunting, and shooting – have arguably experienced the greatest amount of continuity and the smallest amount of change since 1945.

These summaries reflect the way in which this book has been structured as a thematic work of synthesis. The danger of approaching any historical subject thematically is that it can fracture the lived experience while it attempts to clarify the interconnections between parts of that experience. This is an unfortunate side effect of a historical approach that is necessary if we are to see links and trends that narrative history alone cannot show. However, it is worth restating that the approach chosen in this book is honestly seen as one of convenience. In reality, the historical individuals – named and anonymous – who have been covered in this history did not participate in sport through neatly compartmentalised aspects of themselves, appearing as a gendered subject in a tennis match before taking on a national identity to watch cricket. A real example can illustrate the problems of such a division: heptathlete Denise Lewis can be presented at different times as a female athlete, a black athlete, a British and English athlete, an athlete from a specific class background, a beneficiary of state investment in sport, and a commercial agent, but she is really all of these things, and more. Each participant, spectator, administrator, planner, and television executive is working within a broad context of opportunities and constraints which intermesh on the lines of the themes surveyed in this study.

Appendix

The growing historical awareness of sport

In the Introduction, I outlined the kinds of sources I had used for this study. Academic sports history has been the basic genre, but other forms of writing about sport histories have also been used, particularly popular historical writing. While not all of the texts used satisfy the historian's demand for contexts and bibliographies, they are evidence of an important trend: a growing popular interest in the history of sport. In this appendix, I want to outline and exemplify some of the different areas of what we can broadly call historiography in which this interest has manifested itself recently: academic history; popular history; museums; and television and film. I hope that this brief review will help to establish greater links between sometimes disparate modes of historical research and thinking.

The first front, that of academic history, now involves numerous media. It has specific journals (the *International Journal of the History of Sport* and *The Sports Historian*), and monograph series published by Manchester and Leicester Universities' publishing houses. Its conference network involves the British Society of Sports History and its overseas counterparts, and it benefits from specialised research units which work in and around sports history, including the Sir Norman Chester Centre for Football Research at the University of Leicester, the Football Research Unit at the University of Liverpool, and the International Centre for Sports History and Culture at De Montfort University. In higher education, courses based on sports history now vie as options with other new histories as well as older themes: one recent estimate by Wray Vamplew – significantly the UK's first Professor of Sports History – claims that 400 courses cover sports history. It is supported by the monumental bibliographical work of Cox,[1] through the publicity service provided by the Association of Sports Historians, and through the Internet.[2] In addition, existing literature is increasingly

being listed in specialised bibliographies and source lists, such as
Seddon's *A Football Compendium* for the British Library,[3] and Cox's
ongoing British Sports History Bibliographical Series.[4]

Academic sports history, however, inevitably remains a minority
affair, and we need to broaden our view to see other fronts on which
opportunities for sports history research now exist. The types of historiography associated with the Association of Sports Historians (ASH),
which sees itself as 'a grass-roots organisation giving as much encouragement as possible to the "amateur" or "local" sports historian',[5]
should be considered. ASH has created points of contact between
enthusiasts in separate sports and localities, and established opportunities for publication through *Sporting Heritage* and the *ASH Newsletter*.
Although much of this work could still be characterised as 'little more
than the book of Chronicles or the book of Numbers',[6] the specialised
and local knowledge that its authors bring to bear have made it a
significant part of the expansion of sports history. Similarly, the popular
sports history of the sport-specific book has a place here, offering narratives and images of how sports have developed, and while such
examples as Rendall's *The Chequered Flag* and Spencer's *A Century of Polo*
may lack the rigour of the academic, the growth of this sector must be
taken seriously as part of the mushrooming of sports history.[7]

Such writing has been supplemented by a new kind of popular
sports history since the late 1980s, the personal histories that have no
pretence of authority but plenty of authenticity. Geoffrey Moorhouse's
1989 series of connected essays, *At The George and other essays on Rugby
League*, offered a taste of the new genre.[8] Moorhouse mixed personal
history – 'Some games you inherit at birth, but I chose Rugby league'[9] –
with critical historical and social observation on the game's development in England and abroad. The genre took off with Nick Hornby's
Fever Pitch, a critical autobiographical account of one fan's long-term
support for Arsenal FC which attempts to convey the highs as well as
the lows of such an involvement. Hornby explores the history of
Arsenal from the late 1960s purely from his own perspective, as 'an
attempt to gain some kind of an angle on my obsession'.[10] There is no
pretence at giving a comprehensive history of the club: he claims, for
example, that Arsenal winning the Double in 1971 'doesn't really have
much place in my story' as he 'missed it all'.[11] Laura Thompson, a journalist who grew up in a greyhound-racing family, used a similar
approach in *The Dogs*,[12] although unlike Hornby, she did explore the
sport's long-term history. Hornby was quoted approvingly on the dustjacket, which led one reviewer to speculate that the book 'may be

destined to be dubbed *Fever Bitch*,[13] but the mix of memory and researched history ensured the book's success on its own terms. Charles Sprawson's lyrical *Haunts of the Black Masseur* was more ambitious, offering critical essays on the meaning of swimming in different historical cultures, but again it was shot through with personal perspectives, as in his own memories of swimming the Hellespont in the chapter on 'The Byronic Tradition'.[14] A final entrant to this batch is Marcus Berkmann's *Rain Men* on cricket, again tellingly advertised as 'Cricket's *Fever Pitch*, but without the boring bits about Arsenal'.[15] Such writing, treading the line between journalism, literature, and history, was consolidated in 1996 with the publication of a selection of new sports writing co-edited by Hornby.[16] While it is too soon to tell the exact direction of this genre of sports history writing, it has set precedents for popular history, and has injected useful amounts of self-criticism and irony into a field of historical writing in which authors have frequently failed to position themselves. For our immediate purposes, the emergence of this strand of writing in the 1990s is further evidence of the burgeoning interest that sport and its followers have in history.

These different trends of historical writing about sport from non-academic perspectives have all been part of a process whereby sports history has become more accessible to a wider audience than could be met by academic historians or by statisticians. Despite some of the problems of perspective and context, the *Fever Pitch* effect, along with the academic work, has helped to create a balance. Overall, popular sports history is a necessary and dynamic part of sport's post-war development, and it has helped to confirm for increasing numbers of followers a sense of tradition and place in sport. While it may not be as critical as many academics would wish, its importance cannot be denied, and it serves a crucial function of providing detailed factual information, especially at the local level, of a kind that the academic would not usually have time to collate.

A third front on which we can see interest and opportunity for sports history is in the setting of museums and heritage sites. This has never been as strong a tradition in the UK as in Europe or the USA, where national sports museums and individual sports' halls of fame are long-established parts of the public landscape of sport. While they, like some of the less critical popular writing, can sometimes lack integrity and lose sight of contexts, they have been essential for maintaining artefacts as well as a sense of place and tradition for contemporary sports audiences. In the UK, the main trend has been for individual sports to establish their own museum spaces, often within the headquarters of the governing body or leading club, which has then been marketed as a way of raising funds. The All England Lawn Tennis and Croquet Club runs its tennis museum at Wimbledon, for example, as does the Marylebone Cricket Club at Lord's. Other stadia have developed this approach, with Wembley and Cardiff Arms Park both offering tours: the latter's includes not just the changing rooms and grandstand, but also a visit to 'Rugby Memorabilia' and the trophy room.[17] Finally, and perhaps most significantly for the wider appreciation of sports history, there has been the staging of sport exhibitions by mainstream museums. On the assumption that only the dedicated follower of the appropriate sport would make a special visit to Wimbledon, Lord's, or Cardiff Arms Park, these kind of exhibitions are designed to reach wider audiences, including those interested in history who may not previously have considered sports history. Some examples of this kind of approach in the 1990s have been 'The Homes of Football' at the Museum of Reading in 1996, and 'Sporting Life' at the Old Grammar School Museum, Hull, from 1995 to 1996. The latter, which included artefacts from local and national figures (such as Clive Sullivan and Linford Christie), was also used as a focus for debate and discussion about the role of sport in the museum by the Social History Curators Group. Other important exhibitions in this context have been the London Transport Museum's display of sporting posters, and the Photographers' Gallery's 1992 exhibition of Julian Germain's 'In Soccer Wonderland'.[18]

This is clearly a trend which reflects a growing interest in, and awareness of, the history of sport. It has been criticised by some academic sports historians for the lack of planning that is evident. Cox, for example, has warned against some of the collections which have claimed to be museums: the titles, he claims, reflect 'little more than the delusions (of grandeur) of their owners'.[19] Pointing to uncoordinated plans for national football museums in Carlisle, Glasgow, and Sheffield, he called for integration and concentration to avoid the collections being diluted and to protect 'the remnants of our sporting heritage'.[20] Coming within a year of Christie's first auction of football memorabilia,[21] this call was well timed, although its effects remain to be seen. However, it is difficult to ignore the proliferation of interest in history that these initiatives at club, local, and national level signify.

Finally, television and feature films have offered increasing scope for the public exploration of sports history. Arguably, these are the most important of all the genres, as more people watch television programmes and films than read history books or visit specialised museums. Documentaries and documentary series have supplemented the popular and academic sports history discussed above. These have particularly been prevalent around the Olympic Games: in 1988, for example, the build-up to the Seoul Olympics included a Thames documentary history of the men's 100 metres, *The Fastest Men on Earth*, by a series of portraits of different countries' Olympic legends, *For the Honour of their Country*, and by an attempt at demythologising by Channel 4, *The Games in Question*. Other sports have also been subject to this kind of historical examination. Football earned two prestigious BBC documentaries in 1995: *Kicking and Screaming* on the game in the UK, and *Football Fussball Voetball* on European football as part of the build-up for the 1996 European Championships. BBC 2's 1996 *Clash of the Titans* analysed a number of contests and rivalries from the 1970s and 1980s, including John McEnroe and Bjorn Borg, and Sebastian Coe and Steve Ovett. Wimbledon's Number One Court was remembered at the time of its last tournament before demolition with *Chalk Flew Up* in 1996. Significantly, a number of these examples spawned books, suggesting assumed markets in popular sports history: Duncanson's *The Fastest Men on Earth*[22] – clearly aimed at the imminent Seoul Olympics with its concluding emphasis on Ben Johnson – Taylor and Ward's *Kicking and Screaming*,[23] and Cameron's *Football Fussball Voetball*[24] are examples of this. A slight twist to this genre was given in 1996 by Channel 4's *The Greatest*, an interactive discussion of great sportsmen and women of the twentieth century in which panellists discussed and audiences voted for the best from Bobby Moore to Muhammad Ali. While there have been many differences between these examples, both in production values and in intended audiences, they have had enough common ground in terms of historical research, the use of archive footage, and the use of interviews, either specially commissioned or from old tapes. Moreover, many of them have been made from critical standpoints, thus assuming that their audiences will not be satisfied merely with the Chronicles and Numbers approach. These trends in television thus link back to the growth of a critical historiography of sport, whilst also fitting into the general, popular interest in the history of sport. Key feature films have also brought past sportsmen and women to life, most successfully for British sport in *Chariots of Fire* (1980), a romanticised account of athletes Harold Abrahams and Eric Liddell at the 1924 Olympic Games. Other films here that have been based upon real sporting events have included *True Blue* (1996) on the Oxford and Cambridge Boat Race, and *Those Glory, Glory Days* (1984) on a group of teenage girls supporting Tottenham Hotspur through their Double-winning season of 1960–1. There is clearly scope for a critical study of this genre.

The widespread interest in the history of sport that these different forms demonstrate is crucial. Whereas sport has long been seen in common-sense ideology as something that should be enjoyed at face value, the growth of historical interest in sport has set up an alternative view. Now, far from trying to maintain an idealised sporting present in which social, economic, and political pressures are not felt, but in which tradition and nostalgia are unproblematic features, more and more people are prepared to think critically about where sport has come from. For this to work, long-term views are essential: contemporary practices in sports are incomprehensible unless we consider their historical roots in nineteenth-century public schools and in pre-industrial popular settings. However, as this study has shown, we also need to bear in mind more recent history: commercial sponsorship, state involvement, gendered practices, globalism, and so much more must be firmly located within specific historical developments of the last sixty years. By approaching this historically, we can gain perspective and a sense of context and causation. As the quotations from Tony Blair and the 1996 England football anthem showed in the Introduction, a sense of the past is ever present in contemporary sports discourse. By building on this with a sense of history, our understanding of sport can only be enhanced.

Notes

INTRODUCTION

1   T. Blair, 'Stan's my man', *New Statesman and Society*, 20 January 1995, p. 19. For a historical appraisal of Matthews, see T. Mason, 'Stanley Matthews', in R. Holt (ed.), *Sport and the Working Class in Modern Britain*, Manchester, Manchester University Press, 1990, pp. 159–78.

2   D. Baddiel and F. Skinner/Lightning Seeds, 'Three Lions', Epic, 1996.

3   Quoted in D. Marqusee, *Anyone But England: cricket and the national malaise*, London, Verso, 1994, pp. 15–16.

4   For an analysis of the links between football and popular culture, including music, in the 1980s and early 1990s, see S. Redhead, *Football With Attitude*, Manchester, Wordsmith, 1991.

5   A. Frean, 'Editor rebuked as Euro 96 jingoism angers readers', *The Times*, 25 June 1996, p. 1.

6   A. Robson, 'Introduction', in A. M. C. Thorburn, *The Scottish Rugby Union: official history*, Edinburgh, Scottish Rugby Union/Collins, 1985, p. xii.

7   E. Midwinter, *The Illustrated History of County Cricket*, London, Kingswood, 1992, p. 91.

8   L. P. Hartley, *The Go-Between*, London, Hamish Hamilton, 1953, p. 9.

9   T. Mason, *Sport in Britain*, London, Faber and Faber, 1988, p. 7.

10 H. Evans, 'Foreword', in D. Smith and G. Williams, *Fields of Praise: the official centenary history of the Welsh Rugby Union 1881–1981*, Cardiff, University of Wales Press, 1980, p. v.

11 H. Perkin, 'Sport and society: Empire into Commonwealth', in J. A. Mangan and R. B. Small (eds), *Sport, Culture, Society: international historical and sociological perspectives*, London, Spon, 1986, p. 3.

12 N. Blain and R. Boyle, 'Battling along the boundaries: the marking of Scottish identity in sports journalism', in G. Jarvie and G. Walker (eds), *Scottish Sport in the Making of the Nation: ninety-minute patriots?*, Leicester, Leicester University Press, 1994, p. 136.

13 B. Houlihan, *The Government and Politics of Sport*, London, Routledge, 1991, p. 10.

14 See in particular K. Morgan, *The People's Peace: British history 1945–1990*, Oxford, Oxford University Press, 1992; A. Marwick, *British Society since 1945*, Harmondsworth, Penguin, 1982. A concise account can be found in

E. Royle, 'Trends in post-war British social history', in J. Obelkevich and P. Catterall (eds), *Understanding Post-War British Society*, London, Routledge, 1994, pp. 9–18.

15 Royle, 'Trends in post-war British social history', p. 9.

16 R. Gruneau, *Class, Sports, and Social Development*, Amherst, MA, University of Massachusetts Press, 1983, p. 53.

17 R. Holt, *Sport and the British: a modern history*, Oxford, Oxford University Press, 1989, p. 3.

18 D. Brailsford, *Sport, Time and Society: the British at play*, London, Routledge, 1991.

19 J. Maguire, 'American labour migrants, globalization and the making of English basketball', in J. Bale and J. Maguire (eds), *The Global Sports Arena: athletic talent migration in an interdependent world*, London, Frank Cass, 1994, pp. 226–55.

20 See R. Cox, *Sport in Britain: a bibliography of historical publications 1800–1988*, Manchester, Manchester University Press, 1991. The section on 'nation-wide histories of sport' (pp. 4–20) indicates the favoured periods: while the sixteenth and seventeenth centuries had forty-five entries between them, the eighteenth and nineteenth centuries had 221. The twentieth century had fifty three.

21 Examples of books in this series that contain significant amounts of historical material include Jarvie and Walker (eds), *Scottish Sport*; R. Taylor, *Football and its Fans: supporters and their relations with the game 1885–1985*, Leicester, Leicester University Press, 1992; and S. Wagg (ed.), *Giving the Game Away: football, politics and culture on five continents*, London, Leicester University Press, 1995.

22 P. Calvocoressi, *The British Experience 1945–75*, Harmondsworth, Pelican, 1979; Marwick, *British Society since 1945*, p. 78; G. Arnold, *Britain since 1945: choice, conflict and change*, London, Blandford, 1989; M. Pugh, *State and Society: British political and social history 1870–1992*, London, Edward Arnold, 1994, pp. 69–70.

23 G. Whannel, *Blowing the Whistle: the politics of sport*, London, Pluto Press, 1983, p. 115.

24 K. Robbins, *The Eclipse of a Great Power: Modern Britain, 1870–1975*, London, Longman, 1983, especially pp. 326–30.

25 Morgan, *The People's Peace*, pp. 257–8, 341.

26 A. Marwick, *British Society since 1945*, third edition, Harmondsworth, Penguin, 1996, pp. 316–17, 347–50.

27 J. Oakland, *British Civilization: an introduction*, third edition, London, Routledge, 1995, p. 318.

28 C. Brackenbridge and D. Woodward, 'Gender inequalities in leisure and sport in post-war Britain', in Obelkevich and Catterall (eds), *Understanding Post-War British Society*, p. 192.

29 J. A. Mangan, 'Series editor's foreword', in N. Fishwick, *English Football and Society, 1910–1950*, Manchester, Manchester University Press, 1989, p. vi.

30 W. Baker, 'The state of British sport history', *Journal of Sport History*, 1983, vol. 10, no. 1, pp. 53–66; P. Bailey, 'Leisure, culture and the historian: reviewing the first generation of leisure historiography in Britain', *Leisure Studies*, 1989, vol. 8, pp. 107–27; R. Cox, 'A brief history of British sports

history', *Physical Education Review*, 1992, vol. 15, no. 3, pp. 119–26; J. A. Mangan, 'The social history of sport: reflections on some recent British developments in research and teaching', in D. L. Vanderwerken (ed.), *Sport in the Classroom: teaching sport-related courses in the humanities*, London, Associated University Press, 1990, pp. 61–74; R. Malcolmson, 'Sport in society: a historical perspective', *British Journal of Sports History*, 1984, vol. 1, no. 1, pp. 60–72; G. Redmond, 'Sport history in academe: reflections on a half-century of peculiar progress', *British Journal of Sports History*, 1984, vol. 1, no. 1, pp. 24–40; B. Stoddart, 'Historical dimensions in the British sports experience: a review article', *Sporting Traditions*, 1991, vol. 7, part 2, pp. 207–13.

31 Cox, *Sport in Britain*; R. Cox, *History of Sport: a guide to the literature and sources of information*, Frodsham, Sports History Publishing, 1994; R. Cox, *Index to Sporting Manuscripts in the U.K.*, Frodsham, Sports History Publishing, 1995; R. Cox, *Bibliography of British Sporting Biography*, Frodsham, Sports History Publishing, 1995; R. Cox, *The Internet as a Resource for the Sports Historian*, Frodsham, Sports History Publishing, 1995. See also his annual bibliographies in the *International Journal of the History of Sport*.

32 See, for example, J. Maguire, 'The commercialization of English elite basketball 1972–1988: a figurational approach', *International Review for the Sociology of Sport*, 1988, vol. 23, no. 4, pp. 305–23; J. Maguire, 'More than a sporting touchdown: the making of American Football in England 1982–1990', *Sociology of Sport Journal*, 1990, vol. 7, no. 3, pp. 213–37.

33 T. Mason, 'Foreword', in Cox, *Index to Sporting Manuscripts*, p. vi.

34 H. Spencer, *A Century of Polo*, Cirencester, World Polo Associates, 1994, p. 10.

35 R. Holt, 'Introduction', in Holt (ed.), *Sport and the Working Class*, p. 1.

36 G. Whannel, *Fields in Vision: television sport and cultural transformation*, London, Routledge, 1992; S. Barnett, *Games and Sets: the changing face of sport on television*, London, British Film Institute, 1990; E. Cashmore, …*and there was television*, London, Routledge, 1994; J. Chandler, *Television and National Sport: the United States and Britain*, Urbana, IL, University of Illinois Press, 1988.

37 J. Bale, *Landscapes of Modern Sport*, Leicester, Leicester University Press, 1994; L. Allison, 'Sport as an environmental issue', in L. Allison (ed.), *The Changing Politics of Sport*, pp. 207–32; G. Jarvie, 'Dependency, cultural identity and sporting landlords: a Scottish case-study', *British Journal of the History of Sport*, 1986, vol. 3, no. 1, pp. 42–54; G. Jarvie, 'Royal games, sport and the politics of the environment', in Jarvie and Walker (eds), *Scottish Sport*, pp. 154–72.

1 SPORT, POLITICS, AND THE STATE

1 N. Macfarlane with M. Herd, *Sport and Politics: a world divided*, London, Willow, 1986, p. 7.

2 B. Houlihan, *The Government and Politics of Sport*, London, Routledge, 1991, p. 5.

3 Ibid., p. 1.

4 John Hargreaves, 'The state and sport: programmed and non-programmed intervention in Britain', in L. Allison (ed.), *The Politics of Sport*, Manchester, Manchester University Press, 1986, p. 249.

5 Allison, *Politics of Sport*; L. Allison (ed.), *The Changing Politics of Sport*, Manchester, Manchester University Press, 1993.

6 L. Allison, 'Preface', in Allison, *Changing Politics of Sport*, p. ix.

7 R. Thomas, 'Hunting: a sporting or political issue?', in Allison, *Politics of Sport*, pp. 174–97; L. Allison, 'Sport as an environmental issue', in Allison, *Changing Politics of Sport*, pp. 207–32.

8 I. Henry, *The Politics of Leisure Policy*, Basingstoke, Macmillan, 1993.

9 John Hargreaves, *Sport, Power and Culture: a social and historical analysis of popular sports in Britain*, Cambridge, Polity, 1986; D. Hart-Davis, *Hitler's Games: the 1936 Olympics*, New York, Harper and Row, 1986; C. Hill, *Horse Power: the politics of the turf*, Manchester, Manchester University Press, 1988.

10 D. Howell, *Made in Birmingham*, London, Queen Anne Press, 1990; Macfarlane with Herd, *Sport and Politics*; J. Coghlan with I. Webb, *Sport and British Politics since 1960*, Basingstoke, Falmer, 1990.

11 See R. Cox, *History of Sport: a guide to the literature and sources of information*, Frodsham, British Society of Sports History/Sports History Publishing, 1994, p. 39, for a general introduction.

12 K. Foster, 'Sporting autonomy and the law', in Allison, *Politics of Sport*, pp. 49–65; 'Developments in sporting law', in Allison, *Changing Politics of Sport*, pp. 105–24; E. Grayson, *Sport and the Law*, second edition, London, Butterworths, 1994.

13 Coghlan with Webb, *Sport and British Politics*, p. x.

14 Ibid., p. 5.

15 F. Bruno, *Eye of the Tiger: my life*, London, Weidenfeld and Nicolson, 1992, p. 32.

16 Quoted in F. Keating, 'A disgrace, a waste, a fiasco and a bloody good riddance', *The Guardian*, 14 February 1990, p. 15.

17 J. Arlott, 'Up to Players to restore cricket's reputation', *The Guardian*, April 1969 (no exact date). Reprinted in D. R. Allen (ed.), *Arlott on Cricket: his writings on the game*, London, Willow, 1984, p. 208.

18 See D. Brailsford, *Sport, Time and Society: the British at play*, London, Routledge, 1991, pp. 30–45, for a broad view with plenty of examples.

19 M. Polley, 'The Foreign Office and international sport, 1918–948', PhD thesis, University of Wales, 1991.

20 See M. Clapson, *A Bit of a Flutter: popular gambling and English society, c.1823–1961*, Manchester, Manchester University Press, 1992; R. Munting, 'Social opposition to gambling in Britain: a historical overview', *International Journal of the History of Sport*, 1993, vol. 10, no. 3, pp. 295–312.

21 Coghlan with Webb, *Sport and British Politics*, p. 5. For a history of the first forty years of the CCRPT (renamed the Central Council of Physical Recreation (CCPR) in 1944), see H. J. Evans, *Service to Sport: the story of the CCPR, 1937–1975*, London, Pelham, 1975.

22 Grayson, *Sport and the Law*, pp. 40–1.

23 See S. Jones, *Sport, Politics and the Working Class: organised labour and sport in interwar Britain*, Manchester, Manchester University Press, 1988, pp. 142–6.

24 See ibid., pp. 181–6.

25 L. Allison, 'Sport and politics', in Allison, *Politics of Sport*, p. 17.

26 Ibid., p. 12.
27 Ibid., p. 16.
28 M. Collins and H. Jones, 'The economics of sport: sport as an industry', in A. Tomlinson (ed.), *Sport in Society: policy, politics and culture*, Brighton, Leisure Studies Association, 1990, p. 69.
29 For general overviews, see K. Morgan, *The People's Peace: British history 1945–1990*, Oxford, Oxford University Press, 1990, pp. 29–70; A. Sked and C. Cook, *Post-War Britain: a political history, 1945–1992*, fourth edition, Harmondsworth, Penguin, 1993, pp. 23–86.
30 Henry, *Politics of Leisure Policy*, pp. 15–22.
31 J. Sugden and A. Bairner, ' "Ma, there's a helicopter on the pitch!"': sport, leisure, and the state in Northern Ireland', *Sociology of Sport Journal*, 1992, vol. 9, no. 2, p. 157.
32 Committee on the Youth Service in England and Wales, *The Youth Service in England and Wales*, London, HMSO, 1960; Wolfenden Committee on Sport, *Sport and the Community*, London, Central Council of Physical Recreation, 1960.
33 Wolfenden Committee, *Sport and the Community*, p. 7.
34 Physical Education Department, University of Birmingham, *Britain in the World of Sport: an examination of the factors involved in participation in competitive international sport*, [S. l.], Physical Education Association for Great Britain and Northern Ireland, 1956, p. 13.
35 John Hargreaves, 'The state and sport', p. 243.
36 G. Whannel, *Blowing the Whistle: the politics of sport*, London, Pluto Press, 1993, p. 88.
37 For the significance of voluntarism and amateurism in the immediate post-war period, see N. Baker, 'The amateur ideal in a society of equality: change and continuity in post-Second World War British sport, 1945–48', *International Journal of the History of Sport*, 1995, vol. 12, no. 1, pp. 99–126.
38 D. Kirk and R. Tinning (eds), *Physical Education, Curriculum and Culture: critical issues in the contemporary crisis*, Basingstoke, Falmer, 1990.
39 See S. Barnett, *Games and Sets: the changing face of sport on television*, London, British Film Institute, 1990; G. Whannel, *Fields in Vision: television sport and cultural transformation*, London, Routledge, 1992.
40 Howell, *Made in Birmingham*, p. 111; Coghlan with Webb, *Sport and British Politics*, pp. 12–14; Lord Hailsham, *A Sparrow's Flight*, London, Collins, 1990, pp. 332–3, 335–7.
41 H. Wilson, *The Labour Government 1964–1970: a personal record*, London, Weidenfeld and Nicolson/Michael Joseph, 1971, p. 10.
42 Ibid., p. 59. See also Howell, *Made in Birmingham*, p. 155.
43 See Coghlan with Webb, *Sport and British Politics*, Appendix 2, pp. 272–4, for the inaugural membership and terms of reference of the Sports Council, and Howell, *Made in Birmingham*, pp. 146–9, for an insight into the selection of the members.
44 Coghlan with Webb, *Sport and British Politics*, Appendix 2, pp. 272–4.
45 C. Chataway, *A Better Country*, London, Conservative Political Centre, 1966, pp. 44–7.
46 Coghlan with Webb, *Sport and British Politics*; Houlihan, *The Government and*

Politics of Sport, Chapter 4; John Hargreaves, 'The state and sport', pp. 242–61.

47 Howell, *Made in Birmingham*, p. 217.

48 The text of the Royal Charter is printed in Coghlan with Webb, *Sport and British Politics*, Appendix 1, pp. 267–71.

49 Department of the Environment, *Sport and Recreation* (Cmnd. 6200), London, HMSO, 1975, p. 3. See also P. McIntosh and V. Charlton, *The Impact of Sport For All Policy 1966–1984 and a Way Forward*, London, Sports Council, 1985, p. 15; and Coghlan with Webb, *Sport and British Politics*, Appendix 5, pp. 285–7 for a summary.

50 Department of the Environment, *Sport and Recreation*, p. 18. See also P. Taylor, 'The production of sporting excellence in England: a mixed economy problem', in Tomlinson (ed.), *Sport in Society*, p. 19.

51 Quoted in McIntosh and Charlton, *Impact of Sport For All*, p. 19.

52 Sugden and Bairner, '"Ma, there's a helicopter on the pitch!"', pp. 157–8. See also J. Sugden and A. Bairner, *Sport, Sectarianism and Society in a Divided Ireland*, Leicester, Leicester University Press, 1993, pp. 111–24.

53 Quoted in Sugden and Bairner, *Sport, Sectarianism and Society*, p. 115.

54 For the issue of leisure centres and 'demographic polarisation' in Northern Ireland, see ibid., pp. 116–21; Sugden and Bairner, '"Ma, there's a helicopter on the pitch!"', pp. 159–61. For the flag-flying incidents, see C. Knox, 'Political symbolism and leisure provision in Northern Ireland local government', *Local Government Studies*, 1986, vol. 12, no. 5, pp. 42–6.

55 Houlihan, *Government and Politics*, p. 99. See also M. Tomlinson, 'State intervention in voluntary sport: the inner city policy context', *Leisure Studies*, 1987, vol. 6, pp. 329–45. For a view of targeting facilities at inner city areas, see J. Parry and N. Parry, 'Sport and the black experience', in G. Jarvie (ed.), *Sport, Racism and Ethnicity*, London, Falmer, 1991, pp. 165–7.

56 Howell, *Made in Birmingham*, p. 111.

57 Hailsham, *Sparrow's Flight*, p. 335.

58 Ibid., p. 336.

59 Quoted in Grayson, *Sport and the Law*, p. 43.

60 Ibid., p. 51.

61 Ibid., pp. 458–9.

62 B. Houlihan, 'The politics of sports policy in Britain: the examples of football hooliganism and drug abuse', in Tomlinson (ed.), *Sport in Society*, p. 31.

63 Macfarlane with Herd, *Sport and Politics*, p. 60.

64 Grayson, *Sport and the Law*, p. 49.

65 For a discussion of this group's work, see Houlihan, *Government and Politics*, pp. 30–2.

66 Quoted in ibid., p. 37.

67 Ibid., pp. 36–40.

68 John Hargreaves, 'The state and sport', p. 225.

69 Henry, *Politics of Leisure Policy*, p. 90.

70 M. Collins, 'Shifting icebergs: the public, private and voluntary sectors in British sport', in Tomlinson (ed.), *Sport in Society*, p. 9.

71 Houlihan, *Government and Politics*, Chapter 3.

72 Ibid., pp. 51–2.
73 Knox, 'Political symbolism', p. 37.
74 For the impact of Thatcherism on local government provision, see Henry, *Politics of Leisure Policy*, Chapter 4; Houlihan, *Government and Politics*, pp. 73–81.
75 Collins, 'Shifting icebergs', pp. 3–4.
76 Henry, *Politics of Leisure Policy*, pp. 106–8.
77 Tomlinson, 'State intervention in voluntary sport', p. 340.
78 M. Clapson, *A Bit of a Flutter*, pp. 66–7, 122–8; W. Vamplew, *The Turf: a social and economic history of horse racing*, London, Allen Lane, 1976, pp. 68–73.
79 For a detailed discussion of the background to the Act and its passage, see Hill, *Horse Power*, Chapters 2 and 3. Clapson, *A Bit of a Flutter*, provides a good general account of gambling with various insights on the 1960 Act.
80 See Houlihan, 'The politics of sports policy', pp. 32–8, for an overview of policy initiatives and the difficulties of implementation.
81 K. Foster, 'Developments in sporting law', pp. 119–20.
82 R. Thomas, *The Politics of Hunting*, Aldershot, Gower, 1983; Thomas, 'Hunting', p. 186. See also M. Billett, *A History of English Country Sports*, London, Robert Hale, 1994, p. 20.
83 R. Worcester, 'Scenting dissent', *New Statesman and Society*, 21 April 1995, p. 22.
84 K. Foster, 'Sporting autonomy', pp. 49–65.
85 M. Polley, 'Olympic diplomacy: the British Government and the projected 1940 Olympic Games', *International Journal of the History of Sport*, 1992, vol. 9, no. 2, pp. 169–87.
86 For general discussions of the history of this issue, see R. Nixon, *Homelands, Harlem and Hollywood: South African culture and the world beyond*, London, Routledge, 1994, Chapter 5; A. Guelke, 'The politicisation of South African sport', in Allison, *Politics of Sport*, pp. 118–48; A. Guelke, 'Sport and the end of *apartheid*', in Allison, *Changing Politics of Sport*, pp. 151–70. For a survey of post-apartheid developments, see D. Booth, 'United sport: an alternative hegemony in South Africa?', *International Journal of the History of Sport*, 1995, vol. 12, no. 3, pp. 105–24.
87 T. Huddleston, *Naught for your Comfort*, London, Collins, 1956, pp. 201–2.
88 A. Guelke, 'Politicisation of South African sport', p. 123.
89 For accounts of the affair, see B. D'Oliveira with P. Murphy, *Time to Declare: an autobiography*, London, Dent, 1980; P. Hain, *Don't Play with Apartheid: the background to the Stop the Seventy Tour Campaign*, London, George Allen and Unwin, 1971; Howell, *Made in Birmingham*, pp. 200–9; J. Bailey, *Conflicts in Cricket*, London, Kingswood, 1989, pp. 48–54; Guelke, 'Politicisation of South African sport', pp. 130–1; D. Marqusee, *Anyone But England: cricket and the national malaise*, London, Verso, 1994, pp. 187–8.
90 Quoted in G. Howat, *Learie Constantine*, London, George Allen and Unwin, 1975, p. 204.
91 Quoted in Guelke, 'Politicisation of South African sport', p. 131.
92 Howell, *Made in Birmingham*, pp. 200–9.
93 Nixon, *Homelands, Harlem and Hollywood*, p. 142.
94 D. Smith and G. Williams, *Fields of Praise: the official history of the Welsh*

Rugby Union 1881–1981, Cardiff, University of Wales Press, 1980, pp. 404–5.

95 *The Times*, 6 May 1970: reprinted in M. Williams (ed.), *The Way to Lord's: cricketing letters to The Times*, London, Willow, 1983, p. 79.

96 Wilson, *The Labour Government*, pp. 783–5.

97 Quoted in Macfarlane with Herd, *Sport and Politics*, p. 110. See also A. Payne, 'The international politics of the Gleneagles Agreement', *The Round Table*, 1991, no. 320, pp. 417–30.

98 For a detailed discussion of the Moscow debate, see C. Hill, *Olympic Politics*, Manchester, Manchester University Press, 1992, pp. 120–55. Lord Killanin gives a detailed insider's account in *My Olympic Years*, London, Secker & Warburg, 1983, pp. 164–219.

99 M. Thatcher, *The Downing Street Years*, London, HarperCollins, 1993, p. 88.

100 Quoted in Macfarlane with Herd, *Sport and Politics*, p. 222.

101 Quoted in ibid., p. 224.

102 Thatcher, *Downing Street Years*, p. 88.

103 D. Wallechinsky, *The Complete Book of the Olympics*, revised edition, Harmondsworth, Penguin, 1988, p. xiii.

104 Hill, *Olympic Politics*, p. 152.

2 SPORT, THE NATION, AND THE WORLD

1 H. O'Donnell, 'Mapping the mythical: a geopolitics of national sporting stereotypes', *Discourse and Society*, 1994, vol. 5, no. 3, p. 353.

2 M. Billig, *Banal Nationalism*, London, Sage, 1995.

3 B. Anderson, *Imagined Communities: reflections on the origin and spread of nationalism*, London, Verso, 1983.

4 J. Tuck, 'Patriots, barbarians, gentlemen and players: rugby union and national identity in Britain since 1945', *Sporting Heritage*, 1996, no. 2, pp. 25–36.

5 J. Maguire, 'Sport, identity politics, and globalization: diminishing contrasts and increasing varieties', *Sociology of Sport Journal*, 1994, vol. 11, no. 4, p. 423.

6 F. Wheen, 'The athletic fallacy', in A. McLellan (ed.), *Nothing Sacred: the new cricket culture*, London, Two Heads, 1996, p. 107.

7 Maguire, 'Sport, identity politics, and globalization', pp. 415–21.

8 I. Buchanan, *British Olympians: a hundred years of gold medallists*, Enfield, Guinness, 1991.

9 H. Moorhouse, 'One state, several countries: soccer and nationality in a "United" Kingdom', *International Journal of the History of Sport*, 1995, vol. 12, no. 2, pp. 55–74; J. Sugden and A. Bairner, 'Ireland and the World Cup: "two teams in Ireland, there's only two teams in Ireland . . . "', in J. Sugden and A. Tomlinson (eds), *Hosts and Champions: soccer cultures, national identities and the USA World Cup*, Aldershot, Arena, 1994, pp. 119–40; S. Wagg, 'The missionary position: football in the societies of Britain and Ireland', in S. Wagg (ed.), *Giving the Game Away: football, politics and culture on five continents*, London, Leicester University Press, 1995, pp. 1–23.

10 K. McCarra, 'Sport in Scotland', in P. Scott (ed.), *Scotland: a concise cultural history*, Edinburgh, Mainstream, 1993, p. 279.

11 G. Oliver, *The Guinness Record of World Soccer: the history of the game in over 150 countries*, Enfield, Guinness, 1992, p. 524.

12 See A. Blake, *The Body Language: the meaning of modern sport*, London, Lawrence and Wishart, 1996, pp. 88–112.

13 D. Wallechinsky, *The Complete Book of the Olympics*, Harmondsworth, Penguin, 1988, p. 145.

14 G. Jarvie and G. Walker, 'Ninety minute patriots? Scottish sport in the making of the nation', in G. Jarvie and G. Walker (eds), *Scottish Sport in the Making of the Nation: ninety minute patriots?*, Leicester, Leicester University Press, 1994, p. 8.

15 Ibid., p. 3.

16 J. Maguire and J. Bale, 'Postscript: an agenda for research on sports labour migration', in J. Bale and J. Maguire (eds), *The Global Sports Arena: athletic talent migration in an interdependent world*, London, Frank Cass, 1994, p. 284.

17 E. Hobsbawm, *Nations and Nationalism since 1780: programme, myth, reality*, Cambridge, Cambridge University Press, 1990, p. 143.

18 Exceptions include work on sports in which England has had a specific identity apart from Wales, Scotland, and (Northern) Ireland. C. Critcher, 'Putting on the style: aspects of recent English football', in J. Williams and S. Wagg (eds), *British Football and Social Change: getting into Europe*, Leicester, Leicester University Press, 1991, pp. 67–84; C. Critcher, 'England and the World Cup: World Cup willies, English football and the myth of 1966', in Sugden and Tomlinson (eds), *Hosts and Champions*, pp. 77–92; D. Marqusee, *Anyone But England: cricket and the national malaise*, London, Verso, 1994.

19 R. Holt, *Sport and the British: a modern history*, Oxford, Oxford University Press, 1989, p. 262.

20 A. M. C. Thorburn, *The Scottish Rugby Union: official history*, Edinburgh, Scottish Rugby Union/Collins, 1985; D. Smith and G. Williams, *Fields of Praise: the official history of the Welsh Rugby Union 1881–1981*, Cardiff, University of Wales Press, 1980.

21 C. Short, *The Ulster GAA Story, 1884–1984*, [S. l.], Ulster Committee GAA, 1984; C. Short, P. Murray, and J. Smith, *Ard Mhacha 1884–1984: a century of progress*, Armagh, Armagh County Board GAA, 1985.

22 G. Jarvie, 'Highland Gatherings, historical sociology and sport', in J. A. Mangan and R. B. Small (eds), *Sport, Culture, Society: international historical and sociological perspectives*, London, Spon, 1986, p. 69.

23 H. Moorhouse, 'Professional football and working class culture: English theories and Scottish evidence', *Sociological Review*, 1984, vol. 32, no. 2, pp. 285–315.

24 H. Moorhouse, 'Repressed nationalism and professional football: Scotland versus England', in Mangan and Small (eds), *Sport, Culture, Society*, pp. 52–9; H. Moorhouse, 'Scotland against England: football and popular culture', *International Journal of the History of Sport*, 1987, vol. 4, no. 2, pp. 189–202; H. Moorhouse, ' "We're off to Wembley!": The history of a Scottish event and the sociology of football hooliganism', in D. McCrone, S. Kendrick, and P. Straw (eds), *The Making of Scotland: nation, culture and social change*, Edinburgh, Edinburgh University Press/British Sociological Association, 1989, pp. 207–27; H. Moorhouse, 'Shooting stars: footballers

and working-class culture in twentieth-century Scotland', in R. Holt (ed.), *Sport and the Working Class in Modern Britain*, Manchester, Manchester University Press, 1990, pp. 179–97; H. Moorhouse, 'On the periphery: Scotland, Scottish football and the new Europe', in Williams and Wagg (eds), *British Football and Social Change*, pp. 201–19; H. Moorhouse, 'Blue bonnets over the border: Scotland and the migration of footballers', in Bale and Maguire (eds), *The Global Sports Arena*, pp. 78–96; H. Moorhouse, 'From zines like these? Fanzines, tradition and identity in Scottish football', in Jarvie and Walker (eds), *Scottish Sport*, pp. 173–94.

25 B. Murray, *The Old Firm: sectarianism, sport and society in Scotland*, Edinburgh, John Donald, 1984; G. P. T. Finn, 'Racism, religion and social prejudice: Irish Catholic clubs, soccer and Scottish society – I The historical roots of prejudice', *International Journal of the History of Sport*, 1991, vol. 8, no. 1, pp. 72–95; G. P. T. Finn, 'Racism, religion and social prejudice: Irish Catholic clubs, soccer and Scottish society – II Social identities and conspiracy theories', *International Journal of the History of Sport*, 1991, vol. 8, no. 3, pp. 370–97; G. P. T. Finn, 'Faith, hope and bigotry: case studies of anti-Catholic prejudice in Scottish soccer and society', in Jarvie and Walker (eds), *Scottish Sport*, pp. 91–112; J. Bradley, 'Football in Scotland: a history of political and ethnic identity', *International Journal of the History of Sport*, 1995, vol. 12, no. 1, pp. 81–98; J. Bradley, 'Integration or assimilation? Scottish society, football and Irish immigrants', *International Journal of the History of Sport*, 1996, vol. 13, no. 2, pp. 61–79; G. Jarvie, 'Dependency, cultural identity and sporting landlords: a Scottish case-study', *British Journal of the History of Sport*, 1986, vol. 3, no. 1, pp. 42–54; G. Jarvie, 'Highland Gatherings', pp. 68–75; G. Jarvie, *Highland Games: the making of the myth*, Edinburgh, Edinburgh University Press, 1991; G. Jarvie, 'Sport, nationalism and cultural identity', in L. Allison (ed.), *The Changing Politics of Sport*, Manchester, Manchester University Press, 1993, pp. 58–83; G. Jarvie, 'Royal games, sport and the politics of the environment', in Jarvie and Walker (eds), *Scottish Sport*, pp. 154–72.

26 Jarvie and Walker (eds), *Scottish Sport*.

27 Jarvie, 'Highland Gatherings', p. 69.

28 H. Moorhouse, '"We're off to Wembley!"'; G. Walker, '"There's not a team like the Glasgow Rangers": football and religious identity in Scotland', in G. Walker and T. Gallagher (eds), *Sermons and Battle Hymns: protestant popular culture in modern Scotland*, Edinburgh, Edinburgh University Press, 1990, pp. 137–59.

29 McCarra, 'Sport in Scotland'.

30 For a concise overview, and guidance to more specialised work on the GAA, see Holt, *Sport and the British*, pp. 238–46.

31 J. Sugden and A. Bairner, 'Northern Ireland: sport in a divided society', in L. Allison (ed.), *The Politics of Sport*, Manchester, Manchester University Press, 1986, pp. 90–117; J. Sugden and A. Bairner, '"Ma, there's a helicopter on the pitch!" Sport, leisure and the state in Northern Ireland', *Sociology of Sport Journal*, 1992, vol. 9, no. 2, pp. 154–66; J. Sugden and A. Bairner, *Sport, Sectarianism and Society in a Divided Ireland*, Leicester, Leicester University Press, 1993; J. Sugden and A. Bairner, 'National identity, community relations and the sporting life in Northern Ireland', in Allison

(ed.), *Changing Politics of Sport*, pp. 171–206; J. Sugden and A. Bairner, 'Ireland and the World Cup'.

32 Smith and Williams, *Fields of Praise*; D. Smith, 'People's theatre: a century of Welsh rugby', *History Today*, 1981, vol. 31, no. 3, pp. 31–6; D. Smith, 'Focal heroes: a Welsh fighting class', in Holt (ed.), *Sport and the Working Class*, pp. 198–217; G. Williams, 'From Grand Slam to Great Slump: economy, society and rugby football in Wales during the Depression', *Welsh History Review*, 1983, vol. 11, no. 3, pp. 339–57; G. Williams, ' "How amateur was my valley?" Professional sport and national identity in Wales, 1890–1914', *British Journal of Sports History*, 1983, vol. 2, no. 3, pp. 248–69; G. Williams, *1905 and All That: essays on rugby football, sport and Welsh society*, Llandysul, Gomer, 1991; G. Williams, 'The Road to Wigan Pier revisited: the migration of Welsh rugby talent since 1918', in Bale and Maguire (eds), *The Global Sports Arena*, pp. 25–38.

33 G. Jarvie and J. Maguire, *Sport and Leisure in Social Thought*, London, Routledge, 1994, p. 153.

34 Maguire, 'Sport, identity politics, and globalization', p. 398.

35 For a concise overview, see Jarvie and Maguire, *Sport and Leisure*, pp. 230–63. A collection of historical and sociological essays on one of the key themes in the sports globalisation debate, that of athletic labour migration, with a useful theoretical introduction and a research agenda, is Bale and Maguire (eds), *The Global Sports Arena*. A whole issue of the *Sociology of Sport Journal* (vol. 11, no. 4) was given over to the debate in 1994.

36 Williams, 'The Road to Wigan Pier revisited'; H. Moorhouse, 'Blue bonnets over the border'.

37 See, for example, J. Maguire, 'More than a sporting touchdown: the making of American Football in England 1982–1990', *Sociology of Sport Journal*, 1990, vol. 7, no. 3, pp. 213–37; J. Maguire, 'American labour migrants, globalization and the making of English basketball', in Bale and Maguire (eds), *The Global Sports Arena*, pp. 226–56; J. Maguire, 'Sport, identity politics, and globalization'.

38 Sugden and Tomlinson (eds), *Hosts and Champions*. Their ongoing work on world football is flagged in J. Sugden and A. Tomlinson, 'A gulf in class?', *When Saturday Comes*, February 1997, no. 120, pp. 36–7.

39 A. Tomlinson and G. Whannel (eds), *Five Ring Circus: money, power and politics at the Olympic Games*, London, Pluto, 1984; A. Tomlinson and G. Whannel (eds), *Off The Ball: the football World Cup*, London, Pluto, 1986.

40 This subject has a vast literature. For an introduction, see the following two volumes of essays. J. A. Mangan (ed.), *Pleasure, Profit, Proselytism: British culture and sport at home and abroad, 1700–1914*, London, Frank Cass, 1988; J. A. Mangan (ed.), *The Cultural Bond: sport, empire, society*, London, Frank Cass, 1992.

41 Maguire, 'Sport, identity politics, and globalization', p. 406.

42 A. Krüger, 'On the origin of the notion that sport serves as a means of national representation', *History of European Ideas*, 1993, vol. 16, no. 4–6, p. 863.

43 See Wallechinsky, *Complete Book of the Olympics*, pp. xiii–iv, and B. Glanville, *The History of the World Cup*, revised edition, London, Faber and Faber, 1980.

44 Wallechinsky, *Complete Book of the Olympics*, p. xii.
45 J. Sugden and A. Tomlinson, 'Soccer culture, national identity and the World Cup', in Sugden and Tomlinson (eds), *Hosts and Champions*, pp. 4–6.
46 B. Murray, *Football: a history of the world game*, London, Scolar, 1994, pp. 166–74. For detailed records of all international, continental, and national competitions, see Oliver, *World Soccer*.
47 R. Gate, *Rugby League: an illustrated history*, London, Arthur Barker, 1989, pp. 94, 99, 102.
48 D. Wyatt, *Rugby Disunion: the making of three world cups*, London, Vista, 1995, p. 17.
49 For a discussion of how the 'Austerity Olympics' were received, see N. Baker, 'Olympics or Tests: the disposition of the British sporting public, 1948', *Sporting Traditions*, 1994, vol. 11, no. 1, pp. 57–74.
50 C. Leatherdale, *England's Quest for the World Cup: a complete record*, London, Methuen, 1984, pp. 4–5.
51 A. Tomlinson, 'Going global: the FIFA story', in Tomlinson and Whannel (eds), *Off The Ball*, p. 88.
52 M. Golesworthy, *Encyclopaedia of Cricket*, sixth edition, London, Robert Hale, 1977, p. 182.
53 Oliver, *World Soccer*, p. 163.
54 Tomlinson, 'Going global', pp. 89–93.
55 J. Arlott, *The Oxford Companion to Sports and Games*, Oxford, Oxford University Press, 1975, p. 903.
56 S. Wagg, *The Football World: a contemporary social history*, Brighton, Harvester, 1984, p. 77.
57 Critcher, 'England and the World Cup', p. 79.
58 N. Blain and R. Boyle, 'Battling along the boundaries: the marking of Scottish identity in sports journalism', in Jarvie and Walker (eds), *Scottish Sport*, p. 129.
59 Wagg, *The Football World*, p. 78.
60 Walter Winterbottom, quoted in R. Taylor and A. Ward, *Kicking and Screaming: an oral history of football in England*, London, Robson, 1995, p. 89.
61 W. Meisl, *Soccer Revolution*, London, Phoenix, 1955, p. 38.
62 L. Shackleton, *Clown Prince of Soccer: his autobiography*, London, Kaye, 1955, p. 78.
63 C. Critcher, 'Football since the war', in J. Clarke, C. Critcher, and R. Johnson (eds), *Working Class Culture: studies in history and theory*, London, Hutchinson, 1979, especially pp. 179–82.
64 Critcher, 'England and the World Cup', p. 80.
65 J. Clarke and C. Critcher, '1966 and all that: England's World Cup victory', in Tomlinson and Whannel (eds), *Off The Ball*, pp. 112–26; Critcher, 'Football since the war', pp. 180–2.
66 Thorburn, *Scottish Rugby Union*, p. 45.
67 Smith and Williams, *Fields of Praise*, pp. 371–417.
68 Gate, *Rugby League*, pp. 128, 130.
69 C. Hill, *Olympic Politics*, Manchester, Manchester University Press, 1992, pp. 90–119.
70 J. Maguire and J. Bale, 'Introduction: sports labour migration in the global arena', in Bale and Maguire (eds), *The Global Sports Arena*, pp. 1–21.

71　T. Mason, 'The Bogotá affair', in Bale and Maguire (eds), *The Global Sports Arena*, p. 39.

72　Ibid., p. 41.

73　R. Sissons, *The Players: a social history of the professional cricketer*, London, Kingswood, 1988, pp. 306–7.

74　Ibid.; Marqusee, *Anyone but England*, pp. 104–10.

75　See, for example, Marqusee, *Anyone but England*, pp. 204–6 on the Gatting tour of 1990.

76　J. Maguire, 'The commercialization of English elite basketball 1972–1988: a figurational approach', *International Review for the Sociology of Sport*, 1988, vol. 23, no. 4, pp. 305–23; Maguire, 'More than a sporting touchdown'; Maguire, 'American labour migrants'.

77　Maguire, 'American labour migrants', especially pp. 233–9.

78　Ibid., p. 245.

79　Dave West, quoted in ibid., p. 244.

80　S. Genest, 'Skating on thin ice? The international migration of Canadian ice hockey players', in Bale and Maguire (eds), *The Global Sports Arena*, p. 116.

81　G. Moorhouse, *A People's Game: the centenary history of Rugby League, 1895–1995*, London, Hodder and Stoughton, 1995, p. 226. See also Gate, *Rugby League*, p. 91.

82　Gate, *Rugby League*, pp. 107–8.

83　Editorial, 'Pitch Babel', *The Times*, 17 August 1996, p. 19.

84　S. Barnett, *Games and Sets: the changing face of sport on television*, London, British Film Institute, 1990, p. 69. For Channel 4's role in launching American football in the UK, see Maguire, 'More than a sporting touchdown'.

85　G. Whannel, *Fields in Vision: television sport and cultural transformation*, London, Routledge, 1992, pp. 114–15.

86　A. Briggs, 'The media and sport in the global village', in R. Wilcox (ed.), *Sport in the Global Village*, Morgantown, WV, Fitness Information Technology, 1994, p. 20.

87　Jarvie and Maguire, *Sport and Leisure*, p. 147.

88　Ibid., p. 153.

89　H. F. Moorhouse, ' "We're off to Wembley!" ', p. 215.

90　Sugden and Bairner, 'National identity', p. 192.

91　J. Coghlan with I. Webb, *Sport and British Politics since 1960*, Basingstoke, Falmer, 1990, pp. 24–31; Sugden and Bairner, *Sport, Sectarianism and Society*, pp. 100–4.

92　Sugden and Bairner, 'Ireland and the World Cup', especially pp. 121–6; H. Moorhouse, 'One state, several countries'.

93　J. Lowerson, 'Golf and the making of myths', in Jarvie and Walker (eds), *Scottish Sport*, p. 78.

94　Ibid., p. 85.

95　H. Moorhouse, 'From zines like these?', p. 191. Emphasis in original.

96　Finn, 'Racism, religion and social prejudice I'; Finn, 'Racism, religion and social prejudice II'; Finn, 'Faith, hope and bigotry'; Murray, *The Old Firm*.

97　H. Moorhouse, 'From zines like these?', p. 185.

98　Quoted in Walker, ' "There's not a team like the Glasgow Rangers" ', p. 143.

99   R. Holt, 'The king over the border: Denis Law and Scottish football', in Jarvie and Walker (eds), *Scottish Sport*, p. 61.
100 H. Moorhouse, 'Blue bonnets over the border', p. 93.
101 Holt, *Sport and the British*, p. 246.
102 Smith, 'People's theatre', p. 34.
103 Quoted in Smith and Williams, *Fields of Praise*, p. 314.
104 Gate, *Rugby League*, p. 94; G. Moorhouse, *A People's Game*, pp. 243–4.
105 Sugden and Bairner, *Sport, Sectarianism and Society*, p. 29.
106 Sugden and Bairner, 'Northern Ireland: sport in a divided society', pp. 94–9. For an official history, see Short, *Ulster GAA Story*.
107 Sugden and Bairner, 'Northern Ireland: sport in a divided society', p. 95.
108 Short, Murray, and Smith, *Ard Mhacha 1884–1984*, p. 223.
109 Quoted in Sugden and Bairner, '"Ma, there's a helicopter on the pitch!"', p. 162.
110 Short, Murray, and Smith, *Ard Mhacha 1884–1984*, p. 200.
111 Sugden and Bairner, 'Northern Ireland: sport in a divided society', p. 95.
112 McCarra, 'Sport in Scotland', p. 288.
113 D. Whitson, 'Pressures on regional games in a dominant metropolitan culture: the case of shinty', *Leisure Studies*, 1983, vol. 2, no. 2, pp. 139–54.
114 I. Cameron, quoted in ibid., p. 153.
115 Jarvie, *Highland Games*.
116 Quoted in Jarvie and Walker, 'Ninety minute patriots?', p. 1.
117 Ibid., p. 2.
118 H. Moorhouse, 'Blue bonnets over the border', p. 95.
119 Holt, *Sport and the British*, p. 237.
120 Gordon Brown, quoted in Tuck, 'Patriots, barbarians, gentlemen and players', p. 28.
121 Quoted in Maguire, 'Sport, identity politics, and globalization', pp. 411–2.
122 H. Moorhouse, '"We're off to Wembley!"', pp. 208–9.
123 R. Giulianotti, 'Football and the politics of carnival: an ethnographic study of Scottish fans in Sweden', *International Review for the Sociology of Sport*, 1995, vol. 30, no. 2, pp. 202–3. See also R. Giulianotti, 'Scoring away from home: a statistical study of Scotland football fans at international matches in Romania and Sweden', *International Review for the Sociology of Sport*, 1994, vol. 29, no. 2, pp. 171–200.
124 Smith and Williams, *Fields of Praise*, p. 375.
125 Jarvie and Walker, 'Ninety minute patriots?', pp. 4–5. The quotation is from a report in *The Guardian*.
126 Sugden and Bairner, 'National identity', pp. 192–3.
127 Sugden and Bairner, 'Northern Ireland: sport in a divided society', p. 90.
128 Ibid., p. 91.
129 A. Bairner, 'Football and the idea of Scotland', in Jarvie and Walker (eds), *Scottish Sport*, p. 10.

3 SPORT, COMMERCE, AND SPONSORSHIP

1   E. Cashmore, *... and there was television*, London, Routledge, 1994, p. 143.
2   E. Midwinter, *The Illustrated History of County Cricket*, London, Kingswood,

1992, p. 80. See also C. Gratton and P. Taylor, *Sport and Recreation: an economic analysis*, London, Spon, 1985, pp. 225, 229.

3 E. Cashmore, *Making Sense of Sports*, second edition, London, Routledge, 1996, p. 174.

4 T. Mason, *Only A Game? Sport in the modern world*, Cambridge, Cambridge University Press, 1993, pp. 18–19.

5 G. Wright, *Betrayal: the struggle for cricket's soul*, London, Witherby, 1993, pp. 15–16.

6 D. Cohen, 'The Sky's the limit', in A. McLellan (ed.), *Nothing Sacred: the new cricket culture*, London, Two Heads, 1996, p. 138.

7 See M. Polley, 'Great Britain and the Olympic Games, 1896–1908', in C. C. Eldridge (ed.), *Empire, Politics and Popular Culture: essays in eighteenth and nineteenth century British history*, Lampeter, Trivium, 1989, p. 106.

8 W. Vamplew, *The Turf: a social and economic history of horse-racing*, London, Allen Lane, 1976; W. Vamplew, *Pay Up and Play the Game: professional sport in Britain 1875–1914*, Cambridge, Cambridge University Press, 1988; J. Walvin, *The People's Game: a social history of English football*, London, Allen Lane, 1975; T. Mason, *Association Football and English Society, 1863–1915*, Brighton, Harvester, 1980; A. J. Arnold, *A Game That Would Pay: a business history of professional football in Bradford*, London, Duckworth, 1988; M. Clapson, *A Bit of a Flutter: popular gambling and English society c. 1823–1961*, Manchester, Manchester University Press, 1992.

9 H. A. Harris, *Sport in Britain: its origins and development*, London, Stanley Paul, 1975, p. 222.

10 D. Brailsford, *British Sport: a social history*, Cambridge, Lutterworth, 1992; R. Holt, *Sport and the British: a modern history*, Oxford, Oxford University Press, 1989, especially pp. 280–326; T. Mason, *Sport in Britain*, London, Faber and Faber, 1988, especially pp. 1–7.

11 Cashmore, *Making Sense of Sports*, p. 173.

12 Henley Centre, *The Economic Impact of Sport in the UK*, London, Sports Council, 1992, pp. vii, 28.

13 W. Meisl, *Soccer Revolution*, London, Phoenix Sports Books, 1955, pp. 11–16.

14 G. Whannel, *Blowing the Whistle: the politics of sport*, London, Pluto Press, 1983, p. 58.

15 Mason, *Only A Game?*, p. 33.

16 *Independent on Sunday*, 1 September 1996, pp. 29, 31.

17 *Independent on Sunday*, 15 October 1995, p. 24.

18 P. Lovesey, *The Official Centenary History of the Amateur Athletic Association*, Enfield, Guinness Superlatives, 1979, p. 122; J. Crump, 'Athletics', in T. Mason (ed.), *Sport in Britain: a social history*, Cambridge, Cambridge University Press, 1989, p. 65.

19 J. Arlott, *The Oxford Companion to Sports and Games*, Oxford, Oxford University Press, 1975, p. 1042.

20 G. Moorhouse, *A People's Game: the centenary history of Rugby League, 1895–1995*, London, Hodder and Stoughton, 1995, p. 280; R. Gate, *Rugby League: an illustrated history*, London, Arthur Barker, 1989, p. 122.

21 T. Mason, 'Football', in Mason (ed.), *Sport in Britain*, p. 166.

22 E. Dunning and K. Sheard, *Barbarians, Gentlemen and Players: a sociological*

study of the development of rugby football, Oxford, Martin Robertson, 1979, p. 253.

23 N. Smith, *Queen of Games: the history of croquet*, London, Weidenfeld and Nicolson, 1991, pp. 148–9.

24 W. Vamplew, 'Horse-racing', in Mason (ed.), *Sport in Britain*, p. 222.

25 Central Council of Physical Recreation, *Committee of Enquiry into Sports Sponsorship: The Howell Report*, London, Central Council of Physical Recreation, 1983.

26 D. Howell, *Made in Birmingham*, London, Queen Anne Press, 1990, p. 347.

27 Moorhouse, *People's Game*, pp. 363–4; Gate, *Rugby League*, pp. 89, 97, 105.

28 Jack Williams, 'Cricket', in Mason (ed.), *Sport in Britain*, p. 121; Midwinter, *County Cricket*, p. 74; K. Sandiford, 'The professionalization of modern cricket', *British Journal of Sports History*, 1985, vol. 2, no. 3, p. 273.

29 Mason, 'Football', p. 165.

30 Ibid. See also I. Taylor, 'Professional sport and the recession: the case of British soccer', *International Review for the Sociology of Sport*, 1984, vol. 19, no. 1, especially pp. 13–20.

31 Sandiford, 'Professionalization of modern cricket', p. 273.

32 Dunning and Sheard, *Barbarians, Gentlemen and Players*, pp. 229–31.

33 Gate, *Rugby League*, p. 105.

34 E. Dunning, P. Murphy, and John Williams, *The Roots of Football Hooliganism: an historical and sociological study*, London, RKP, 1988, p. 133.

35 S. Barnett, *Games and Sets: the changing face of sport on television*, London, British Film Institute, 1990, pp. 9–18; G. Whannel, *Fields in Vision: television sport and cultural transformation*, London, Routledge, 1992, pp. 80–1. For independent television, see B. Sendall, *Independent Television in Britain: Volume I, Origin and Foundation, 1946–62*, London, Macmillan, 1982; B. Sendall, *Independent Television in Britain: Volume II, Expansion and Change, 1958–68*, London, Macmillan, 1983; J. Potter, *Independent Television in Britain: Volume III, Politics and Control, 1968–1980*, London, Macmillan, 1988. For the BBC in this period see A. Briggs, *The History of Broadcasting in the United Kingdom: Volume IV, Sound and Vision*, Oxford, Oxford University Press, 1979.

36 G. Whannel, *Fields in Vision*, p. 81; J. Maguire, 'More than a sporting touchdown: the making of American Football in England 1982–1990', *Sociology of Sport Journal*, 1990, vol. 7, no. 3, pp. 213–37. For Channel 4, see G. Whannel, *Sport on 4*, London, Windsor, 1988.

37 S. Garfield, *The Wrestling*, London, Faber and Faber, 1996.

38 Mason, 'Football', p. 165.

39 C. Brookes, *English Cricket: the game and its players through the ages*, London, Weidenfeld and Nicolson, 1978, p. 156.

40 Smith, *Queen of Games*, p. 146.

41 Gratton and Taylor, *Sport and recreation*, pp. 217–27.

42 Central Council of Physical Recreation, *Howell Report*, p. 77.

43 Mason, *Sport in Britain*, p. 5.

44 C. Critcher, 'Media spectacles: sport and mass communication', in A. Cashdan and M. Jordin (eds), *Studies in Communication*, Oxford, Blackwell, 1987, p. 142.

45 Gratton and Taylor, *Sport and recreation*, p. 223.

46 N. Wilson, *The Sports Business: the men and the money*, London, Piatkus, 1988, p. 163.
47 Gratton and Taylor, *Sport and recreation*, p. 220. For a wider consideration of tobacco advertising that includes a discussion of sports sponsorship, see S. Chapman, *Great Expectorations: advertising and the tobacco industry*, London, Comedia, 1986.
48 Cashmore, *Making Sense of Sports*, p. 187.
49 J. Lowerson, 'Golf', in Mason (ed.), *Sport in Britain*, p. 211.
50 Gate, *Rugby League*, p. 144.
51 See Mason, *Sport in Britain*, p. 5; Gratton and Taylor, *Sport and recreation*, pp. 222–6.
52 Mason, *Sport in Britain*, p. 89.
53 Taylor, 'Professional sport and the recession', p. 11; Mason, 'Football', pp. 163–7; T. Arnold, 'Rich man, poor man: economic arrangements in the Football League', in John Williams and S. Wagg (eds), *British Football and Social Change: getting into Europe*, Leicester, Leicester University Press, 1991, pp. 51–2. For an account of the Tottenham experience based largely on the views of the Chairman, Irving Scholar, see N. Wilson, *The Sports Business: the men and the money*, London, Piatkus, 1988, pp. 109–24.
54 See J. Brower, 'Professional sports team ownership: fun, profit and ideology of the power elite', *Journal of Sport and Social Issues*, 1976, vol. 1, no. 1, pp. 16–51.
55 Sandiford, 'Professionalization of modern cricket', p. 272.
56 Quoted in Vamplew, 'Horse-racing', p. 239; W. Vamplew, *The Turf*, p. 238.
57 C. Critcher, 'Football since the war', in J. Clarke, C. Critcher, and R. Johnson (eds), *Working Class Culture: studies in history and theory*, London, Hutchinson, 1979, p. 171. See also Chapter 5 below.
58 K. Brady, *Brady Plays the Blues: my diary of the season*, London, Pavilion, 1995, picture caption 6. See also pp. 25–35 for an account of her arrival and first impressions on the amateur administrative structures in place.
59 T. Mason, 'Football', p. 166.
60 A. Longmore, 'Football puts its shirt on profit', *The Times*, 19 December 1994, p. 27.
61 C. Hill, *Olympic Politics*, Manchester, Manchester University Press, 1992, pp. 74–81.
62 N. Wilson, *Sports Business*, pp. 33–46.
63 J. Maguire, 'More than a sporting touchdown: the making of American Football in England 1982–1990', *Sociology of Sport Journal*, 1990, vol. 7, no. 3, pp. 226–7.
64 W. Vamplew, 'Horse-racing', p. 226.
65 Christopher Gorringe, Chief Executive of the AELTCC, quoted in Wilson, *Sports Business*, p. 46.
66 S. Inglis, *Football Grounds of Britain*, third edition, London, CollinsWillow, 1996, pp. 104–13, 144, 405.
67 S. Kelner, *To Jerusalem and Back*, London, Macmillan, 1996, p. 76.
68 G. Moorhouse, *People's Game*, p. 280.
69 Inglis, *Football Grounds*, p. 202; Gate, *Rugby League*, p. 135.
70 Moorhouse, *People's Game*, pp. 295–6; Gate, *Rugby League*, pp. 134–5.

71 A. Baker, 'Hall's city of sporting dreams', *Independent on Sunday*, 8 October 1995, p. 24.
72 Sir B. Batsford, *The Times*, 14 June 1974, reprinted in M. Williams (ed.), *The Way to Lord's: cricketing letters to The Times*, London, Willow, 1983, p. 123.
73 Quoted in D. Marqusee, *Anyone But England: cricket and the national malaise*, London, Verso, 1994, p. 15.
74 Gratton and Taylor, *Sport and Recreation*, p. 227.
75 Ibid., p.229.
76 S. O'Hagan, 'Home truths for a tournament too far', *Independent on Sunday*, 15 October 1995, p. 24.
77 Jack Williams, 'Cricket', p. 124.
78 J. Arlott, 'Merits of the over-limit game are clear', *Cricket Spotlight*, 1972, reprinted in D. R. Allen (ed.), *Arlott on Cricket: his writings on the game*, London, Fontana, 1985, p. 216.
79 Smith, *Queen of Games*, p. 148.
80 Dunning and Sheard, *Barbarians, Gentlemen and Players*, pp. 248–50.

4 SPORT AND GENDER

1 See E. Cashmore, *United Kingdom? Class, race and gender since the war*, London, Unwin Hyman, 1989, part 3.
2 M. Messner and D. Sabo, 'Introduction: toward a critical feminist reappraisal of sport, men, and the gender order', in M. Messner and D. Sabo (eds), *Sport, Men, and the Gender Order: critical feminist perspectives*, Champaign, IL, Human Kinetics, 1990, p. 9.
3 A. Dewar, 'Sexual oppression in sport: past, present, and future alternatives', in A. Ingham and J. Loy (eds), *Sport in Social Development: traditions, transitions and transformations*, Champaign, IL, Human Kinetics, 1993, p. 167.
4 See E. Cashmore, *Making Sense of Sports*, second edition, London, Routledge, 1996, p. 130, for a graph illustrating comparative marathon performances.
5 Jennifer Hargreaves, *Sporting Females: critical issues in the history and sociology of women's sport*, London, Routledge, 1994, p. 155.
6 John Williams and J. Woodhouse, 'Can play, will play? Women and football in Britain', in John Williams and S. Wagg (eds), *British Football and Social Change: getting into Europe*, Leicester, Leicester University Press, 1991, p. 85.
7 See M. Simpson, *Male Impersonators: men performing masculinity*, London, Cassell, 1994, p. 91. I am grateful to Jude Davies for this reference.
8 R. Holt, *Sport and the British: a modern history*, Oxford, Oxford University Press, 1989, p. 8.
9 Quoted in J. Coakley, *Sport in Society: issues and controversies*, fifth edition, St Louis, Mosby, 1994, p. 226.
10 C. Parratt, 'From the history of women in sport to women's sport history: a research agenda', in D. M. Costa and S. R. Guthrie (eds), *Women and Sport: interdisciplinary perspectives*, Champaign, IL, Human Kinetics, 1994, p. 8.

11 Compare D. Frith, *The Golden Age of Cricket, 1890–1914*, London, Lutterworth, 1978, with claims for 'the Golden Age' in R. Flint and N. Rheinberg, *Fair Play: the story of women's cricket*, London, Angus and Robertson, 1976, p. 37.

12 E. Dunning, 'Sport as a male preserve: notes on the social sources of masculine identity and its transformations', *Theory, Culture and Society*, 1986, vol. 3, no. 1, p. 79.

13 For critical introductions to feminist theory as it has been applied to sport, see Jennifer Hargreaves, *Sporting Females*, pp. 25–41; G. Jarvie and J. Maguire, *Sport and Leisure in Social Thought*, London, Routledge, 1994, pp. 161–82.

14 Coakley, *Sport in Society*, p. 209.

15 M. Shoebridge, *Women in Sport: a select bibliography*, London, Mansell, 1987.

16 See, for example, G. Lerner, *The Majority Finds its Past: placing women in history*, New York, Oxford University Press, 1979; R. Bridenthal and C. Koonz (eds), *Becoming Visible: women in European history*, Boston, Houghton Mifflin, 1977; S. Rowbotham, *Hidden from History*, London, Pluto, 1973.

17 Jennifer Hargreaves, *Sporting Females*. Her bibliography provides an excellent guide to the literature.

18 Parratt, 'From the history of women in sport', p. 6.

19 A. Blue, *Grace Under Pressure: the emergence of women in sport*, London, Sidgwick and Jackson, 1987, pp. xii, 187–91.

20 Quoted on ibid., dustjacket.

21 K. Dyer, *Catching Up the Men: women in sport*, London, Junction Books, 1982, p. 3.

22 B. Birkett and B. Peascod, *Women Climbing: 200 years of achievement*, London, A & C Black, 1989; A. Martin, *The Equestrian Woman*, New York, Paddington, 1979; C. Ramsden, *Ladies in Racing: sixteenth century to the present day*, London, Stanley Paul, 1973.

23 E. P. Thompson, *The Making of the English Working Class*, revised edition, Harmondsworth, Penguin, 1980, p. 12.

24 See Jennifer Hargreaves, *Sporting Females*, pp. 26–9. For a general overview of theorising women in sport, see Parratt, 'From the history of women in sport', pp. 5–14; Dewar, 'Sexual oppression in sport', pp. 147–66.

25 Jennifer Hargreaves, *Sporting Females*, p. 1.

26 Dewar, 'Sexual oppression in sport', p. 158.

27 Costa and Guthrie (eds), *Women and Sport*.

28 P. Willis, 'Women in sport in ideology', in Jennifer Hargreaves (ed.), *Sport, culture and ideology*, London, RKP, 1982, p. 117. Emphasis in original.

29 M. Roper and J. Tosh, 'Introduction: historians and the politics of masculinity', in M. Roper and J. Tosh (eds), *Manful Assertions: masculinities in Britain since 1800*, London, Routledge, 1991, p. 1.

30 Quoted in N. Fishwick, *English Football and Society, 1910–1950*, Manchester, Manchester University Press, 1989, p. 147.

31 Quoted in S. Garfield, *The Wrestling*, London, Faber and Faber, 1996, pp. 105–6.

32 See, for example, E. Dunning, P. Murphy, and J. Williams, *The Roots of Football Hooliganism: an historical and sociological study*, London, RKP, 1988;

P. Murphy, J. Williams, and E. Dunning, 'Life with the Kingsley Lads: community, masculinity and football', in *Football on Trial: spectator violence and development in the football world*, London, Routledge, 1990, pp. 129–66.

33 See, for example, J. A. Mangan, 'Duty unto death: English masculinity and militarism in the age of New Imperialism', *International Journal of the History of Sport*, 1995, vol. 12, no. 2, pp. 10–38; J. A. Mangan, '"Muscular, Militaristic and Manly": the British middle-class hero as moral messenger', *International Journal of the History of Sport*, 1996, vol. 13, no. 1, pp. 28–47; J. A. Mangan, 'Games field and battlefield: a romantic alliance in verse and the creation of militaristic masculinity', in J. Nauright and T. Chandler (eds), *Making Men: rugby and masculine identity*, London, Frank Cass, 1996, pp. 140–57.

34 J. A. Mangan and J. Walvin (eds), *Manliness and Morality: middle-class masculinity in Britain and America, 1800–1940*, Manchester, Manchester University Press, 1987.

35 T. Chandler and J. Nauright, 'Introduction: rugby, manhood and identity', in Nauright and Chandler (eds), *Making Men*, p. 1.

36 M. Messner, *Power at Play: sports and the problem of masculinity*, Boston, Beacon Press, 1992; Messner and Sabo (eds), *Sport, Men and the Gender Order*; B. Pronger, *The Arena of Masculinity: sports, homosexuality, and the meaning of sex*, London, GMP, 1990; M. Simpson, 'Big tits! Masochism and transformation in bodybuilding' and 'Active sports: the anus and its goal-posts', in *Male Impersonators*, pp. 21–44, 69–93.

37 Coakley, *Sport in Society*, p. 226.

38 Pronger, *The Arena of Masculinity*, p. 125.

39 Simpson, 'Active sports'.

40 Cashmore, *Making Sense of Sports*, p. 119.

41 Jennifer Hargreaves, *Sporting Females*, p. 8.

42 Quoted in Blue, *Grace Under Pressure*, p. 44.

43 J. A. May, 'The lady champions', in A. Elliott and J. A. May, *A History of Golf*, London, Chancellor, 1994, p. 166.

44 Williams and Woodhouse, 'Can play, will play?'.

45 Dyer, *Catching up the Men*, p. 205.

46 Jennifer Hargreaves, *Sporting Females*, pp. 143–4.

47 Quoted in Blue, *Grace Under Pressure*, p. 72.

48 British Olympic Association, *Great Britain and the Olympic Games*, London, British Olympic Association, 1987, p. 33.

49 Flint and Rheinberg, *Fair Play*, pp. 47–9.

50 A. Turnbull, *Running Together: every woman's running guide*, London, Unwin, 1986, p. 61.

51 Quoted in ibid., pp. 19, 41.

52 See Jennifer Hargreaves, *Sporting Females*, pp. 145–73; G. Whannel, 'Building our bodies to beat the best: notes on sport, work and fitness chic', in A. Tomlinson (ed.), *Sport in Society: policy, politics and culture*, Brighton, Leisure Studies Association, 1990, pp. 119–27.

53 M. MacNeill, 'Active women, media representations, and ideology', in J. Harvey and H. Cantelon (eds), *Not Just a Game: essays in Canadian sport sociology*, Ottawa, University of Ottawa Press, 1988, p. 200.

54 Flint and Rheinberg, *Fair Play*, pp. 28–33, 149–51.

55 Ibid., pp. 168–72.

56 Williams and Woodhouse, 'Can play, will play?', p. 101.

57 Jennifer Hargreaves, *Sporting Females*, pp. 287–8.

58 Ramsden, *Ladies in Racing*, p. 119.

59 Quoted in Martin, *The Equestrian Woman*, p. 199.

60 Quoted in Ramsden, *Ladies in Racing*, p. 116.

61 Quoted in ibid., p. 119.

62 Ibid., pp. 154–66; Martin, *The Equestrian Woman*, pp. 204–9.

63 Quoted in Williams and Woodhouse, 'Can play, will play?', p. 98.

64 Title IX of the 1972 Education Amendments Act stated that 'No person in the United States shall, on the basis of sex, be excluded from participation, be denied the benefits of, or be subjected to any discrimination under any educational program or activity receiving federal financial assistance.' (Quoted in Dyer, *Catching up the Men*, p. 116.) For critical discussions of its application to sport, see Coakley, *Sport in Society*, pp. 217–18; Cashmore, *Making Sense of Sports*, pp. 133–4.

65 Garfield, *The Wrestling*, p. 114.

66 A. Little, *Wimbledon Compendium 1991*, Wimbledon, All England Lawn Tennis and Croquet Club, 1991, p. 122. For a wider discussion of differential prize money, see D. Marple, 'Tournament earnings and performance differentials between the sexes in professional golf and tennis', *Journal of Sport and Social Issues*, 1983, vol. 7, no. 1, pp. 1–14.

67 N. Smith, *Queen of Games: the history of croquet*, London, Weidenfeld and Nicolson, 1991, pp. 168–9.

68 Ibid., p. 54.

69 D. Wallechinsky, *The Complete Book of the Olympics*, revised edition, Harmondsworth, Penguin, 1988, pp. 243, 247, 251. See also Martin, *The Equestrian Woman*, pp. 17–18, 210.

70 K. Summerfield and A. White, 'Korfball: a model of egalitarianism?', *Sociology of Sport Journal*, 1989, vol. 6, no. 2, p. 150. See also B. Crum, 'A critical analysis of Korfball as a non-sexist sport', *International Review for the Sociology of Sport*, 1988, vol. 23, no. 3, pp. 233–43; Jennifer Hargreaves, *Sporting Females*, pp. 248–50. For a description and history of Korfball, see J. Arlott (ed.), *The Oxford Companion to Sports and Games*, Oxford, Oxford University Press, 1975, pp. 582–4.

71 Sports Council, *Women and Sport: policy and frameworks for action*, London, Sports Council, 1993.

72 G. Whannel, *Blowing the Whistle: the politics of sport*, London, Pluto Press, 1983, p. 78.

73 B. Houlihan, *The Government and Politics of Sport*, London, Routledge, 1991, p. 16.

74 J. Coakley and A. White, 'Making decisions: gender and sport participation among British adolescents', *Sociology of Sport Journal*, 1992, vol. 9, no. 1, pp. 20–35.

75 Sports Council, *Women and Sport*, p. 43.

76 S. Alexander, 'Gender bias in British television coverage of major athletics championships', *Women's Studies International Forum*, 1994, vol. 17, no. 6,

pp. 647–54. See also G. Whannel, *Fields in Vision: television sport and cultural transformation*, London, Routledge, 1992, pp. 126–9.

77 M. Dunne, 'An introduction to some of the images of sport in girls' comics and magazines', in Centre for Contemporary Cultural Studies, *Sporting Fictions*, Birmingham, University of Birmingham, 1982, p. 36–59. See also Jennifer Hargreaves, *Sporting Females*, pp. 149–50.

78 Quoted in Flint and Rheinberg, *Fair Play*, p. 50.

79 Quoted in Whannel, *Fields in Vision*, p. 127.

80 C. Hendrie and L. Brannan, 'Ride into history', *Mail on Sunday*, 19 May 1996, p. 96. I am grateful to Karen Winterson for this reference.

81 Blue, *Grace Under Pressure*, p. 13.

82 Quoted in Whannel, *Fields in Vision*, p. 128.

83 Sports Council, *Women and Sport*, p. 23.

84 B. Johnston, 'Foreword', in Flint and Rheinberg, *Fair Play*, p. 10.

85 Quoted in Williams and Woodhouse, 'Can play, will play?', p. 98.

86 Quoted in Whannel, *Fields in Vision*, p. 127.

87 Flint and Rheinberg, *Fair Play*, p. 173.

88 M. Savidge, 'Stuff the sandwiches', in A. McLellan (ed.), *Nothing Sacred: the new cricket culture*, London, Two Heads, 1996, p. 74.

89 Jennifer Hargreaves, *Sporting Females*, p. 287.

90 Messner and Sabo (eds), *Sport, Men, and the Gender Order*.

91 Dunning, 'Sport as a male preserve', p. 79.

92 Nauright and Chandler (eds), *Making Men*.

93 Little, *Wimbledon Compendium*, p. 122.

94 Roper and Tosh, 'Introduction', p. 1.

95 W. Hicks, 'Coronation year'; 'Take a hint from the stars'; R. McWhirter, 'Young men turn to rugby', in W. Hicks (ed), *News Chronicle Boys' Book of All Sports*, London, News Chronicle Book Department, undated (1953/4), pp. 6, 66, 154–9.

96 Quoted in L. Leaman, 'Sport and the feminist novel', in Centre for Contemporary Cultural Studies, *Sporting Fictions*, p. 279.

97 Garfield, *The Wrestling*, pp. 36–43.

98 Quoted in S. Wagg, *The Football World: a contemporary social history*, Brighton, Harvester, 1984, p. 143.

99 P. White and A. Vagi, 'Rugby in the 19th-Century British boarding-school system: a feminist psychoanalytic perspective', in Messner and Sabo (eds), *Sport, Men, and the Gender Order*, pp. 67–78; Dunning, 'Sport as a male preserve'.

100 Dunning, Murphy, and Williams, *The Roots of Football Hooliganism*.

101 Holt, *Sport and the British*, p. 8.

102 *Bee-sotted*, no. 6, undated, no page numbers.

103 Dunning, 'Sport as a male preserve', p. 84. See also White and Vagi, 'Rugby in the 19th-Century British boarding-school system', pp. 75–7.

104 Quoted in G. Smith (ed.), *Take the Ball and Run: a rugby anthology*, London, Pavilion, 1991, p. 131.

105 Simpson, 'Big tits!'; Simpson, 'Active sports'; B. Pronger, 'Gay jocks: a phenomenology of gay men in athletics', in Messner and Sabo (eds) *Sport, Men, and the Gender Order*, pp. 141–52; B. Pronger, *The Arena of Masculinity*.

106 See R. Nixon, *Homelands, Harlem and Hollywood: South African culture and the world beyond*, London, Routledge, 1994, p. 136.
107 'What are you looking at?', *Independent on Sunday, Real Life*, 13 August 1995, p. 6.

5 SPORT, SOCIAL CLASS, AND PROFESSIONAL STATUS

1 A. Hopcraft, *The Football Man: people and passions in soccer*, London, Simon & Schuster, 1988, p. 179.
2 John Hargreaves, *Sport, Power and Culture: a social and historical analysis of popular sports in Britain*, Cambridge, Polity, 1986.
3 For concise critical analyses of class divisions in post-war Britain, see E. Cashmore, *United Kingdom? Class, race and gender since the war*, London, Unwin Hyman, 1989, pp. 13–76; R. Hudson and A. Williams, *Divided Britain*, second edition, Chichester, Wiley, 1995, pp. 50–132.
4 I. Reid, *Social Class Differences in Britain: life-chances and life-styles*, third edition, London, Fontana, 1989, p. xxv.
5 Ibid., pp. 27–90.
6 T. Mason, *Association Football and English Society, 1863–1915*, Hassocks, Harvester, 1980; W. Vamplew, *The Turf: a social and economic history of horse racing*, London, Allen Lane, 1976; P. Bailey, *Leisure and Class in Victorian England: rational recreation and the contest for control, 1830–1885*, London, RKP, 1978; John Hargreaves, *Sport, Power and Culture*; S. Jones, *Workers at Play: a social and economic history of leisure 1918–1939*, London, RKP, 1986; S. Jones, *Sport, Politics and the Working Class: organised labour and sport in interwar Britain*, Manchester, Manchester University Press, 1988; J. Lowerson, *Sport and the English Middle Class 1870–1914*, Manchester, Manchester University Press, 1993.
7 R. Holt, *Sport and the British: a modern history*, Oxford, Oxford University Press, 1989.
8 R. Holt, 'Introduction', in R. Holt (ed.), *Sport and the Working Class in Modern Britain*, Manchester, Manchester University Press, 1990, p. 1.
9 P. Bourdieu, 'Sport and social class', *Social Science Information*, 1978, vol. 17, no. 6, pp. 832–3.
10 B. Dabscheck, 'Defensive Manchester: a history of the Professional Footballers Association', in R. Cashman and M. McKernan (eds), *Sport in History: the making of modern sporting history*, St Lucia, University of Queensland Press, 1979, pp. 227–57.
11 S. Wagg, *The Football World: a contemporary social history*, Brighton, Harvester, 1984, pp. 101–20; S. Redhead, 'The legalisation of the professional footballer: a study of some aspects of the legal status and employment conditions of Association Football players in England and Wales from the late nineteenth century to the present day', PhD thesis, School of Law, University of Warwick, 1984; '"You've really got a hold on me": footballers in the market', in A. Tomlinson and G. Whannel (eds), *Off The Ball: the football World Cup*, London, Pluto, 1986, pp. 54–66.
12 Quoted in Wagg, *The Football World*, p. 117.
13 L. Shackleton, *Clown Prince of Soccer: his autobiography*, London, Nicholas Kaye, 1955, p. 17.
14 Quoted in R. Taylor and A. Ward, *Kicking and Screaming: an oral history of*

football in England, London, Robson, 1995, pp. 80–1. See also T. Mason, 'The Bogotá affair', in J. Bale and J. Maguire (eds), *The Global Sports Arena: athletic talent migration in an interdependent world*, London, Frank Cass, 1994, pp. 39–48.

15 Wagg, *The Football World*, p. 116. Redhead links the name change itself to the players' perceived change in status: Redhead, 'The legalisation of the professional footballer', p. 115.

16 See Redhead, 'The legalisation of the professional footballer', pp. 104–45; Wagg, *The Football World*, pp. 101–20. For Jimmy Hill's own account of the dispute and its context, see Jimmy Hill, *Striking for Soccer*, London, Peter Davies, 1961. Useful reflections on the dispute from Hill, Goodhart, and others involved can be found in Taylor and Ward, *Kicking and Screaming*, pp. 151–8.

17 Quoted in Taylor and Ward, *Kicking and Screaming*, p. 154.

18 G. Eastham, *Determined to Win*, London, Stanley Paul, 1964, p. 79.

19 Ibid., p. 118.

20 B. Dabscheck, 'Player associations and professional team sports', *Labour and Society*, 1979, vol. 4, no. 3, p. 234.

21 Redhead, 'The legalisation of the professional footballer', p. 127. See also Wagg, *The Football World*, p. 120; Redhead, '"You've really got a hold on me"', pp. 55–6.

22 Transfer figures taken from B. Bateson and A. Sewell (eds), *News of the World Football Annual, 1989–90*, London, Invincible, 1990, pp. 245–8.

23 Wagg, *The Football World*, p. 102.

24 T. Mason, 'Football', in T. Mason (ed.), *Sport in Britain*, Cambridge, Cambridge University Press, 1989, pp. 162–3.

25 Dabscheck, 'Player associations', pp. 234–5.

26 C. Critcher, 'Football since the war', in J. Clarke, C. Critcher, and R. Johnson (eds), *Working Class Culture: studies in history and theory*, London, Hutchinson, 1979, p. 164. See Redhead, 'The legalisation of the professional footballer', pp. 149–50, for a critique of Critcher's model.

27 Critcher, 'Football since the war' p. 167.

28 H. Davies, *The Glory Game*, London, Sphere, 1973, p. 8.

29 Ibid., p. 312.

30 P. Douglas, *The Football Industry*, London, George Allen and Unwin, 1973, pp. 127–8.

31 Ibid., p. 118.

32 Redhead, 'The legalisation of the professional footballer', p. 146.

33 Ibid., p. 150. Emphasis in original.

34 R. Sissons, *The Players: a social history of the professional cricketer*, London, Kingswood, 1988, p. 274. See also K. Sandiford, 'The professionalization of modern cricket', *British Journal of Sports History*, 1985, vol. 2, no. 3, p. 271.

35 Holt, *Sport and the British*, p. 292; Sandiford, 'Professionalization of modern cricket', p. 271.

36 R. Bowen, *Cricket: a history of its growth and development throughout the world*, London, Eyre and Spottiswoode, 1970, p. 207.

37 C. Brookes, *English Cricket: the game and its players through the ages*, London, Weidenfeld and Nicolson, 1978, p. 157.

38 Sissons, *The Players*, pp. 280–2.
39 D. Marqusee, *Anyone But England: cricket and the national malaise*, London, Verso, 1994, p. 124. See also Sissons, *The Players*, pp. 287–92.
40 J. Arlott, 'Growth of the Cricketers' Association', *The Cricketer*, March 1979; reprinted in D. R. Allen (ed.), *Arlott on Cricket: his writings on the game*, London, Fontana, 1985, p. 220. See also Sandiford, 'Professionalization of modern cricket', pp. 281–2.
41 Marqusee, *Anyone But England*, pp. 104–10.
42 G. Moorhouse, *A People's Game: the centenary history of Rugby League, 1895–1995*, London, Hodder and Stoughton, 1995, p. 299.
43 F. Perry, *An Autobiography*, London, Arrow, 1984, pp. 85–6.
44 Jimmy Hill, *Striking for Soccer*, p. 122.
45 Wagg, *The Football World*, p. 123.
46 T. Mason, 'Football', p. 163; Wagg, *The Football World*, p. 145.
47 F. Keating. 'Over to you, Bill', *The Guardian*, 17 October 1995, Section 2, p. 5.
48 E. Dunning and K. Sheard, *Barbarians, Gentlemen and Players: a sociological study of the development of rugby football*, Oxford, Martin Robertson, 1979, pp. 232–68.
49 G. Williams, 'Rugby Union', in Mason (ed.), *Sport in Britain*, p. 333.
50 D. Smith and G. Williams, *Fields of Praise: the official history of the Welsh Rugby Union 1881–1981*, Cardiff, University of Wales Press, 1980, p. 417.
51 Moorhouse, *A People's Game*, pp. 292–3.
52 Dunning and Sheard, *Barbarians, Gentlemen and Players*, p. 260.
53 Quoted in D. Hands, 'RFU men call for Carling apology', *The Times*, 5 May 1995, p. 48.
54 Sandiford, 'Professionalization of modern cricket', p. 272.
55 J. Crump, 'Athletics', in Mason (ed.), *Sport in Britain*, p. 75.
56 Ibid., p. 56.
57 John Hargreaves, *Sport, Power and Culture*, pp. 111–12.
58 T. Veblen, *The Theory of the Leisure Class*, London, Unwin, 1970.
59 See, for example, R. Gruneau, *Class, Sports, and Social Development*, Amherst, MA, University of Massachusetts Press, 1983.
60 Bourdieu, 'Sport and social class'. For a critical discussion of Bourdieu's work and its application to sport, see G. Jarvie and J. Maguire, *Sport and Leisure in Social Thought*, London, Routledge, 1994, pp. 183–210.
61 Gruneau, *Class, Sports*, p. 53.
62 Bourdieu, 'Sport and social class', p. 834.
63 J.-M. Brohm, *Sport: a prison of measured time*, London, Ink Links, 1978. See especially 'Twenty theses on sport', pp. 175–82.
64 John Hargreaves, *Sport, Power and Culture*, p. 99.
65 Vamplew, *The Turf*, p. 12.
66 John Hargreaves, *Sport, Power and Culture*.
67 Bourdieu, 'Sport and social class', p. 820.
68 R. Carr, *English Fox Hunting: a history*, revised edition, London, Weidenfeld and Nicolson, 1986, pp. 230–46.
69 'A-hunting we will go', *Class War*, undated [1985], no page number.
70 T. Carroll, *Diary of a Fox-Hunting Man*, London, Futura, 1984, p. 130.

71   C. McKenzie, 'The origins of the British Field Sports Society', *International Journal of the History of Sport*, 1996, vol. 13, no. 2, p. 185.

72   Sports Council, *A Digest of Sports Statistics for the UK*, third edition, London, Sports Council, 1991, p. 143. For a detailed discussion of class politics and property relations in Scotland, see G. Jarvie, 'Dependency, cultural identity and sporting landlords: a Scottish case-study', *British Journal of Sports History*, 1986, vol. 3, no. 1, pp. 42–54.

73   Sports Council, *Digest of Sports Statistics*, p. 124.

74   B. Stoddart, 'Golf international: considerations of sport in the global marketplace', in R. Wilcox (ed.), *Sport in the Global Village*, Morgantown, WV, Fitness Information Technology, 1994, p. 30.

75   Sports Council, *Digest of Sports Statistics*, pp. 154–5.

76   Dunning and Sheard, *Barbarians, Gentlemen and Players*, p. 240.

77   Holt, *Sport and the British*, p. 133.

78   R. Holt, 'Working class football and the city: the problem of continuity', *British Journal of Sports History*, 1986, vol. 3, no. 1, pp. 5–17.

79   J. Clarke, 'Football and working class fans: tradition and change', in R. Ingham (ed.), *'Football Hooliganism': the wider context*, London, Inter-Action Inprint, 1978, pp. 49–50; emphasis in original. See also I. Taylor, '"Football Mad": a speculative sociology of football hooliganism', in E. Dunning (ed.), *The Sociology of Sport: a selection of readings*, London, Frank Cass, 1971, pp. 352–77; I. Taylor, 'On the sports violence question: soccer hooliganism revisited', in Jennifer Hargreaves (ed.), *Sport, Culture and Ideology*, London, RKP, 1982, pp. 152–96; I. Taylor, 'Class, violence and sport: the case of soccer hooliganism in Britain', in H. Cantelon and R. Gruneau (eds), *Sport, Culture and the Modern State*, Toronto, University of Toronto Press, 1982, pp. 39–96. This approach is summarised and critically considered in E. Dunning, P. Murphy, and John Williams, *The Roots of Football Hooliganism: an historical and sociological study*, London, RKP, 1988, pp. 23–31. For Taylor's response, see I. Taylor, 'Putting the boot into a working-class sport: British soccer after Bradford and Brussels', *Sociology of Sport Journal*, 1987, vol. 4, no. 2, pp. 176–9.

80   Dunning, Murphy, and Williams, *The Roots of Football Hooliganism*, p. 30.

81   Ibid.; John Williams, E. Dunning, and P. Murphy, *Hooligans Abroad*, second edition, London, Routledge, 1989; P. Murphy, John Williams, and E. Dunning, *Football on Trial: spectator violence and development in the football world*, London, Routledge, 1990; John Williams, 'Having an away day: English football spectators and the hooligan debate', in John Williams and S. Wagg (eds), *British Football and Social Change: getting into Europe*, Leicester, Leicester University Press, 1991, pp. 160–84.

82   Dunning, Murphy, and Williams, *The Roots of Football Hooliganism*, pp. 186–91.

83   Taylor, 'Putting the boot in', p. 175.

84   Olly Croft, quoted in J. Duncan, 'Darts swept from the board', *The Guardian*, 14 February 1996, p. 27. I am grateful to Neil Curtin for this reference.

85   G. Beattie, *On The Ropes: boxing as a way of life*, London, Victor Gollancz, 1996.

86   S. Garfield, *The Wrestling*, London, Faber and Faber, 1996.

87 Gruneau, *Class, Sports*, p. 75, citing A. Giddens.
88 I. MacQuillin, 'Who's afraid of the Barmy Army', in A. McLellan (ed.), *Nothing Sacred: the new cricket culture*, London, Two Heads, 1996, pp. 37–54.
89 Bourdieu, 'Sport and social class', p. 835.

6 SPORT AND ETHNICITY

1 Quoted in D. Hill, *"Out Of His Skin": the John Barnes phenomenon*, London, Faber and Faber, 1989, p. 125. See also D. Hill, 'Black on red', *New Society*, 11 December 1987, pp. 19–21.
2 For an agenda on using 'physicality' as a way of analysing the links between gender and race in sport, see S. Birrell, 'Racial relations theories and sports: suggestions for a more critical analysis', *Sociology of Sport Journal*, 1989, vol. 6, no. 3, p. 222.
3 K. Mercer, *Welcome to the Jungle: new positions in black cultural studies*, London, Routledge, 1994, pp. 178–9.
4 For a critical discussion of 'the Tebbit test', see D. Marqusee, *Anyone But England: cricket and the national malaise*, London, Verso, 1994, pp. 137–41. The book's title is taken from Labour MP Dennis Skinner's response to the question of who he would support in a Test Match: see p. 250.
5 E. Cashmore, *United Kingdom? Class, race and gender since the war*, London, Unwin Hyman, 1989, p. 122. See also J. Coakley, *Sport in Society: issues and controversies*, fifth edition, St Louis, Mosby, 1994, pp. 240–2, for a brief overview.
6 R. Hudson and A. Williams, *Divided Britain*, second edition, Chichester, John Wiley, 1995, p. 177.
7 Coakley, *Sport in Society*, pp. 240–2.
8 Quoted in K. Malik, 'Minorities face soccer "wall"', *Independent on Sunday*, 17 September 1995, p. 9.
9 P. Fryer, *Staying Power: the history of black people in Britain*, London, Pluto, 1984, pp. xi, 1–2.
10 C. Holmes, 'Immigration', in T. Gourvish and A. O'Day (eds), *Britain Since 1945*, London, Macmillan, 1991, pp. 209–11.
11 Fryer, *Staying Power*, pp. 372–99; C. Holmes, *John Bull's Island: immigration and British society, 1871–1971*, Basingstoke, Macmillan, 1988; Holmes, 'Immigration'; C. Holmes, *A Tolerant Country? Immigrants, refugees and minorities in Britain*, London, Faber and Faber, 1991; Cashmore, *United Kingdom?*, pp. 79–158; Hudson and Williams, *Divided Britain*, pp. 177–217; P. Rich, *Race and Empire in British Politics*, second edition, Cambridge, Cambridge University Press, 1990, pp. 145–200.
12 E. Cashmore, *Making Sense of Sports*, second edition, London, Routledge, 1996, p. 104.
13 B. Carrington, T. Chivers, and T. Williams, 'Gender, leisure and sport: a case-study of young people of South Asian descent', *Leisure Studies*, 1987, vol. 6, pp. 265–79; R. Dixey, 'Asian women and sport: the Bradford experience', *British Journal of Physical Education*, 1982, vol. 13, no. 4, pp. 108, 114; S. Fleming, 'Sport, schooling and Asian male youth culture', in G. Jarvie (ed.), *Sport, Racism and Ethnicity*, London, Falmer, 1991, pp. 30–57; S. Fleming, *"Home and Away": sport and South Asian male youth*, Aldershot,

Ashgate, 1995; A. Lyons, *Asian Women and Sport*, London, Sports Council, 1988; G. Verma and D. Darby, *Winners and Losers: ethnic minorities in sport and recreation*, London, Falmer, 1994.

14 Malik, 'Minorities face soccer "wall"'; A. Lyons, 'Missing in action', *When Saturday Comes*, April 1995, no. 110, pp. 6–7.

15 H. Edwards, *The Revolt of the Black Athlete*, New York, Free Press, 1969; J. Scott, *The Athletic Revolution*, New York, Free Press, 1971.

16 S. Birrell, 'Racial relations theories and sports', p. 214. For a concise overview of the American research, particularly on stacking and centrality, see J. Maguire, 'Sport, racism and British society: a sociological study of England's élite male Afro/Caribbean soccer and Rugby Union players', in Jarvie (ed.), *Sport, Racism and Ethnicity*, pp. 97–9.

17 See Cashmore, *Making Sense of Sports*, pp. 104–6.

18 See Coakley, *Sport in Society*, pp. 239–73, for an overview of the issues.

19 Holmes, 'Immigration', p. 215.

20 J. Parry and N. Parry, 'Sport and the black experience', in Jarvie (ed.), *Sport, Racism and Ethnicity*, p. 150.

21 E. Cashmore, *Black Sportsmen*, London, RKP, 1982; *Making Sense of Sports*, pp. 97–116.

22 J. Maguire, 'Race and position assignment in English soccer: a preliminary analysis of ethnicity and sport in Britain', *Sociology of Sport Journal*, 1988, vol. 5, pp. 257–69; Maguire, 'Sport, racism and British society'; M. Melnick, 'Racial segregation by playing position in the English Football League: some preliminary observations', *Journal of Sport and Social Issues*, 1988, vol. 12, no. 2, pp. 122–30.

23 T. Mason, *Sport in Britain*, London, Faber and Faber, 1988, pp. 15–17.

24 Jarvie (ed.), *Sport, Racism and Ethnicity*.

25 Jeff Hill, 'Cricket and the imperial connection: overseas players in Lancashire in the inter-war period', in J. Bale and J. Maguire (eds), *The Global Sports Arena: athletic talent migration in an interdependent world*, London, Frank Cass, 1994, pp. 49–62; P. Vasali, 'Colonialism and football: the first Nigerian tour to Britain', *Race and Class*, 1995, vol. 36, no. 4, pp. 55–70. A concise summary of his research on the history of black footballers is provided in P. Vasali, 'Men out of time', *When Saturday Comes*, October 1993, no. 80, pp. 8–10.

26 M. Rivlin, 'Albert Memorial', *When Saturday Comes*, November 1995, no. 105, p. 10. See also 'Remember Albert', *Picture This*, BBC 2, 27 August 1996.

27 Holmes, *A Tolerant Country?*, p. 4.

28 Hudson and Williams, *Divided Britain*, p. 14.

29 Fryer, *Staying Power*, pp. 445–54; P. Gilroy, 'Frank Bruno or Salman Rushdie', in *Small Acts: thoughts on the politics of Black cultures*, London, Serpent's Tail, 1993, pp. 86–94.

30 J. Parry, *Participation by Black and Ethnic Minorities in Sport and Recreation: a review of literature*, London, London Research Centre, 1989.

31 Quoted in A. Longmore, *Viv Anderson*, London, Heinemann, 1988, p. xiv.

32 See Cashmore, *Black Sportsmen*, pp. 11–36, for a historical overview.

33 Jeff Hill, 'Cricket and the imperial connection'. For Constantine, see G. Howat, *Learie Constantine*, London, George Allen and Unwin, 1975.

34 C. L. R. James, *Beyond a Boundary*, London, Stanley Paul, 1963, p. 127.
35 Quoted in Cashmore, *Black Sportsmen*, p. 25.
36 Cashmore, *United Kingdom?*, pp. 79–80.
37 W. Daniel, *Racial Discrimination in England*, Harmondsworth, Penguin, 1968, p. 209.
38 For a concise summary of the legislation and wider issues, see Holmes, 'Immigration'.
39 E. Cashmore, 'The race season', *New Statesman and Society*, 1 June 1990, p. 10.
40 F. Bruno, *Eye of the Tiger: my life*, London, Weidenfeld and Nicolson, 1992, p. 96; L. Christie, *To Be Honest With You*, London, Michael Joseph, 1995, p. 37.
41 S. Shipley, 'Boxing', in T. Mason (ed.), *Sport in Britain: a social history*, Cambridge, Cambridge University Press, 1989, pp. 103–4; Cashmore, *Black Sportsmen*, p. 25.
42 BBBC rules, quoted in Cashmore, *Black Sportsmen*, p. 27.
43 Cashmore, *Black Sportsmen*, pp. 25–6. See also J. Birtley, *The Tragedy of Randolph Turpin*, London, New English Library, 1975; P. Walsh, *Men of Steel: the lives and times of boxing's middleweight champions*, London, Robson, 1993, pp. 149–56.
44 J. Harding, *Lonsdale's Belt: the story of boxing's greatest prize*, London, Robson, 1994, p. 272.
45 Quoted in Cashmore, *Black Sportsmen*, p. 76.
46 P. Hain, *Don't Play with Apartheid: the background to the Stop The Seventy Tour Campaign*, London, George Allen and Unwin, 1971, pp. 218–19.
47 See P. Thomas, 'Kicking racism out of football: a supporter's view', *Race and Class*, 1995, vol. 36, no. 4, pp. 95–101.
48 R. Haynes, *The Football Imagination: the rise of football fanzine culture*, Aldershot, Arena, 1995, pp. 131–42.
49 Thomas, 'Kicking racism out of football', p. 96.
50 Shipley, 'Boxing', pp. 99–103.
51 Quoted in Cashmore, *Black Sportsmen*, p. 26.
52 P. Lovesey, *The Official Centenary History of the Amateur Athletic Association*, Enfield, Guinness, 1979, pp. 93–8; Cashmore, *Black Sportsmen*, pp. 26–7.
53 Quoted in Cashmore, *Black Sportsmen*, p. 135.
54 Christie, *To Be Honest*, p. 34.
55 Shipley, 'Boxing', pp. 100–3; Cashmore, *Black Sportsmen*, p. 28.
56 Harding, *Lonsdale's Belt*, p. 272.
57 Cashmore, *Making Sense of Sports*, p. 99.
58 Quoted in Harding, *Lonsdale's Belt*, p. 278.
59 Vasali, 'Men out of time'; Vasali, 'Colonialism and football'.
60 B. Woolnough, *Black Magic: England's black footballers*, London, Pelham, 1983, p. 164.
61 See Longmore, *Viv Anderson*, pp. 7–16, for Anderson's family background and childhood.
62 Woolnough, *Black Magic*, p. 8.
63 Maguire, 'Race and position assignment', p. 262; Maguire, 'Sport, racism and British society', p. 104.
64 J. Latus, *Hard Road to the Top: the Clive Sullivan story*, Hull, Boulevard

Publications, 1973; G. Moorhouse, *A People's Game: the centenary history of Rugby League 1895–1995*, London, Hodder and Stoughton, 1995, p. 286.

65 A. McLellan, *The Enemy Within: the impact of overseas players on English cricket*, London, Blandford, 1994.

66 N. Scott and N. Cook, *England Test Cricket: the years of indecision, 1981–92*, London, Kingswood, 1992, pp. 29–31; Longmore, *Viv Anderson*, p. 11.

67 Quoted in Longmore, *Viv Anderson* p. 1.

68 Gilroy, 'Frank Bruno or Salman Rushdie', p. 87.

69 Bruno, *Eye of the Tiger*, p. 33.

70 R. Majors, 'Cool pose: black masculinity and sports', in M. Messner and D. Sabo (eds), *Sport, Men and the Gender Order: critical feminist perspectives*, Champaign, IL, Human Kinetics, 1990, pp. 109–14.

71 S. Small, *Racialised Barriers: the black experience in the United States and England in the 1980s*, London, Routledge, 1994, pp. 74–5.

72 R. Holt, *Sport and the British: a modern history*, Oxford, Oxford University Press, 1989, p. 303.

73 Coakley, *Sport in Society*, pp. 262–6. See also Cashmore, *Making Sense of Sports*, p. 104; Mason, *Sport in Britain*, pp. 13–18.

74 J. Walvin, *Football and the Decline of Britain*, London, Macmillan, 1986, pp. 72–4.

75 Coakley, *Sport in Society*, p. 243. See Cashmore, *Black Sportsmen*, pp. 42–56, for a critique of 'that black magic of nature'.

76 Quoted in Scott, *The Athletic Revolution*, p. 81.

77 Quoted in N. Ascherson, 'Once they blamed breast-feeding. New racists just measure the tendons', *Independent on Sunday*, 17 September 1995, p. 20.

78 Melnick, 'Racial segregation by playing position in the English Football League'.

79 Maguire, 'Sport, racism and British society', p. 106.

80 Maguire, 'Race and position assignment in English soccer'.

81 Maguire, 'Sport, racism and British society', p. 113.

82 Ibid., p. 120.

83 Quoted in Cashmore, *Black Sportsmen*, p. 45.

84 Cashmore, 'The race season'.

85 Quoted in M. Brown, 'The chosen few', *When Saturday Comes*, December 1995, no. 106, p. 26.

86 Vasali, 'Men out of time'.

87 Maguire, 'Sport, racism and British society', p. 121.

88 Quoted in Cashmore, *Making Sense of Sports*, p. 109.

89 Quoted in Howat, *Learie Constantine*, pp. 136–7.

90 Quoted in Cashmore, *Black Sportsmen*, p. 180.

91 Christie, *To Be Honest*, p. 10.

92 Bruno, *Eye of the Tiger*, p. 95.

93 Hill, *"Out of his Skin"*, pp. 70–1.

94 Walvin, *Football*, p. 75.

95 R. Taylor and A. Ward, *Kicking and Screaming: an oral history of football in England*, London, Robson, 1995, pp. 257–8.

96 Thomas, 'Kicking racism out of football', p. 96.

97 E. Dunning, P. Murphy, and John Williams, *The Roots of Football Hooliganism: an historical and sociological study*, London, RKP, 1988,

pp. 181–3; I. Taylor, 'Professional sport and the recession: the case of British soccer', *International Review for the Sociology of Sport*, 1984, vol. 19, no. 1, pp. 18–20.

98 Longmore, *Viv Anderson*, p. 103; Woolnough, *Black Magic*, p. 166.

99 Maguire, 'Sport, racism and British society', pp. 116–17.

100 Quoted in Marqusee, *Anyone But England*, p. 143.

101 For a discussion of the media's coverage of one notorious match in 1987 when John Barnes was abused throughout by Everton supporters, see Hill, *"Out of His Skin"*, pp. 135–42.

CONCLUSION

1 Quoted in S. Kelner, *To Jerusalem and Back*, London, Macmillan, 1996, pp. 161, 167.

2 For a critical introduction to sport and post-modernism, see G. Jarvie and J. Maguire, *Sport and Leisure in Social Thought*, London, Routledge, 1994, pp. 211–29. A brief summary is given in L. Allison, 'The changing context of sporting life', in L. Allison (ed.), *The Changing Politics of Sport*, Manchester, Manchester University Press, 1993, pp. 10–11.

3 See Jarvie and Maguire, *Sport and Leisure*, pp. 12–13 for a concise summary of the features of industrial sport. Dunning and Sheard's schema, 'The structural properties of folk-games and modern sports', is an excellent introduction to the changes involved: E. Dunning and K. Sheard, *Barbarians, Gentlemen and Players: a sociological study of the development of rugby football*, Oxford, Martin Robertson, 1979, pp. 33–4.

4 Quoted in J. Maguire, 'American labour migrants, globalization and the making of English basketball', in J. Bale and J. Maguire (eds), *The Global Sports Arena: athletic talent migration in an interdependent world*, London, Frank Cass, 1994, p. 245.

5 A. Briggs, 'The media and sport in the global village', in R. Wilcox (ed.), *Sport in the Global Village*, Morgantown, WV, Fitness Information Technology, 1994, p. 5.

6 G. Jarvie, 'Dependency, cultural identity and sporting landlords: a Scottish case-study', *British Journal of Sports History*, 1986, vol. 3, no. 1, p. 48.

APPENDIX: THE GROWING HISTORICAL AWARENESS OF SPORT

1 See, for example, R. Cox, *Sport in Britain: a bibliography of historical publications 1800–1988*, Manchester, Manchester University Press, 1991, as well as his annual bibliographies in the *International Journal of the History of Sport* and *The Sports Historian*.

2 R. Cox, *The Internet as a Resource for the Sports Historian*, Frodsham, Sports History Publishing, 1995; S. Bailey, 'Sport history and the Internet', *Sporting Heritage*, nd [1995/6], no. 1, pp. 115–16.

3 P. Seddon (compiler), *A Football Compendium: a comprehensive guide to the literature of Association Football*, London, British Library, 1995.

4 R. Cox, *History of Sport: a guide to the literature and sources of information*,

Frodsham, Sports History Publishing, 1994; R. Cox, *Index to Sporting Manuscripts in the UK*, Frodsham, Sports History Publishing, 1995; R. Cox, *Bibliography of British Sporting Biography*, Frodsham, Sports History Publishing, 1995.

5   'A.S.H. News', *Association of Sports Historians Newsletter*, July 1996, p. 3.

6   R. Holt, *Sport and the British: a modern history*, Oxford, Oxford University Press, 1989, p. 2.

7   I. Rendall, *The Chequered Flag: 100 years of motor racing*, London, Weidenfeld and Nicolson, 1993; H. Spencer, *A Century of Polo*, Cirencester, World Polo Associates, 1994.

8   G. Moorhouse, *At the George and other essays on Rugby League*, London, Sceptre, 1989.

9   Moorhouse, 'Class of '46', in ibid., p. 12.

10 N. Hornby, *Fever Pitch: a fan's life*, London, Gollancz, 1992, p. 11.

11 Ibid., p. 44.

12 L. Thompson, *The Dogs: a personal history of greyhound racing*, London, Chatto and Windus, 1994.

13 S. Hey, 'With flying collars', *Independent on Sunday, Review*, 23 January 1994, p. 35.

14 C. Sprawson, *Haunts of the Black Masseur: the swimmer as hero*, London, Jonathan Cape, 1992, pp. 102–32.

15 M. Berkmann, *Rain Men: the madness of cricket*, London, Abacus, 1995.

16 N. Coleman and N. Hornby (eds), *The Picador Book of Sports Writing*, London, Picador, 1996.

17 Welsh Rugby Union, undated publicity leaflet, 'Cardiff Arms Park – The Inside Story'.

18 The exhibition was reworked and published as J. Germain, *In Soccer Wonderland*, London, Booth–Clibborn Editions, 1994.

19 R. Cox, 'Sports archives, libraries and museums in the UK – what should be the policy?', *The Sports Historian*, 1996, no. 16, p. 156.

20 Ibid., p. 159.

21 Christie's publicity leaflet, 'Football Memorabilia', 1995.

22 N. Duncanson, *The Fastest Men on Earth: the 100m Olympic champions*, London, Willow, 1988.

23 R. Taylor and A. Ward, *Kicking and Screaming: an oral history of football in England*, London, Robson, 1995.

24 C. Cameron, *Football Fussball Voetball: the European Game 1956–Euro 96*, London, BBC Books, 1995.

Bibliography

Alexander, S., 'Gender bias in British television coverage of major athletics championships', *Women's Studies International Forum*, 1994, vol. 17, no. 6, pp. 647–54.

Allen, D. R. (ed.), *Arlott on Cricket: his writings on the game*, London, Fontana, 1985.

Allison, L. (ed.), *The Politics of Sport*, Manchester, Manchester University Press, 1986.

—, 'Sport and politics', in L. Allison (ed.), *The Politics of Sport*, Manchester, Manchester University Press, 1986, pp. 1–26.

— (ed.), *The Changing Politics of Sport*, Manchester, Manchester University Press, 1993.

—, 'The changing context of sporting life', in L. Allison (ed.), *The Changing Politics of Sport*, Manchester, Manchester University Press, 1993, pp. 1–14.

—, 'Sport as an environmental issue', in L. Allison (ed.), *The Changing Politics of Sport*, Manchester, Manchester University Press, 1993, pp. 207–32.

Anderson, B., *Imagined Communities: reflections on the origin and spread of nationalism*, London, Verso, 1983.

Arlott, J., *The Oxford Companion to Sports and Games*, Oxford, Oxford University Press, 1975.

Arnold, A., *A Game That Would Pay: a business history of professional football in Bradford*, London, Duckworth, 1988.

—, 'Rich man, poor man: economic arrangements in the Football League', in John Williams and S. Wagg (eds), *British Football and Social Change: getting into Europe*, Leicester, Leicester University Press, 1991, pp. 48–63.

Arnold, G., *Britain since 1945: choice, conflict and change*, London, Blandford, 1989.

Ascherson, N., 'Once they blamed breast-feeding. New racists just measure the tendons', *Independent on Sunday*, 17 September 1995, p. 20.

Association of Sports Historians Newsletter, July 1996.

Bailey, J., *Conflicts in Cricket*, London, Kingswood, 1989.

Bailey, P., *Leisure and Class in Victorian England: rational recreation and the contest for control, 1830–1885*, London, RKP, 1978.

—, 'Leisure, culture and the historian: reviewing the first generation of leisure historiography in Britain', *Leisure Studies*, 1989, vol. 8, pp. 107–27.

Bailey, S., 'Sport history and the Internet', *Sporting Heritage*, nd [1995/6], no. 1, pp. 115–16.

Bairner, A., 'Football and the idea of Scotland', in G. Jarvie and G. Walker (eds), *Scottish Sport in the Making of the Nation: ninety minute patriots?*, Leicester, Leicester University Press, 1994, pp. 9–26.

Baker, A., 'Hall's city of sporting dreams', *Independent on Sunday*, 8 October 1995, p. 24.

Baker, N., 'Olympics or Tests: the disposition of the British sporting public, 1948', *Sporting Traditions*, 1994, vol. 11, no. 1, pp. 57–74.

—, 'The amateur ideal in a society of equality: change and continuity in post-Second World War British sport, 1945–48', *International Journal of the History of Sport*, 1995, vol. 12, no. 1, pp. 99–126.

Baker, W. J., 'The state of British sport history', *Journal of Sport History*, 1983, vol. 10, no. 1, pp. 53–66.

Bale, J., *Landscapes of Modern Sport*, Leicester, Leicester University Press, 1994.

Bale, J. and Maguire, J. (eds), *The Global Sports Arena: athletic talent migration in an interdependent world*, London, Frank Cass, 1994.

Barnett, S., *Games and Sets: the changing face of sport on television*, London, British Film Institute, 1990.

Bateson, B. and Sewell, A. (eds), *News of the World Football Annual, 1989–90*, London, Invincible, 1990.

Beattie, G., *On The Ropes: boxing as a way of life*, London, Victor Gollancz, 1996.

Bee-sotted, no. 6, undated.

Berkmann, M., *Rain Men: the madness of cricket*, London, Abacus, 1995.

Billett, M., *A History of English Country Sports*, London, Robert Hale, 1994.

Billig, M., *Banal Nationalism*, London, Sage, 1995.

Birkett, B. and Peascod, B., *Women Climbing: 200 years of achievement*, London, A & C Black, 1989.

Birrell, S., 'Racial relations theories and sports: suggestions for a more critical analysis', *Sociology of Sport Journal*, 1989, vol. 6, no. 3, pp. 212–27.

Birtley, J., *The Tragedy of Randolph Turpin*, London, New English Library, 1975.

Blain, N. and Boyle, R., 'Battling along the boundaries: the marking of Scottish identity in sports journalism', in G. Jarvie and G. Walker (eds), *Scottish Sport in the Making of the Nation: ninety-minute patriots?*, Leicester, Leicester University Press, 1994, pp. 125–41.

Blain, N., Boyle, R., and O'Donnell, H., *Sport and National Identity in the European Media*, Leicester, Leicester University Press, 1993.

Blair, T., 'Stan's my man', *New Statesman and Society*, 20 January 1995, p. 19.

Blake, A., *The Body Language: the meaning of modern sport*, London, Lawrence and Wishart, 1996.

Blue, A., *Grace Under Pressure: the emergence of women in sport*, London, Sidgwick and Jackson, 1987.

Booth, D., 'United sport: an alternative hegemony in South Africa?', *International Journal of the History of Sport*, 1995, vol. 12, no. 3, pp. 105–24.

Bourdieu, P., 'Sport and social class', *Social Science Information*, 1978, vol. 17, no. 6, pp. 819–40.

Bowen, R., *Cricket: a history of its growth and development throughout the world*, London, Eyre and Spottiswoode, 1970.

Brackenbridge, C. and Woodward, D., 'Gender inequalities in leisure and sport in post-war Britain', in J. Obelkevich and P. Catterall (eds), *Understanding Post-War British Society*, London, Routledge, 1994, pp. 192–203.

Bradley, J., 'Football in Scotland: a history of political and ethnic identity', *International Journal of the History of Sport*, 1995, vol. 12, no. 1, pp. 81–98.

—, 'Integration or assimilation? Scottish society, football and Irish immigrants', *International Journal of the History of Sport*, 1996, vol. 13, no. 2, pp. 61–79.

Brady, K., *Brady Plays the Blues: my diary of the season*, London, Pavilion, 1995.

Brailsford, D., *Sport, Time and Society: the British at play*, London, Routledge, 1991.

—, *British Sport: a social history*, Cambridge, Lutterworth, 1992.

Bridenthal, R. and Koonz, C. (eds), *Becoming Visible: women in European history*, Boston, Houghton Mifflin, 1977.

Briggs, A., *The History of Broadcasting in the United Kingdom: Volume IV, Sound and Vision*, Oxford, Oxford University Press, 1979.

—, 'The media and sport in the global village', in R. Wilcox (ed.), *Sport in the Global Village*, Morgantown, WV, Fitness Information Technology, 1994, pp. 5–20.

British Olympic Association, *Great Britain and the Olympic Games*, London, British Olympic Association, 1987.

Brohm, J.-M., *Sport: a prison of measured time*, London, Ink Links, 1978.

Brookes, C., *English Cricket: the game and its players through the ages*, London, Weidenfeld and Nicolson, 1978.

Brower, J., 'Professional sports team ownership: fun, profit, and ideology of the power elite', *Journal of Sport and Social Issues*, 1976, vol. 1, no. 1, pp. 16–51.

Brown, M., 'The chosen few', *When Saturday Comes*, no. 106, December 1995, p. 26.

Bruno, F., *Eye of the Tiger: my life*, London, Weidenfeld and Nicolson, 1992.

Buchanan, I., *British Olympians: a hundred years of gold medallists*, Enfield, Guinness, 1991.

Calvocoressi, P., *The British Experience 1945–75*, Harmondsworth, Pelican, 1979.

Cameron, C., *Football Fussball Voetball: the European Game 1956–Euro 96*, London, BBC Books, 1995.

Cantelon, H. and Gruneau, R. (eds), *Sport, Culture and the Modern State*, Toronto, University of Toronto Press, 1982.

Carr, R., *English Fox Hunting: a history*, revised edition, London, Weidenfeld and Nicolson, 1986.

Carrington, B., Chivers, T., and Williams, T., 'Gender, leisure and sport: a case-study of young people of South Asian descent', *Leisure Studies*, 1987, vol. 6, pp. 265–79.

Carroll, T., *Diary of a Fox-Hunting Man*, London, Futura, 1984.

Cashman, R. and McKernan, M. (eds), *Sport in History: the making of modern sporting history*, St Lucia, University of Queensland Press, 1979.

Cashmore, E., *Black Sportsmen*, London, RKP, 1982.

—, *United Kingdom? Class, race and gender since the war*, London, Unwin Hyman, 1989.

—, 'The race season', *New Statesman and Society*, 1 June 1990, pp. 10–11.

—, *... and there was television*, London, Routledge, 1994.

—, *Making Sense of Sports*, second edition, London, Routledge, 1996.

Central Council of Physical Recreation, *Committee of Enquiry into Sports Sponsorship: The Howell Report*, London, Central Council of Physical Recreation, 1983.

Centre for Contemporary Cultural Studies, *Sporting Fictions*, Birmingham, University of Birmingham, 1982.

Chandler, J., *Television and National Sport: the United States and Britain*, Urbana, IL, University of Illinois Press, 1988.

Chapman, S., *Great Expectorations: advertising and the tobacco industry*, London, Comedia, 1986.

Chataway, C., *A Better Country*, London, Conservative Political Centre, 1966.

Christie, L., *To Be Honest With You*, London, Michael Joseph, 1995.

Clapson, M., *A Bit of a Flutter: popular gambling and English society, c.1823–1961*, Manchester, Manchester University Press, 1992.

Clarke, J., 'Football and working class fans: tradition and change', in R. Ingham (ed.), *'Football Hooliganism': the wider context*, London, Inter-Action Inprint, 1978, pp. 37–60.

Clarke, J. and Critcher, C., '1966 and all that: England's World Cup victory', in A. Tomlinson and G. Whannel (eds), *Off The Ball: the football World Cup*, London, Pluto, 1986, pp. 112–26.

Clarke, J., Critcher, C., and Johnson, R. (eds), *Working Class Culture: studies in history and theory*, London, Hutchinson, 1979.

Class War, 'A-hunting we will go', undated [1985].

Coakley, J., *Sport in Society: issues and controversies*, fifth edition, St Louis, Mosby, 1994.

Coakley, J. and White, A., 'Making decisions: gender and sport participation among British adolescents', *Sociology of Sport Journal*, 1992, vol. 9, no. 1, pp. 20–35.

Coghlan, J. with Webb, I., *Sport and British Politics since 1960*, Basingstoke, Falmer, 1990.

Cohen, D., 'The Sky's the limit', in A. McLellan (ed.), *Nothing Sacred: the new cricket culture*, London, Two Heads, 1996, pp. 136–45.

Coleman, N. and Hornby, N. (eds), *The Picador Book of Sports Writing*, London, Picador, 1996.

Collins, M., 'Shifting icebergs: the public, private and voluntary sectors in British sport', in A. Tomlinson (ed.), *Sport in Society: policy, politics and culture*, Brighton, Leisure Studies Association, 1990, pp. 1–12.

Collins, M. and Jones, H., 'The economics of sport: sport as an industry', in A. Tomlinson (ed.), *Sport in Society: policy, politics and culture*, Brighton, Leisure Studies Association, 1990, pp. 68–79.

Committee on the Youth Service in England and Wales, *The Youth Service in England and Wales*, London, HMSO, 1960.

Costa, D. M. and Guthrie, S. R. (eds), *Women and Sport: interdisciplinary perspectives*, Champaign, IL, Human Kinetics, 1994.

Cox, R., *Sport in Britain: a bibliography of historical publications 1800–1988*, Manchester, Manchester University Press, 1991.

—, 'A brief history of British sports history', *Physical Education Review*, 1992, vol. 15, no. 3, pp. 119–26.

—, *History of Sport: a guide to the literature and sources of information*, Frodsham, British Society of Sports History/Sports History Publishing, 1994.

—, *The Internet as a Resource for the Sports Historian*, Frodsham, Sports History Publishing, 1995.

—, *Index to Sporting Manuscripts in the UK*, Frodsham, Sports History Publishing, 1995.

—, *Bibliography of British Sporting Biography*, Frodsham, Sports History Publishing, 1995.

—, 'Sports archives, libraries and museums in the UK – what should be the policy?', *The Sports Historian*, 1996, no. 16, pp. 156–9.

Critcher, C., 'Football since the war', in J. Clarke, C. Critcher, and R. Johnson (eds), *Working Class Culture: studies in history and theory*, London, Hutchinson, 1979, pp. 161–84.

—, 'Media spectacles: sport and mass communication', in A. Cashdan and M. Jordin (eds), *Studies in Communication*, Oxford, Blackwell, 1987, pp. 131–50.

—, 'Putting on the style: aspects of recent English football', in John Williams and S. Wagg (eds), *British Football and Social Change: getting into Europe*, Leicester, Leicester University Press, 1991, pp. 67–84.

—, 'England and the World Cup: World Cup willies, English football and the myth of 1966', in J. Sugden and A. Tomlinson (eds), *Hosts and Champions: soccer cultures, national identities and the USA World Cup*, Aldershot, Arena, 1994, pp. 77–92.

Crum, B., 'A critical analysis of Korfball as a non-sexist sport', *International Review for the Sociology of Sport*, 1988, vol. 23, no. 3, pp. 233–43.

Crump, J., 'Athletics', in T. Mason (ed.), *Sport in Britain: a social history*, Cambridge, Cambridge University Press, 1989, pp. 44–77.

Dabscheck, B., 'Defensive Manchester: a history of the Professional Footballers Association', in R. Cashman and M. McKernan (eds), *Sport in History: the making of modern sporting history*, St Lucia, University of Queensland Press, 1979, pp. 227–57.

—, 'Player associations and professional team sports', *Labour and Society*, 1979, vol. 4, no. 3, pp. 225–39.

Daniel, W., *Racial Discrimination in England*, Harmondsworth, Penguin, 1968.

Davies, H., *The Glory Game*, London, Sphere, 1973.

Department of the Environment, *Sport and Recreation* (Cmnd. 6200), London, HMSO, 1975.

Dewar, A., 'Sexual oppression in sport: past, present, and future alternatives', in A. Ingham and J. Loy (eds), *Sport in Social Development: traditions, transitions, and transformations*, Champaign, IL, Human Kinetics, 1993, pp. 147–66.

Dixey, R., 'Asian women and sport: the Bradford experience', *British Journal of Physical Education*, 1982, vol. 13, no. 4, pp. 108, 114.

D'Oliveira, B. with Murphy, P., *Time to Declare: an autobiography*, London, Dent, 1980.

Douglas, P., *The Football Industry*, London, George Allen and Unwin, 1973.

Duncan, J., 'Darts swept from the board', *The Guardian*, 14 February 1996, p. 27.

Duncanson, N., *The Fastest Men on Earth: the 100m Olympic champions*, London, Willow, 1988.

Dunne, M., 'An introduction to some of the images of sport in girls' comics and magazines', in Centre for Contemporary Cultural Studies, *Sporting Fictions*, Birmingham, University of Birmingham, 1982, pp. 36–59.

Dunning, E. (ed.), *The Sociology of Sport: a selection of readings*, London, Frank Cass, 1971.

—, 'Sport as a male preserve: notes on the social sources of masculine identity and its transformations', *Theory, Culture and Society*, vol. 3, no. 1, 1986, pp. 79–90.

Dunning, E. and Sheard, K., *Barbarians, Gentlemen and Players: a sociological study of the development of rugby football*, Oxford, Martin Robertson, 1979.

Dunning, E., Murphy, P., and Williams, John, *The Roots of Football Hooliganism: an historical and sociological study*, London, RKP, 1988.

Dunning, E., Maguire, J., and Pearton, R. (eds), *The Sports Process: a comparative and developmental approach*, Champaign, IL, Human Kinetics, 1993.

Dyer, K., *Catching Up the Men: women in sport*, London, Junction Books, 1982.

Eastham, G., *Determined to Win*, London, Stanley Paul, 1964.

Edwards, H., *The Revolt of the Black Athlete*, New York, Free Press, 1969.

Elliott, A., and May, J. A., *A History of Golf*, London, Chancellor, 1994.

Evans, H. J., *Service to Sport: the story of the CCPR, 1937–1975*, London, Pelham, 1975.

Finn, G. P. T., 'Racism, religion and social prejudice: Irish Catholic clubs, soccer and Scottish society – I The historical roots of prejudice', *International Journal of the History of Sport*, 1991, vol. 8, no. 1, pp. 72–95.

—, 'Racism, religion and social prejudice: Irish Catholic clubs, soccer and Scottish society – II Social identities and conspiracy theories', *International Journal of the History of Sport*, 1991, vol. 8, no. 3, pp. 370–97.

—, 'Faith, hope and bigotry: case studies of anti-Catholic prejudice in Scottish soccer and society', in G. Jarvie and G. Walker (eds), *Scottish Sport in the Making of the Nation: ninety minute patriots?*, Leicester, Leicester University Press, 1994, pp. 91–112.

Fishwick, N., *English Football and Society, 1910–1950*, Manchester, Manchester University Press, 1989.

Fleming, S., 'Sport, schooling and Asian male youth culture', in G. Jarvie (ed.), *Sport, Racism and Ethnicity*, London, Falmer, 1991, pp. 30–57.

—, *"Home and Away": sport and South Asian male youth*, Aldershot, Ashgate, 1995.

Flint, R. H., *Heyhoe! The autobiography of Rachael Heyhoe Flint*, London, Pelham, 1978.

Flint, R. H., and Rheinberg, N., *Fair Play: the story of women's cricket*, London, Angus and Robertson, 1976.

Foster, K., 'Sporting autonomy and the law', in L. Allison (ed.), *The Politics of Sport*, Manchester, Manchester University Press, 1986, pp. 49–65.

—, 'Developments in sporting law', in L. Allison (ed.), *The Changing Politics of Sport*, Manchester, Manchester University Press, 1993, pp. 105–24.

Frean, A., 'Editor rebuked as Euro 96 jingoism angers readers', *The Times*, 25 June 1996, p. 1.

Frith, D., *The Golden Age of Cricket, 1890–1914*, London, Lutterworth, 1978.

Fryer, P., *Staying Power: the history of black people in Britain*, London, Pluto, 1984.

Garfield, S., *The Wrestling*, London, Faber and Faber, 1996.

Gate, R., *Rugby League: an illustrated history*, London, Arthur Barker, 1989.

Genest, S., 'Skating on thin ice? The international migration of Canadian ice hockey players', in J. Bale and J. Maguire (eds), *The Global Sports Arena: athletic talent migration in an interdependent world*, London, Frank Cass, 1994, pp. 112–25.

Germain, J., *In Soccer Wonderland*, London, Booth–Clibborn Editions, 1994.

Gilroy, P., *Small Acts: thoughts on the politics of black cultures*, London, Serpent's Tail, 1993.

Giulianotti, R., 'Scoring away from home: a statistical study of Scotland football fans at international matches in Romania and Sweden', *International Review for the Sociology of Sport*, 1994, vol. 29, no. 2, pp. 171–200.

—, 'Football and the politics of carnival: an ethnographic study of Scottish fans in Sweden', *International Review for the Sociology of Sport*, 1995, vol. 30, no. 2, pp. 191–223.

Glanville, B., *The History of the World Cup*, revised edition, London, Faber and Faber, 1980.

Goldlust, J., *Playing for Keeps: sport, the media and society*, Melbourne, Longman Cheshire, 1987.

Golesworthy, M., *Encyclopaedia of Cricket*, sixth edition, London, Robert Hale, 1977.

Gourvish, T. and O'Day, A. (eds), *Britain Since 1945*, London, Macmillan, 1991.

Gratton, C. and Taylor, P., *Sport and Recreation: an economic analysis*, London, Spon, 1985.

Grayson, E., *Sport and the Law*, second edition, London, Butterworths, 1994.

Gruneau, R., *Class, Sports, and Social Development*, Amherst, MA, University of Massachusetts Press, 1983.

Guelke, A., 'The politicisation of South African sport', in L. Allison (ed.), *The Politics of Sport*, Manchester, Manchester University Press, 1986, pp. 118–48.

—, 'Sport and the end of *apartheid*', in L. Allison (ed.), *The Changing Politics of Sport*, Manchester, Manchester University Press, 1993, pp. 151–70.

Hailsham, Lord, *A Sparrow's Flight*, London, Collins, 1990.

Hain, P., *Don't Play with Apartheid: the background to the Stop The Seventy Tour Campaign*, London, George Allen and Unwin, 1971.

Hands, D., 'RFU men call for Carling apology', *The Times*, 5 May 1995, p. 48.

Harding, J., *Lonsdale's Belt: the story of boxing's greatest prize*, London, Robson, 1994.

Hargreaves, Jennifer (ed.), *Sport, culture and ideology*, London, RKP, 1982.

—, *Sporting Females: critical issues in the history and sociology of women's sport*, London, Routledge, 1994.

Hargreaves, John, 'The state and sport: programmed and non-programmed intervention in Britain', in L. Allison (ed.), *The Politics of Sport*, Manchester, Manchester University Press, 1986, pp. 242–61.

—, *Sport, Power and Culture: a social and historical analysis of popular sports in Britain*, Cambridge, Polity, 1986.

Harris, H. A., *Sport in Britain: its origins and development*, London, Stanley Paul, 1975.

Hart-Davis, D., *Hitler's Games: the 1936 Olympics*, New York, Harper and Row, 1986.

Hartley, L.P., *The Go-Between*, London, Hamish Hamilton, 1953

Harvey, J. and Cantelon, H. (eds), *Not Just a Game: essays in Canadian sport sociology*, Ottawa, University of Ottawa Press, 1988.

Haynes, R., *The Football Imagination: the rise of football fanzine culture*, Aldershot, Arena, 1995.

Hendrie, C. and Brannan, L., 'Ride into history', *Mail on Sunday*, 19 May 1996, pp. 96–7.

Henley Centre, *The Economic Impact of Sport in the UK*, London, Sports Council, 1992.

Henry, I., *The Politics of Leisure Policy*, Basingstoke, Macmillan, 1993.

Hey, S., 'With flying collars', *Independent on Sunday, Review*, 23 January 1994, p. 35.

Hicks, W. (ed.), *News Chronicle Boys' Book of All Sports*, London, News Chronicle Book Department, undated [1953/4].

Hill, C., *Horse Power: the politics of the turf*, Manchester, Manchester University Press, 1988.

—, *Olympic Politics*, Manchester, Manchester University Press, 1992.

Hill, D., 'Black on red', *New Society*, 11 December 1987, pp. 19–21.

—, *"Out Of His Skin": the John Barnes phenomenon*, London, Faber and Faber, 1989.

Hill, Jeff, 'Cricket and the imperial connection: overseas players in Lancashire in the inter-war period', in J. Bale and J. Maguire (eds), *The Global Sports Arena: athletic talent migration in an interdependent world*, London, Frank Cass, 1994, pp. 49–62.

Hill, Jimmy, *Striking for Soccer*, London, Peter Davies, 1961.

Hobsbawm, E., *Nations and Nationalism since 1780: programme, myth, reality*, Cambridge, Cambridge University Press, 1990.

Holmes, C., *John Bull's Island: immigration and British society, 1871–1971*, Basingstoke, Macmillan, 1988.

—, *A Tolerant Country? Immigrants, refugees and minorities in Britain*, London, Faber and Faber, 1991.

—, 'Immigration', in T. Gourvish and A. O'Day (eds), *Britain Since 1945*, London, Macmillan, 1991, pp. 209–31.

Holt, R., 'Working class football and the city: the problem of continuity', *British Journal of Sports History*, 1986, vol. 3, no. 1, pp. 5–17.

—, *Sport and the British: a modern history*, Oxford, Oxford University Press, 1989.

— (ed.), *Sport and the Working Class in Modern Britain*, Manchester, Manchester University Press, 1990.

—, 'Introduction', in R. Holt (ed.), *Sport and the Working Class in Modern Britain*, Manchester, Manchester University Press, 1990, pp. 1–11.

—, 'King across the Border: Denis Law and Scottish football', in G. Jarvie and G. Walker (eds), *Scottish Sport in the Making of the Nation: ninety minute patriots?*, Leicester, Leicester University Press, 1994, pp. 58–74.

Hopcraft, A., *The Football Man: people and passions in soccer*, London, Simon & Schuster, 1988.

Hornby, N., *Fever Pitch: a fan's life*, London, Victor Gollancz, 1992.

Houlihan, B., 'The politics of sports policy in Britain: the examples of football hooliganism and drug abuse', in A. Tomlinson (ed.), *Sport in Society: policy, politics and culture*, Brighton, Leisure Studies Association, 1990, pp. 27–49.

—, *The Government and Politics of Sport*, London, Routledge, 1991.

Howat, G., *Learie Constantine*, London, George Allen and Unwin, 1975.

Howell, D., *Made in Birmingham*, London, Queen Anne Press, 1990.

Huddleston, T., *Naught for your Comfort*, London, Collins, 1956.

Hudson, R. and Williams, A., *Divided Britain*, second edition, Chichester, John Wiley, 1995.

Ingham, A. and Loy, J. (eds), *Sport in Social Development: traditions, transitions, and transformations*, Champaign, IL, Human Kinetics, 1993.

Ingham, R. (ed.), *'Football Hooliganism': the wider context*, London, Inter-Action Inprint, 1996.

Inglis, S., *Football Grounds of Britain*, third edition, London, CollinsWillow, 1996.

James, C. L. R., *Beyond a Boundary*, London, Stanley Paul, 1963.

Jarvie, G., 'Dependency, cultural identity and sporting landlords: a Scottish case-study', *British Journal of Sports History*, 1986, vol. 3, no. 1, pp. 42–54.

—, 'Highland Gatherings, historical sociology and sport', in J. A. Mangan and R. B. Small (eds), *Sport, Culture, Society: international historical and sociological perspectives*, London, Spon, 1986, pp. 68–75.

—, *Highland Games: the making of the myth*, Edinburgh, Edinburgh University Press, 1991.

— (ed.), *Sport, Racism and Ethnicity*, London, Falmer, 1991.

—, 'Sport, nationalism and cultural identity', in L. Allison (ed.), *The Changing Politics of Sport*, Manchester, Manchester University Press, 1993, pp. 58–83.

—, 'Royal games, sport and the politics of the environment', in G. Jarvie and G. Walker (eds), *Scottish Sport in the Making of the Nation: ninety minute patriots?*, Leicester, Leicester University Press, 1994, pp. 154–72.

Jarvie, G. and Maguire, J., *Sport and Leisure in Social Thought*, London, Routledge, 1994.

Jarvie, G. and Walker, G. (eds), *Scottish Sport in the Making of a Nation: ninety minute patriots?*, Leicester, Leicester University Press, 1994.

—, 'Ninety minute patriots? Scottish sport in the making of the nation', in G. Jarvie and G. Walker (eds), *Scottish Sport in the Making of the Nation: ninety minute patriots?*, Leicester, Leicester University Press, 1994, pp. 1–8.

Jones, S. G., *Workers at Play: a social and economic history of leisure 1918–1939*, London, RKP, 1986.

—, *Sport, Politics and the Working Class: organised labour and sport in interwar Britain*, Manchester, Manchester University Press, 1988.

Keating, F., 'A disgrace, a waste, a fiasco and a bloody good riddance', *The Guardian*, 14 February 1990, p. 15.

—, 'Over to you, Bill', *The Guardian*, 17 October 1995, Section 2, p. 5.

Kelner, S., *To Jerusalem and Back*, London, Macmillan, 1996.

Killanin, Lord, *My Olympic Years*, London, Secker & Warburg, 1983.

Kirk, D. and Tinning, R. (eds), *Physical Education, Curriculum and Culture: critical issues in the contemporary crisis*, Basingstoke, Falmer, 1990.

Knox, C., 'Political symbolism and leisure provision in Northern Ireland local government', *Local Government Studies*, 1986, vol. 12, no. 5, pp. 37–50.

Krüger, A., 'On the origin of the notion that sport serves as a means of national representation', *History of European Ideas*, 1993, vol. 16, no. 4–6, pp. 863–9.

Latus, J., *Hard Road to the Top: the Clive Sullivan story*, Hull, Boulevard Stadium Publications, 1973.

Leaman, L., 'Sport and the feminist novel', in Centre for Contemporary Cultural Studies, *Sporting Fictions*, Birmingham, University of Birmingham, 1982, pp. 276–89.

Leatherdale, C., *England's Quest for the World Cup: a complete record*, London, Methuen, 1984.

Lerner, G., *The Majority Finds its Past: placing women in history*, New York, Oxford University Press, 1979.

Lewis, T., *Double Century: 200 years of the MCC*, London, Coronet, 1987.

Little, A., *Wimbledon Compendium 1991*, London, All England Lawn Tennis and Croquet Club, 1991.

Longmore, A., *Viv Anderson*, London, Heinemann, 1988.

—, 'Football puts its shirt on profit', *The Times*, 19 December 1994, p. 27.

Lovesey, P., *The Official Centenary History of the Amateur Athletic Association*, Enfield, Guinness Superlatives, 1979.

Lowerson, J., 'Golf', in T. Mason (ed.), *Sport in Britain: a social history*, Cambridge, Cambridge University Press, 1989, pp. 187–214.

—, *Sport and the English Middle Class 1870–1914*, Manchester, Manchester University Press, 1993.

—, 'Golf and the making of myths', in G. Jarvie and G. Walker (eds), *Scottish Sport in the Making of the Nation: ninety minute patriots?*, Leicester, Leicester University Press, 1994, pp. 75–90.

Lyons, A., *Asian Women and Sport*, London, Sports Council, 1988.

—, 'Missing in action', *When Saturday Comes*, April 1995, no. 110, pp. 6–7.

McCarra, K., 'Sport in Scotland', in P. Scott (ed.), *Scotland: a concise cultural history*, Edinburgh, Mainstream, 1993, pp. 279–90.

McCrone, D., Kendrick, S., and Straw, P. (eds), *The Making of Scotland: nation, culture and social change*, Edinburgh, Edinburgh University Press/British Sociological Association, 1989.

Macfarlane, N. with Herd, M., *Sport and Politics: a word divided*, London, Willow, 1986.

McIntosh, P. and Charlton, V., *The Impact of Sport for All Policy 1966–1984 and a Way Forward*, London, Sports Council, 1985.

McKenzie, C., 'The origins of the British Field Sports Society', *International Journal of the History of Sport*, 1996, vol. 13, no. 2, pp. 177–91.

McLellan, A., *The Enemy Within: the impact of overseas players on English cricket*, London, Blandford, 1994.

— (ed.), *Nothing Sacred: the new cricket culture*, London, Two Heads, 1996.

MacNeill, M., 'Active women, media representations, and ideology', in J. Harvey and H. Cantelon (eds), *Not Just a Game: essays in Canadian sport sociology*, Ottawa, University of Ottawa Press, 1988, pp. 195–211.

MacQuillin, I., 'Who's afraid of the Barmy Army', in A. McLellan (ed.), *Nothing Sacred: the new cricket culture*, London, Two Heads, 1996, pp. 37–54.

Maguire, J., 'Race and position assignment in English soccer: a preliminary analysis of ethnicity and sport in Britain', *Sociology of Sport Journal*, 1988, vol. 5, no. 3, pp. 257–69.

—, 'The commercialization of English elite basketball 1972–1988: a figurational approach', *International Review for the Sociology of Sport*, 1988, vol. 23, no. 4, pp. 305–23.

—, 'More than a sporting touchdown: the making of American Football in England 1982–1990', *Sociology of Sport Journal*, 1990, vol. 7, no. 3, pp. 213–37.

—, 'Sport, racism and British society: a sociological study of England's élite male Afro/Caribbean soccer and Rugby Union players', in G. Jarvie (ed.), *Sport, Racism and Ethnicity*, London, Falmer, 1991, pp. 94–123.

—, 'American labour migrants, globalization and the making of English basketball', in J. Bale and J. Maguire (eds), *The Global Sports Arena: athletic talent migration in an interdependent world*, London, Frank Cass, 1994, pp. 226–55.

—, 'Sport, identity politics, and globalization: diminishing contrasts and increasing varieties', *Sociology of Sport Journal*, 1994, vol. 11, no. 4, pp. 398–427.

Maguire, J. and Bale, J., 'Introduction: sports labour migration in the global arena', in J. Bale and J. Maguire (eds), *The Global Sports Arena: athletic talent migration in an interdependent world*, London, Frank Cass, 1994, pp. 1–21.

—, 'Postscript: an agenda for research on sports labour migration', in J. Bale and J. Maguire (eds), *The Global Sports Arena: athletic talent migration in an interdependent world*, London, Frank Cass, 1994, pp. 281–4.

Majors, R., 'Cool pose: black masculinity and sports', in M. Messner and D. Sabo (eds), *Sport, Men and the Gender Order: critical feminist perspectives*, Champaign, IL, Human Kinetics, 1991, pp. 109–14.

Malcolmson, R., 'Sport in society: a historical perspective', *British Journal of Sports History*, 1984, vol. 1, no. 1, pp. 60–72.

Malik, K., 'Minorities face soccer "wall"', *Independent on Sunday*, 17 September 1995, p. 9.

Mangan, J. A. (ed.), *Pleasure, Profit, Proselytism: British culture and sport at home and abroad, 1700–1914*, London, Frank Cass, 1988.

—, 'The social history of sport: reflections on some recent British developments in research and teaching', in D. L. Vanderwerken (ed.), *Sport in the Classroom: teaching sport-related courses in the humanities*, London, Associated University Press, 1990, pp. 61–74.

— (ed.), *The Cultural Bond: sport, empire, society*, London, Frank Cass, 1992.

—, 'Duty unto death: English masculinity and militarism in the age of New Imperialism', *International Journal of the History of Sport*, 1995, vol. 12, no. 2, pp. 10–38.

—, '"Muscular, Militaristic and Manly": the British middle-class hero as moral messenger', *International Journal of the History of Sport*, 1996, vol. 13, no. 1, pp. 28–47.

—, 'Games field and battlefield: a romantic alliance in verse and the creation of militaristic masculinity', in J. Nauright and T. Chandler (eds), *Making Men: rugby and masculine identity*, London, Frank Cass, 1996, pp. 140–57.

Mangan, J. A. and Small, R. B. (eds), *Sport, Culture, Society: international historical and sociological perspectives*, London, Spon, 1986.

Mangan, J. A. and Walvin, J. (eds), *Manliness and Morality: middle-class masculinity in Britain and America, 1800–1940*, Manchester, Manchester University Press, 1987.

Marple, D., 'Tournament earnings and performance differentials between the sexes in professional golf and tennis', *Journal of Sport and Social Issues*, 1983, vol. 7, no. 1, pp. 1–14.

Marqusee, D., *Anyone But England: cricket and the national malaise*, London, Verso, 1994.

Martin, A., *The Equestrian Woman*, New York, Paddington, 1979.

Marwick, A., *British Society since 1945*, Harmondsworth, Penguin, 1982.

—, *British Society since 1945*, third edition, Harmondsworth, Penguin, 1996.

Mason, T., *Association Football and English Society, 1863–1915*, Hassocks, Harvester, 1980.

—, *Sport in Britain*, London, Faber and Faber, 1988.

— (ed.), *Sport in Britain: a social history*, Cambridge, Cambridge University Press, 1989.

—, 'Football', in T. Mason (ed.), *Sport in Britain: a social history*, Cambridge, Cambridge University Press, 1989, pp. 146–86.

—, 'Stanley Matthews', in R. Holt (ed.), *Sport and the Working Class in Modern Britain*, Manchester, Manchester University Press, 1990, pp. 159–78.

—, *Only A Game? Sport in the modern world*, Cambridge, Cambridge University Press, 1993.

—, 'The Bogotá affair', in J. Bale and J. Maguire (eds), *The Global Sports Arena: athletic talent migration in an interdependent world*, London, Frank Cass, 1994, pp. 39–48.

Meisl, W., *Soccer Revolution*, London, Phoenix Sports Books, 1955.

Melnick, M., 'Racial segregation by playing position in the English Football League: some preliminary observations', *Journal of Sport and Social Issues*, 1988, vol. 12, no. 2, pp. 122–30.

Mercer, K., *Welcome to the Jungle: new positions in black cultural studies*, London, Routledge, 1994.

Messner, M., *Power at Play: sports and the problem of masculinity*, Boston, Beacon Press, 1992.

Messner, M. and Sabo, D. (eds), *Sport, Men, and the Gender Order: critical feminist perspectives*, Champaign, IL, Human Kinetics, 1990.

—, 'Introduction: toward a critical feminist reappraisal of sport, men, and the gender order', in M. Messner and D. Sabo (eds), *Sport, Men, and the Gender Order: critical feminist perspectives*, Champaign, IL, Human Kinetics, 1990, pp. 1–15.

Midwinter, E., *The Illustrated History of County Cricket*, London, Kingswood, 1992.

Moorhouse, G., *At the George and other essays on Rugby League*, London, Sceptre, 1989.

—, *A People's Game: the centenary history of Rugby League, 1895–1995*, London, Hodder and Stoughton, 1995.

Moorhouse, H. F., 'Professional football and working class culture: English theories and Scottish evidence', *Sociological Review*, 1984, vol. 32, no. 2, pp. 285–315.

—, 'Repressed nationalism and professional football: Scotland versus England', in J. A. Mangan and R. B. Small (eds), *Sport, Culture, Society: international historical and sociological perspectives*, London, Spon, 1986, pp. 52–9.

—, 'Scotland against England: football and popular culture', *International Journal of the History of Sport*, 1987, vol. 4, no. 2, pp. 189–202.

—, '"We're off to Wembley!": The history of a Scottish event and the sociology of football hooliganism', in D. McCrone, S. Kendrick, and P. Straw (eds), *The Making of Scotland: nation, culture and social change*, Edinburgh, Edinburgh University Press/British Sociological Association, 1989, pp. 207–27.

—, 'Shooting stars: footballers and working-class culture in twentieth-century Scotland', in R. Holt (ed.), *Sport and the Working Class in Modern Britain*, Manchester, Manchester University Press, 1990, pp. 179–97.

—, 'On the periphery: Scotland, Scottish football and the new Europe', in John Williams and S. Wagg (eds), *British Football and Social Change: getting into Europe*, Leicester, Leicester University Press, 1991, pp. 201–19.

—, 'Blue bonnets over the border: Scotland and the migration of footballers', in J. Bale and J. Maguire (eds), *The Global Sports Arena: athletic talent migration in an interdependent world*, London, Frank Cass, 1994, pp. 78–96.

—, 'From zines like these? Fanzines, tradition and identity in Scottish football', in G. Jarvie and G. Walker (eds), *Scottish Sport in the Making of the Nation: ninety minute patriots?*, Leicester, Leicester University Press, 1994, pp. 173–94.

—, 'One state, several countries: soccer and nationality in a "United" Kingdom', *International Journal of the History of Sport*, 1995, vol. 12, no. 2, pp. 55–74.

Morgan, K. O., *The People's Peace: British history 1945–1990*, Oxford, Oxford University Press, 1992.

Munting, R., 'Social opposition to gambling in Britain: a historical overview', *International Journal of the History of Sport*, 1993, vol. 10, no. 3, pp. 295–312.

Murphy, P., Williams, John, and Dunning, E., *Football on Trial: spectator violence and development in the football world*, London, Routledge, 1990.

Murray, B., *The Old Firm: sectarianism, sport and society in Scotland*, Edinburgh, John Donald, 1984.

—, *Football: a history of the world game*, London, Scolar, 1994.

Nauright, J. and Chandler, T. (eds), *Making Men: rugby and masculine identity*, London, Frank Cass, 1996.

Nixon, R., *Homelands, Harlem and Hollywood: South African culture and the world beyond*, London, Routledge, 1994.

Oakland, J., *British Civilization: an introduction*, third edition, London, Routledge, 1995.

Obelkevich, J. and Catterall, P. (eds), *Understanding Post-War British Society*, London, Routledge, 1994.

O'Donnell, H., 'Mapping the mythical: a geopolitics of national sporting stereotypes', *Discourse and Society*, 1994, vol. 5, no. 3, pp. 345–80.

O'Hagan, S., 'Home truths for a tournament too far', *Independent on Sunday*, 15 October 1995, p. 24.

Oliver, G., *The Guinness Record of World Soccer: the history of the game in over 150 countries*, Enfield, Guinness, 1992.

Parratt, C., 'From the history of women in sport to women's sport history: a research agenda', in D. M. Costa and S. R. Guthrie (eds), *Women and Sport: interdisciplinary perspectives*, Champaign, IL, Human Kinetics, 1994, pp. 5–14.

Parry, J., *Participation by Black and Ethnic Minorities in Sport and Recreation: a review of literature*, London, London Research Centre, 1989.

Parry, J. and Parry, N., 'Sport and the black experience', in G. Jarvie (ed.), *Sport, Racism and Ethnicity*, London, Falmer, 1991, pp. 150–74.

Payne, A., 'The international politics of the Gleneagles Agreement', *The Round Table*, 1991, no. 320, pp. 417–30.

Perkin, H., 'Sport and society: Empire into Commonwealth', in J. A. Mangan and R. B. Small (eds), *Sport, Culture, Society: international historical and sociological perspectives*, London, Spon, 1986, pp. 3–5.

Perry, F., *An Autobiography*, London, Arrow, 1984.

Physical Education Department, University of Birmingham, *Britain in the World of Sport: an examination of the factors involved in participation in competitive international sport*, [S. l.], Physical Education Association for Great Britain and Northern Ireland, 1956.

Polley, M., 'Great Britain and the Olympic Games, 1896–1908', in C. C. Eldridge (ed.), *Empire, Politics and Popular Culture: essays in eighteenth and nineteenth century British history*, Lampeter, Trivium, 1989, pp. 98–108.

—, 'The Foreign Office and international sport, 1918–1948', unpublished PhD thesis, University of Wales, 1991.

—, 'Olympic diplomacy: the British Government and the projected 1940 Olympic Games', *International Journal of the History of Sport*, 1992, vol. 9, pp. 169–87.

Potter, J., *Independent Television in Britain: Volume III, Politics and Control, 1968–1980*, London, Macmillan, 1988.

Pronger, B., *The Arena of Masculinity: sports, homosexuality, and the meaning of sex*, London, GMP, 1990.

—, 'Gay jocks: a phenomenology of gay men in athletics', in M. Messner and D. Sabo (eds), *Sport, Men, and the Gender Order: critical feminist perspectives*, Champaign, IL, Human Kinetics, 1990, pp. 141–52.

Pugh, M., *State and Society: British political and social history 1870–1992*, London, Edward Arnold, 1994.

Ramsden, C., *Ladies in Racing: sixteenth century to the present day*, London, Stanley Paul, 1973.

Redhead, S., 'The legalisation of the professional footballer: a study of some aspects of the legal status and employment conditions of Association Football players in England and Wales from the late nineteenth century to the present day', unpublished PhD thesis, University of Warwick, 1984.

—, 'You've really got a hold on me: footballers in the market', in A. Tomlinson and G. Whannel (eds), *Off The Ball: the football World Cup*, London, Pluto, 1986, pp. 54–66.

—, *Football With Attitude*, Manchester, Wordsmith, 1991.

Redmond, G., 'Sport history in academe: reflections on a half-century of peculiar progress', *British Journal of Sports History*, 1984, vol. 1, no. 1, pp. 24–40.

Reid, I., *Social Class Differences in Britain: life-chances and life-styles*, third edition, London, Fontana, 1989.

Rendall, I., *The Chequered Flag: 100 years of motor racing*, London, Weidenfeld and Nicolson, 1993.

Rich, P., *Race and Empire in British Politics*, second edition, Cambridge, Cambridge University Press, 1990.

Rivlin, M., 'Albert Memorial', *When Saturday Comes*, November 1995, no. 105, pp. 10–11.

Robbins, K., *The Eclipse of a Great Power: Modern Britain, 1870–1975*, London, Longman, 1983.

Roper, M. and Tosh, J. (eds), *Manful Assertions: masculinities in Britain since 1800*, London, Routledge, 1991.

—, 'Introduction: historians and the politics of masculinity', in M. Roper and J. Tosh (eds), *Manful Assertions: masculinities in Britain since 1800*, London, Routledge, 1991, pp. 1–24.

Rowbotham, S., *Hidden from History*, London, Pluto, 1973.

Royle, E., 'Trends in post-war British social history', in J. Obelkevich and

P. Catterall (eds), *Understanding Post-War British Society*, London, Routledge, 1994, pp. 9–18.

Sandiford, K., 'The professionalization of modern cricket', *British Journal of Sports History*, 1985, vol. 2, no. 3, pp. 270–89.

Savidge, M., 'Stuff the sandwiches', in A. McLellan (ed.), *Nothing Sacred: the new cricket culture*, London, Two Heads, 1996, pp. 74–83.

Scott, J., *The Athletic Revolution*, New York, Free Press, 1971.

Scott, N. and Cook, N., *England Test Cricket: the years of indecision, 1981–92*, London, Kingswood, 1992.

Scott, P. (ed.), *Scotland: a concise cultural history*, Edinburgh, Mainstream, 1993.

Seddon, P. (compiler), *A Football Compendium: a comprehensive guide to the literature of Association Football*, London, British Library, 1995.

Sendall, B., *Independent Television in Britain: Volume I, Origin and Foundation, 1946–62*, London, Macmillan, 1982.

—, *Independent Television in Britain: Volume II, Expansion and Change, 1958–68*, London, Macmillan, 1983.

Shackleton, L., *Clown Prince of Soccer: his autobiography*, London, Nicholas Kaye, 1955, p. 17.

Shipley, S., 'Boxing', in T. Mason (ed.), *Sport in Britain: a social history*, Cambridge, Cambridge University Press, 1989, pp. 78–115.

Shoebridge, M., *Women in Sport: a select bibliography*, London, Mansell, 1987.

Short, C., *The Ulster GAA Story, 1884–1984*, [S. l.], Ulster Committee GAA, 1984.

Short, C., Murray, P., and Smith, J., *Ard Mhacha 1884–1984: a century of progress*, Armagh County Board GAA, Armagh, 1985.

Simpson, M., *Male Impersonators: men performing masculinity*, London, Cassell, 1994.

Sissons, R., *The Players: a social history of the professional cricketer*, London, Kingswood, 1988.

Sked, A. and Cook, C., *Post-War Britain: a political history, 1945–1992*, fourth edition, Harmondsworth, Penguin, 1993.

Small, S., *Racialised Barriers: the black experience in the United States and England in the 1980s*, London, Routledge, 1994.

Smith, D., 'People's theatre: a century of Welsh rugby', *History Today*, 1981, vol. 31, no. 3, pp. 31–6.

—, 'Focal heroes: a Welsh fighting class', in R. Holt (ed.), *Sport and the Working Class in Modern Britain*, Manchester, Manchester University Press, 1990, pp. 198–217.

Smith, D. and Williams, G., *Fields of Praise: the official history of the Welsh Rugby Union 1881–1981*, Cardiff, University of Wales Press, 1980.

Smith, G. (ed.), *Take the Ball and Run: a rugby anthology*, London, Pavilion, 1991.

Smith, N., *Queen of Games: the history of croquet*, London, Weidenfeld and Nicolson, 1991.

Spencer, H., *A Century of Polo*, Cirencester, World Polo Associates, 1994.

Sports Council, *A Digest of Sports Statistics for the UK*, third edition, London, Sports Council, 1991.

—, *Women and Sport: policy and frameworks for action*, London, Sports Council, 1993.

Sprawson, C., *Haunts of the Black Masseur: the swimmer as hero*, London, Jonathan Cape, 1992.

Stoddart, B., 'Historical dimensions in the British sports experience: a review article', *Sporting Traditions*, 1991, vol. 7, part 2, pp. 207–13.
—, 'Golf international: considerations of sport in the global marketplace', in R. Wilcox (ed.), *Sport in the Global Village*, Morgantown, WV, Fitness Information Technology, 1994, pp. 21–34.
Sugden, J. and Bairner, A., 'Northern Ireland: sport in a divided society', in L. Allison (ed.), *The Politics of Sport*, Manchester, Manchester University Press, 1986, pp. 90–117.
—, ' "Ma, there's a helicopter on the pitch!" Sport, leisure and the state in Northern Ireland', *Sociology of Sport Journal*, 1992, vol. 9, no. 2, pp. 154–66.
—, *Sport, Sectarianism and Society in a Divided Ireland*, Leicester, Leicester University Press, 1993.
—, 'National identity, community relations and the sporting life in Northern Ireland', in L. Allison (ed.), *The Changing Politics of Sport*, Manchester, Manchester University Press, 1993, pp. 171–206.
—, 'Ireland and the World Cup: "two teams in Ireland, there's only two teams in Ireland . . . " ', in J. Sugden and A. Tomlinson (eds), *Hosts and Champions: soccer cultures, national identities and the USA World Cup*, Aldershot, Arena, 1994, pp. 119–40.
Sugden, J. and Tomlinson, A. (eds), *Hosts and Champions: soccer cultures, national identities and the USA World Cup*, Aldershot, Arena, 1994.
—, 'A gulf in class?', *When Saturday Comes*, February 1997, no. 120, pp. 36–7.
Summerfield, K. and White, A., 'Korfball: a model of egalitarianism?', *Sociology of Sport Journal*, 1989, vol. 6, no. 2, pp. 144–51.
Taylor, I., ' "Football Mad": a speculative sociology of football hooliganism', in E. Dunning (ed.), *The Sociology of Sport: a selection of readings*, London, Frank Cass, 1971, pp. 352–77.
—, 'On the sports violence question: soccer hooliganism revisited', in Jennifer Hargreaves (ed.), *Sport, Culture and Ideology*, London, RKP, 1982, pp. 152–96.
—, 'Class, violence and sport: the case of soccer hooliganism in Britain', in H. Cantelon and R. Gruneau (eds), *Sport, Culture and the Modern State*, Toronto, University of Toronto Press, 1982, pp. 39–96.
—, 'Professional sport and the recession: the case of British soccer', *International Review for the Sociology of Sport*, 1984, vol. 19, no. 1, pp. 7–30.
—, 'Putting the boot into a working-class sport: British soccer after Bradford and Brussels', *Sociology of Sport Journal*, 1987, vol. 4, no. 2, pp. 171–91.
Taylor, P., 'The production of sporting excellence in England: a mixed economy problem', in A. Tomlinson (ed.), *Sport in Society: policy, politics and culture*, Brighton, Leisure Studies Association, 1990, pp. 13–26.
Taylor, R., *Football and its Fans: supporters and their relations with the game 1885–1985*, Leicester, Leicester University Press, 1992.
Taylor, R. and Ward, A., *Kicking and Screaming: an oral history of football in England*, London, Robson, 1995.
Thatcher, M., *The Downing Street Years*, London, HarperCollins, 1993.
Thomas, P., 'Kicking racism out of football: a supporter's view', *Race and Class*, 1995, vol. 36, no. 4, pp. 95–101.
Thomas, R., *The Politics of Hunting*, Aldershot, Gower, 1983.
—, 'Hunting: a sporting or political issue?', in L. Allison (ed.), *The Politics of Sport*, Manchester, Manchester University Press, 1986, pp. 174–97.

Thompson, E. P., *The Making of the English Working Class*, revised edition, Harmondsworth, Penguin, 1980.

Thompson, L., *The Dogs: a personal history of greyhound racing*, London, Chatto and Windus, 1994.

Thorburn, A. M. C., *The Scottish Rugby Union: official history*, Edinburgh, Scottish Rugby Union/Collins, 1985.

The Times, 'Pitch Babel', 17 August 1996, p. 19.

Tomlinson, A., 'Going global: the FIFA story', in A. Tomlinson and G. Whannel (eds), *Off The Ball: the football World Cup*, London, Pluto, 1986, pp. 83–98.

— (ed.), *Sport in Society: policy, politics and culture*, Brighton, Leisure Studies Association, 1990.

Tomlinson, A. and Whannel, G. (eds), *Five Ring Circus: money, power and politics at the Olympic Games*, London, Pluto, 1984.

— (eds), *Off The Ball: the football World Cup*, London, Pluto, 1986.

Tomlinson, M., 'State intervention in voluntary sport: the inner city policy context', *Leisure Studies*, 1987, vol. 6, pp. 329–45.

Tuck, J., 'Patriots, barbarians, gentlemen and players: rugby union and national identity in Britain since 1945', *Sporting Heritage*, no. 2, 1996, pp. 25–36.

Turnbull, A., *Running Together: every woman's running guide*, London, Unwin, 1986.

Vamplew, W., *The Turf: a social and economic history of horse racing*, London, Allen Lane, 1976.

—, *Pay Up and Play the Game: professional sport in Britain 1875–1914*, Cambridge, Cambridge University Press, 1988.

—, 'Horse-racing', in T. Mason (ed.), *Sport in Britain: a social history*, Cambridge, Cambridge University Press, 1989, pp. 215–44.

Vanderwerken, D. L. (ed.), *Sport in the Classroom: teaching sport-related courses in the humanities*, London, Associated University Press, 1990.

Vasali, P., 'Men out of time', *When Saturday Comes*, October 1993, no. 80, pp. 8–10.

—, 'Colonialism and football: the first Nigerian tour to Britain', *Race and Class*, 1995, vol. 36, no. 4, pp. 55–70.

Veblen, T., *The Theory of the Leisure Class*, London, Unwin, 1970.

Verma, G. and Darby, D., *Winners and Losers: ethnic minorities in sport and recreation*, London, Falmer, 1994.

Wagg, S., *The Football World: a contemporary social history*, Brighton, Harvester, 1984.

— (ed.), *Giving the Game Away: football, politics and culture on five continents*, London, Leicester University Press, 1995.

—, 'The missionary position: football in the societies of Britain and Ireland', in S. Wagg (ed.), *Giving the Game Away: football, politics and culture on five continents*, London, Leicester University Press, 1995, pp. 1–23.

Walker, G., ' "There's not a team like the Glasgow Rangers": football and religious identity in Scotland', in G. Walker and T. Gallagher (eds), *Sermons and Battle Hymns: Protestant popular culture in modern Scotland*, Edinburgh, Edinburgh University Press, 1990, pp. 137–59.

Walker, G. and Gallagher, T. (eds), *Sermons and Battle Hymns: Protestant popular culture in modern Scotland*, Edinburgh, Edinburgh University Press, 1990.

Wallechinsky, D., *The Complete Book of the Olympics*, revised edition, Harmondsworth, Penguin, 1988.

Walsh, P., *Men of Steel: the lives and times of boxing's middleweight champions*, London, Robson, 1993.

Walvin, J., *The People's Game: a social history of English football*, London, Allen Lane, 1975.

—, *Football and the Decline of Britain*, London, Macmillan, 1986.

Whannel, G., *Blowing the Whistle: the politics of sport*, London, Pluto Press, 1983.

—, *Sport on 4*, London, Channel 4, 1988.

—, 'Building our bodies to beat the best: notes on sport, work and fitness chic', in A. Tomlinson (ed.), *Sport in Society: policy, politics and culture*, Brighton, Leisure Studies Association, 1990, pp. 119–27.

—, *Fields in Vision: television sport and cultural transformation*, London, Routledge, 1992.

Wheen, F., 'The athletic fallacy', in A. McLellan (ed.), *Nothing Sacred: the new cricket culture*, London, Two Heads, 1996, pp. 104–17.

White, P. and Vagi, A., 'Rugby in the 19th-Century British boarding-school system: a feminist psychoanalytic perspective', in M. Messner and D. Sabo (eds), *Sport, Men, and the Gender Order: critical feminist perspectives*, Champaign, IL, Human Kinetics, 1990, pp. 67–78.

Whitson, D., 'Pressures on regional games in a dominant metropolitan culture: the case of shinty', *Leisure Studies*, 1983, vol. 2, no. 2, pp. 130–54.

Wilcox, R. (ed.), *Sport in the Global Village*, Morgantown, WV, Fitness Information Technology, 1994.

Williams, G., 'From Grand Slam to Great Slump: economy, society and rugby football in Wales during the Depression', *Welsh History Review*, 1983, vol. 11, no. 3, pp. 339–57.

—, ' "How amateur was my valley?" Professional sport and national identity in Wales, 1890–1914', *British Journal of Sports History*, 1983, vol. 2, no. 3, pp. 248–69.

—, 'Rugby Union', in T. Mason (ed.), *Sport in Britain: a social history*, Cambridge, Cambridge University Press, 1989, pp. 308–43.

—, *1905 and All That: essays on rugby football, sport and Welsh society*, Llandysul, Gomer, 1991.

—, 'The Road to Wigan Pier revisited: the migration of Welsh rugby talent since 1918', in J. Bale and J. Maguire (eds), *The Global Sports Arena: athletic talent migration in an interdependent world*, London, Frank Cass, 1994, pp. 25–38.

Williams, Jack, 'Cricket', in T. Mason (ed.), *Sport in Britain: a social history*, Cambridge, Cambridge University Press, 1989, pp. 116–45.

Williams, John, 'Having an away day: English football spectators and the hooligan debate', in John Williams and S. Wagg (eds), *British Football and Social Change: getting into Europe*, Leicester, Leicester University Press, 1991, pp. 160–84.

Williams, John and Wagg, S. (eds), *British Football and Social Change: getting into Europe*, Leicester, Leicester University Press, 1991.

Williams, John and Woodhouse, J., 'Can play, will play? Women and football in Britain', in John Williams and S. Wagg (eds), *British Football and Social Change: getting into Europe*, Leicester, Leicester University Press, 1991, pp. 85–108.

Williams, John, Dunning, E., and Murphy, P., *Hooligans Abroad*, second edition, London, Routledge, 1989.

Williams, M. (ed.), *The Way to Lord's: cricketing letters to The Times*, London, Willow, 1983.

Willis, P., 'Women in sport in ideology', in Jennifer Hargreaves (ed.), *Sport, culture and ideology*, London, RKP, 1982, pp. 117–35.

Wilson, H., *The Labour Government 1964–1970: a personal record*, London, Weidenfeld and Nicolson/Michael Joseph, 1971.

Wilson, N., *The Sports Business: the men and the money*, London, Piatkus, 1988.

Wolfenden Committee on Sport, *Sport and the Community*, London, Central Council of Physical Recreation, 1960.

Woolnough, B., *Black Magic: England's black footballers*, London, Pelham, 1983.

Worcester, R., 'Scenting dissent', *New Statesman and Society*, 21 April 1995, pp. 22–3.

Wright, G., *Betrayal: the struggle for cricket's soul*, London, Witherby, 1993.

Wright, P., *On Living in an Old Country: the national past in contemporary Britain*, London, Verso, 1985.

Wyatt, D., *Rugby Disunion: the making of three world cups*, London, Vista, 1995.

Index